FREE SPIRIT
IN ARCHITECTURE

FREE SPIRIT
IN ARCHITECTURE
OMNIBUS VOLUME

EDITED BY ANDREAS PAPADAKIS
GEOFFREY BROADBENT & MAGGIE TOY

AD ACADEMY EDITIONS

Editorial Note

The initial inspiration for this volume began with the Academy Forum on Modern Pluralism, which took place at the Royal Academy of Arts in September 1991, when it was clear from the discussion that a new mood was developing. The theme of pluralism was quickly interpreted as a quest for a new freedom in architectural thinking, and the work collected here wishes to convey this spirit.

Many of the architects included in this volume have participated in the Academy Forums and Symposia and it is through discussions and meetings with them that it has been possible for me to chart and formalise directions in architecture today. I am especially indebted to Peter Eisenman, Daniel Libeskind and Bernard Tschumi who, over the years, have been instrumental in furthering architectural discourse generally, and have always been forthcoming to me with their comments on architecture and theory. Many of the articles and projects have been published in *Architectural Design* and *Art & Design* magazines, but much recent work of the architects involved has been included to bring the presentation up to date.

I should like to express my thanks to the President of the Royal Academy, Sir Roger de Grey, for making it possible for the Academy Symposia to take place, and especially to MaryAnne Stevens for all her support and invaluable help in organising events there. I also wish to thank my co-editor Geoffrey Broadbent who contributed the main essay and Maggie Toy for her research and for collecting much of the material featured here. My thanks also to Andrea Bettella for his imaginative design concept, and to other staff at Academy Editions who have contributed to this volume including John Honderich, who contributed the biographies and worked on project texts, Vivian Constantinopoulos and Meret Gabra-Liddell.   *Andreas Papadakis*

Front cover: Zaha Hadid, Osaka Folly; *p1:* Peter Eisenman, Koizumi Sangyo Building, Tokyo; *p2:* Philippe Starck, Moondog Building, Tokyo; *p3:* Itsuko Hasegawa, House in Nerima; *p4:* Lebbeus Woods, Zagreb Free Zone; *p5:* Günter Behnisch, Postal Museum, Frankfurt; *p8:* Bernard Tschumi, Glass Video Gallery, Groningen

First published in Great Britain in 1992 by
ACADEMY EDITIONS
An imprint of the Academy Group Ltd
A member of the VCH Publishing Group
42 Leinster Gardens London W2 3AN

Distributed to the trade in the USA by
ST MARTIN'S PRESS
175 Fifth Avenue, New York, NY 10010

ISBN 1 85490 129 X (HB)
ISBN 1 85490 130 3 (PB)

Printed and bound in Singapore

CONTENTS

IN DEFENCE OF FREEDOM
ANDREAS PAPADAKIS AND KENNETH POWELL

Architecture is about building for eternity, creating monuments, defying time, enclosing space, taming nature, defining roles, defining rules, controlling humanity, balancing reason and emotion: or rather it *was* once upon a time about all those things. Architecture today is reaching for infinity: breaking the rules, embracing nature (and mankind), letting space, time and emotions flow freely, confusing rather than reassuring us, coalescing past, present and future, even undermining our sense of reality and reason and, above all, of permanence. (The world around us does that, of course, every day.) It is all unsettling, disturbing, infuriating, incomprehensible. It doesn't make sense: complete anarchy appears (to some) to be just around the corner. Such is the price of freedom, of the rebirth of architecture as an art, unfettered by the dogmas and rules of academies and schools of thought. In an age of experiment, the old proprieties no longer apply. The free spirit at work in late 20th-century architecture does not produce buildings which can be formally analysed like the monuments of the past, subject to being looked at and walked around, but not touched or felt or experienced in any 'non-rational' fashion. As Peter Eisenman puts it, the four walls of the building of the future, 'could deal with the possibility of . . . these other discourses, the other affective senses of sound, touch, and of that light lying within the darkness'.

Of course, not *all* architecture in the last decade of the century is like that. There is no lack of architecture which tries to be reassuring, rational, reasonable, but it seems out of joint with the times. Architecture in the 90s is a critical process, from whichever starting point the critique begins. It reflects and draws upon a society in confused transition, as did those other products of architectural radicalism, Neo-Classicism in the late 18th century and the Modern Movement between the two world wars. In all honesty, it can do nothing else. The issue is not style – that debate has run its course – but the reality (or illusion of reality) which underlies mere physical details, whether they be Classical, Post-Modern or High-Tech.

The formulaic divisions of the 1980s – they dominated Europe and the USA but hardly counted beyond – served to imprison architects within prison camps of their own making. The figures whose work is collected together here are the liberators, the architectural resistance movement. They are fighters for freedom, but this does not make them anarchists in the usual pejorative sense. Like all the best anarchists they have a definite, positive sense of the way things should be, but they value freedom more than rules and believe that a little confusion and annoyance is preferable to unquestioning obedience to discredited authority.

Freedom is generally a rather messy business. Lebbeus Woods has spoken of the political context of the new architecture and the 'lie' of professionalism – 'professionalism separates architects from people and their need to change the conditions of their existence . . . Far from protecting the high standards of architecture, this separation impoverishes architectural work, reducing its productions to tokens of power at best – at worst, to instruments of destruction'. The new free spirit represents a broad protest movement. If Woods conceives his architecture as an attack on the social and political status quo, others are more indirectly political. Frank Gehry favours the gently anarchistic approach of buildings that are playful, party places, where the sober-faced citizen is invited to drop his guard and have some fun. Itsuko Hasegawa offers the most radical challenge of all: nature versus the modern city and the need to recast architecture as 'second nature'. Mark Fisher, Nigel Coates and Philippe Starck throw themselves into the market-oriented world of popular music, shopping and 'leisure', seeking subtly to subvert capitalist society from within. Bernard Tschumi's *folies* in Paris's Parc de la Villette are pleasure pavilions for the democratic age, open to all, their exact purpose as indefinite as their form, inviting *homo ludens* to make of them what he will. The aim is to encourage invention and improvisation: the antithesis of the high-minded paternalism of the old Modern Movement, with its clear vision of the way people *should* enjoy themselves.

The generation of Corbusier and Gropius grew up amidst the decaying remains of the 19th-century industrial order, which they wanted to finally bury. Confusion and chaos and squalor were all around and in place of it they proposed light, order, regularity. The Post-Modern world – and we're all Post-Modernists – values a degree of confusion, of irregularity and ad hoc-ness, as a corrective to the failings of a society organised into its own destruction. So the practitioners influenced by the new free spirit revel in the Post-Modern city, in Tokyo above all, seeing in it not just chaos and despair but a hidden order and hope too. The transitory, 'throwaway' society of contemporary Japan has been perhaps the biggest single influence on the new architecture. In the West, architecture is about the only commodity which is not expendable. The 'monumental' philosophy still prevails: everything is built to last. But for what? The monstrous progeny of the economic boom years in the USA and Britain remain to remind us of the shattered certainties of that era. They argue the case for a loose fit society where human activities are less rigidly compartmentalised. Frank Gehry and Eric Owen Moss are among the architects recasting the office block as a multifunctional shed, with areas of activity within in place of the more conventional compartments. The transformation of the office is about more than mere organisational strategy: it reflects a new view of work in society.

The issue of Deconstruction as an influence on these free spirits can hardly be ignored. Yet it has been overworked. The philosophical apparatus of a new school of literary criticism worked well enough as a battering ram against the old presumptions and precepts, yet there has been, perhaps, an excess of theory – as if it was needed as an excuse for abandoning a strictly pragmatic approach to architectural design. The work of two leading exponents of the new architecture underlines how inadequate Deconstruction is as a rationale and container for their work.

Bernard Tschumi's approach to urban design, seen in the Kyoto Station Masterplan and in projects at Karlsruhe and Chartres, is not about arbitrary intervention into established scenes but about a re-assertion of positive qualities of the random, irrational organism that is a city. At La Villette, Tschumi tackled – and broke down – the 20th-century megastructure. His subsequent projects have been part of an attack on the hierarchy and false order of Western cities, urban planning with a distinctly social aim. While Rob and Leon Krier attack the modernist city with the intention of restoring a lost order, Tschumi looks for a new one, to emerge out of a period of liberated confusion. This may sound grossly idealistic, but late 20th-century cities need all the idealism that exists.

Daniel Libeskind, Polish-born and trained in Britain and the USA, has become particularly identified with the rebirth of Berlin. Like the Briton Will Alsop, he responded in an uncompromisingly radical way to the proposed rebuilding of the Potsdamerplatz quarter of the city. Where others (and none more so than the winners of the official competition, Hilmer & Sattler) produced more prescriptive schemes, rich in certainties, Libeskind accepted, embraced Berlin's uneasy dynamism, revelled in its potential as the pivot of a new Europe.

Libeskind declined, however, simply to glorify Berlin – again, like Tschumi, he looks for a new order, not the rebuilding of what is lost. Libeskind is Jewish and the recent history of Berlin has special significance for him. His Jewish Museum project is, beyond question, one of the key architectural enterprises of the 1990s, not a container for artefacts and history, but a living expression of the soul of a race. Libeskind has said that, 'the everyday architect is dead. His body useless unless it becomes manure or kindling for the fire which, after all, is based on what is "no better"'. His vision of architecture is almost apocalyptic, full of portents of the end of architecture 'as a practice of control'. Architectural form can no more be tightly controlled, says Libeskind, than information in the proverbial 'electronic village'.

The new spirit in architecture celebrated here is about freedom above everything else – social responsibility, respect for history and hierarchy, consistency, even logic itself, are secondary considerations. It may be a passing interlude in the evolution of the new architecture of humanism, but it has a vigour, a variety and a sheer honesty which command respect.

WHO ARE THESE SPIRITS WILD AND FREE?
GEOFFREY BROADBENT

It was clear in the early 1980s that new and strange forms of architecture were emerging. Different architects with very different backgrounds seemed to be doing similar things: fragmenting their buildings, placing bits and pieces at odd angles to each other, having one block penetrate another. Often they designed with buildings as 'bars' or 'beams', clashing into one another, and whatever their other qualities or defects – some of them did seem rather antisocial – the results possessed enormous vitality.

The kinds of thing I have in mind include Zaha Hadid's scheme for the Hong Kong Peak Club, and her office block for the Kurfürstendamm in Berlin; schemes for the Parc de la Villette in Paris by Bernard Tschumi, Rem Koolhaas and OMA; housing of various kinds in Berlin by Libeskind, Koolhaas and Eisenman; Eisenman's Wexner Center for the Visual Arts in Columbus, Ohio; his Bio-Centrum for Frankfurt; Coop Himmelblau's Merz School for Stuttgart, their Rooftop Remodelling in Vienna, their Open House at Malibu; and Frank Gehry's own little House at Santa Monica and his Vitra Museum, near Basle.

For her club at the Hong Kong Peak, Zaha Hadid envisaged four great 'beams' of building flying over the city and plunging, at different angles, into the side of the Peak. They were to embed themselves in a man-made, polished granite landscape, at this point containing the social facilities of a club, whereas the beams themselves were given over largely to housing, with studio apartments in the lower two and a gap containing further club facilities (including a swimming pool) skewed back onto the mountain. There were to be larger apartments in the beam above this gap and a luxurious penthouse in the top one. Hadid's Kurfürstendamm offices also started as a beam strung along her long, narrow site, over which a glass-faced 'sail' was to billow out, gaining additional accommodation for the upper floors which got progressively deeper.

Then Daniel Libeskind's first project for Berlin, his massive City Edge project of 1987, was a vast Hadid-like beam some 450 metres long, 10 wide and 20 high, rising upwards from Am Karlsbad (from the site, indeed, of Mies van der Rohe's office) and cantilevering south along Flottwellstrasse at an angle of about six degrees, rising at the far end to some 56 metres. Internally, in section, this beam was to be a maze of interlocking levels, folded concrete slabs and partitions forming the stiffening structure which also contained housing, offices, public administration, shops, cinemas and so on. Libeskind's drawings of the beam show it criss-crossed with networks of fine lines, some of which descend to ground level as delicate supports around the staircases and elevators every 60 metres or so. Despite its defiance of gravity Libeskind's

beam was eminently constructable, indeed construction drawings had been prepared. But the Green Party gained a majority in the Berlin Senate, and the beam was not deemed Green enough.

Not so Bernard Tschumi's Parc de la Villette in Paris. Like Hadid, Tschumi draws elements of his design 'flying' over the site, for he had deconstructed the brief of workshop, gymnasium, and bath facilities, playgrounds, places for exhibitions, concerts, scientific experiments, games and competitions into individual components; they could have been jammed into a large megastructure but that might never have been started, so Tschumi fragmented his brief, scattered the bits and pieces across the site and yet gave coherence to his Parc by having each of them within, or attached to a '*folie*'. These are ten-metre cubes, red-painted, formed of smaller cubes three-by-three in each of the three dimensions, laid at the intersections of a 120-metre grid, eight squares from north to south and five from east to west. Tschumi reasoned, correctly, that one *folie* might get built, as an experiment, and others might follow. He worked out a geometric 'syntax' – a system of rules, by which a *folie* could be built complete as an open 'cage', or built in part with smaller cubes missing. It could be enclosed, in whole or in part, by metal plates to give internal spaces, and there might be metal attachments to the cube – spiral ramps or stairs, water wheels or constructivist sculpture, or else highly geometric granite buildings with quite interchangeable functions such as bar, restaurant, exhibition gallery, a play school and so on.

There are other geometric systems interacting at La Villette: the huge square, circle and triangle to which the landscape is laid, the multiplicity of paths and walkways. Some of these 'lines' follow those geometric forms – Tschumi sees those as 'surfaces' – and others are free to soar and swoop around his *folies* as a '*promenade cinématique*' of the kind which Tschumi himself had described in his *Manhattan Transcripts*,[1] giving one different, multi-sensory experiences as one moves, 'frame by frame', over and around the 'thematic' gardens between the *folies* designed by Tschumi and others. What's more, Tschumi's idea of deconstructing the brief paid off to such an extent that all the *folies* are being completed.

Rem Koolhaas and OMA adopted a similar strategy in their design for La Villette. They divided the Parc into east-west strips intersected by a large north-south mall at a higher level. The strips themselves were given over to thematic gardens, play areas, discovery gardens and so on with kiosks, concession stands and ticket sales booths as appropriate for 'sites within the site', such as a small amphitheatre, chess tables, puppet theatres, platforms,

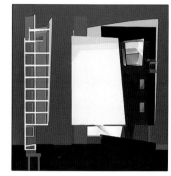

Zaha Hadid, Kurfürstendamm, Berlin

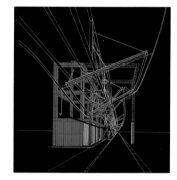

Bernard Tschumi, Parc de la Villette, Paris

Morphosis, Chiba project, Tokyo

13

OMA, Checkpoint Charlie housing, Berlin

Peter Eisenman, Wexner Center for the Visual Arts, Columbus, Ohio

roller skating rinks and so on. Very different from their housing for Checkpoint Charlie in Berlin, designed for the international building exhibition, the Internationale Bauaustellung of 1987. It stands on the Friedrichstrasse, immediately south of Zimmerstrasse where the checkpoint used to be, with a fairly open ground floor, containing small-scale, somewhat sculptural buildings. Over these are three storeys of apartments with horizontal, Corbusian strip windows and set-back penthouses on the upper two floors with a skewed overhanging roof.

This all seems a bit intuitive compared to the geometric rigours of Peter Eisenman's apartment block, just south of OMA's, across the Friedrichstrasse and containing the Museum of the Berlin Wall.[2] This marks a stage in the development of that way of transcending the brief that Eisenman calls 'scaling', which he started in 1978 when, for the first time, he needed to design more than a single house – a site plan, indeed, for Cannaregio Town Square in Venice.[3] He looked for clues in Cannaregio itself but there were few: just canals and an abattoir. But Le Corbusier had used the Cannaregio site for his Venice Hospital and Eisenman took Le Corbusier's grid as a basis for his design. About this time however, Eisenman had started to worry about man's place in the scheme of things; the unquestioned assumption that man is the 'measure of all things'. So he opted for an architecture of 'absence . . . a series of voids . . . holes in the ground' to act as 'metaphors' for his 'displacement' of man's position as the 'centred instrument of measure'. It was in this way that for Eisenman architecture became not something which relates to human scale but simply 'the measure of itself'.

He demonstrated this in his Cannaregio scheme with variations on House 11a, at three different scales, nested inside each other like Russian dolls. The smallest house, some five feet high, could just about be used as a shelter, raising the question, house or model? The second house was of normal size but since the first, nested inside, almost filled its useable space, this 'normal' house also could not be used as such. Was it a house, or a museum with a model house inside? The third house was twice as big as the second, which it contained. So was it a museum containing a real house with a model of a house inside? Or a mausoleum for a museum?

Such 'nesting' of cubes or 'el-shaped' forms occurs in several Eisenman projects, such as the House El Even Odd and House X of 1980, and the Fin d'Ou T Hou S of 1985, as Eisenman continued his musings on 'scaling', questioning how meaning changes with size, and the relevance, if any, of human scale to architecture.[4] Other considerations entered his thinking as he was designing his Housing Block for the IBA in Berlin, 1982-86. This stands on Friedrichstrasse, immediately south of the former Checkpoint Charlie and the line of the notorious Wall.[5] Eisenman saw the Wall as cutting off the centre of Berlin – the Stadtmitte – from the West and turning it into a museum. Friedrichstrasse had been designed by Nering as the major axis of his 17th-century Baroque extension to Berlin, whilst westward of Checkpoint Charlie the Wall ran between two sites of desperation: Hitler's Bunker to the north, the remnant of his Reichschancellory, and the

headquarters of the Gestapo to the south. It is hardly surprising that for Eisenman, a Jew, the site represented brooding memories whilst the Wall, which was still standing, embodied such binary oppositions as 'severance and connection, exclusion and inclusion'. In response Eisenman sought 'to erect the structure of both somewhere and nowhere, to memorialise the place and to deny the efficacy of that memory'.

Eisenman planned to excavate the site, at the Friedrichstrasse/Kochstrasse corner, as a three-dimensional park, exposing layer by layer a history of Berlin; seeing it, indeed, as a Tschumi-like 'palimpsest' with traces of absent walls from three centuries of development. Where there were no actual remains he would build fictitious ones, thereby forming 'a nexus of walls at different levels . . . a complete datum of memory'. Later he was to give the name 'discontinuity' to such references to the past of his sites, not to mention projections into their futures. But much of Berlin's most tragic history had been played out on Nering's grid, up to and including the building of the Wall. So Eisenman 'challenged' this with another grid; that 17th-century Humanist one of Mercator's map projection, from which Nering's skews by some 3.3 degrees. Whilst Eisenman's facades conform to the Nering grid, his main blocks include a five-storey one aligned to the Mercator grid, which starts embedded in the corner and skews out eastwards along the Kochstrasse. And whilst Eisenman's main facades are covered in a 'neutral' grid of small grey tiles, his Mercator elevations, not to mention his site plan, embody 'scaling' of a rather different kind: large 'tartan-gridded' patterns of white and dark grey tiles crossed by an even larger red grid.

So Eisenman's Berlin block offers two of his crucial ideas: the palimpsest of his layering down into the site, and his scaling in site plan and facades – ideas of a kind he was to develop further in his Wexner Center for the Visual Arts, Columbus, for the Ohio State University (1983-89). But of course the Northwest Territory – Ohio – was laid out in Jefferson's time to a grid aligned with Mercator. Columbus itself is a gridded city but it departs from Mercator by 12.25 degrees, and High Street extends some six miles northwest from downtown Columbus on this eccentric line, passing, at about two and a half miles, the university campus. East of High Street the Mercator line has been recaptured for suburban housing and the main entrance to the campus lies opposite 15th Avenue. Just inside the gates there are two large buildings, the Mershon Auditorium and Weigel Hall, both parallel to High Street. Eisenman laid out his site to a huge rectangular grid on the High Street line, fractured by a 'fault' line on Mercator. Parallel to this he extended 15th Avenue past the two auditoria, punctuating his new axis at the gap between them. From this point he projected an axis northwards on the Mercator line, of which the most visible feature is a huge white steel pergola, his 'scaffolding' on a 12-foot grid. Then, just beyond this, he re-erected armoury-like towers in brick to mark the entrance to his Center; so here, as in Berlin, Eisenman has designed history into his new building.

His northward-running axis with its 'scaffolding' leaves long, thin, triangular spaces against the two buildings; that towards the Mershon Auditorium contains the entrance to his (largely underground) library. Indeed, as in Berlin, Eisenman thought of building in an excavation so that his galleries are approached through the new 'armoury' towers down steps to the basement level from where one rises by ramp – parallel to his 'scaffolding' mall – and back up to surface level. Eisenman's galleries are strung along this ramp so, according to position, some are underground and dark whilst others are at ground level, flooded with light through their translucent walls. The highly visible internal frame is built to a 24-foot Mercator grid which clashes, at various points, with walls and other features aligned to High Street. The original armoury had been torn down in 1959 but its brick foundations remained and Eisenman could have built directly onto them. He preferred instead to tidy them up a little so they could be seen as traces, and his replacement towers are 'fractured', peeled-back, not to say abstracted, 'evocations of the old'. His aim was to 'recall' history in modern terms, to offer 'the continuous transformation of a memory – fictive, transformed and continuous'. Later (1987) he was to call such evocative reinterpretations of forms 'self-similarity'.

As for Eisenman's Bio-Centrum in Frankfurt, this is not so much site-derived as stimulated by basic 20th-century biology: Watson and Crick's double helix, the DNA spiral which encodes the basic instructions by which living beings construct themselves. Eisenman took the four components of DNA, modelled by biologists as 'bars' with interlocking ends, convex or concave, V-shaped or curved, and used these as the bases for his blocks of buildings; nine of them, interlocking as do models of DNA. Having set up these basic forms Eisenman then cut through them, with an Ohio State-like mall, adding in certain places smaller versions of themselves.

Of all the architects in this group Eisenman is by far the most 'intellectual', whilst Coop Himmelblau are perhaps the most intuitive. They first emerged as themselves – architects and not just interior designers – in 1981 with their proposals for the Merz School in Stuttgart. They were to provide a multi-purpose room, a utility room, an apartment and dormitories all attached to an existing villa. Since this was an 'open' school they envisaged an 'Open Architecture' based on 'the dissolution and alteration of a house into a confident, bold, open system'.[6] Their extension 'grew' out of the existing school as steel branches supporting dormitories in the form of prefabricated huts protecting the other accommodation. Coop Himmelblau called it the 'Merz Boarding School or How a Fledgling Learns To Fly', so it's hardly surprising that their plan is somewhat bird-like and the section is a living, animate form. As Coop Himmelblau's founding partner, Wolf Prix was to ask:

Have you ever seen a leaping whale? I saw one in San Francisco and it was fantastic. I would like to compare [our] way of drawing with a leaping, champing whale . . . In our creative procedure we try to capture this very instant when the animal is moving from water to air . . .

It's as if one of them were trying to mime their spaces; mould them in the air as the other partner watches and draws, trying to capture on paper the essence of those hand-traced movements. This was nowhere truer than in designing their Open House for Malibu Beach. The client hardly knew what he wanted and Coop Himmelblau were much more concerned with his feelings anyway, his emotional rather than his functional needs. So there was no question of working out a detailed brief, schedule of accommodation and so on. Indeed Coop Himmelblau were determined that nothing should 'lead them astray' from their intuitive feelings; ideas welling up from the subconscious. Their city after all, Vienna, was also the home of Sigmund Freud. The architects were determined not to allow practicalities of structure or construction nor even the process of drawing to distort those evanescent feelings as they welled up, so Prix closed his eyes and used his hands, his gestures, to describe as he says a 'graph of feelings' in a process much like Action Painting.[7] The result was by no means an architectural drawing; it was rather, he says, a 'psychogram' to do with 'rays of light and shadow, brightness and darkness, height and width, whiteness and vaulting, the view (of the sea) and the air.' Then suddenly Prix had the feeling that something was 'right', beginning to hold together; an emotional, rather than a rational decision after which everything fell into place – structure, function, programme, materials and so on. Thus drawing with closed eyes helps Coop Himmelblau capture 'the moment' on paper, or rather the feelings of that moment.

Coop Himmelblau's brilliant engineer Osker Graf deconstructed the psychogram, broke it down into manageable components and reassembled them as a buildable – bridge or aircraft-like – structure. Open House rests, almost floats, on three supporting points with taut bowstring trusses between them, which allow a double shell where the House needs a solid skin and double-glazing where it doesn't, thus providing the basis for a passive solar energy design. Open House was the project, more than any other, which gave Coop Himmelblau the basis for their 'open' design, indeed for their Open Architecture (they derived this title from another distinguished native of Vienna, Karl Popper, and his *Open Society and its Enemies*):[8] 'The client may think he knows how to use the House: this client, unfortunately, died but Kim Bassinger may be interested . . . But after moving in, living there for a while the client's conceptions may well change: where to sleep, where to eat, read and so on.' It's the essence of Coop Himmelblau's Open Architecture that such choices, long term, are wholly the client's. As architects they do not want to impose too much.

By this philosophy, of course, Coop Himmelblau designed their Rooftop Remodelling in Vienna (1983-89). They had to organise a lawyer's office around a meeting room so, as with the Open House, they looked for abstract qualities of light and shadow, of brightness and darkness, height and width, whiteness and vaulting, the view over the rooftops and so on. They were building onto the corner of an existing building and they wanted to find a 'contemporary' solution to that typical Viennese problem, the corner building, on which Rob Krier has waxed so eloquent.[9] They saw this as not so much a matter of analysing proportion,

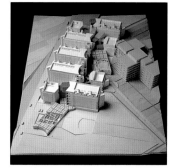

Peter Eisenman, Bio-Centrum, Frankfurt

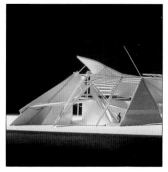

Coop Himmelblau, Open House, Malibu

*Frank Gehry, Loyola Law School,
Los Angeles*

*Frank Gehry, Fish Restaurant,
Kobe*

colour, texture, materials and so on, to build into context as Krier might well have done, but of finding an 'energy line', a line of visual connection between the street corner and the roof, a 'flash of light' from the street crossing the corner transversely and thus creating a new space.[10] So in this design a taut bowstring slashes the corner as the steel spine of a structure which cuts and destroys roof to create a new, light and airy space.

This bowstring forms one of four overlaid structures: the steel and concrete foundations along the original walls; the bowstring itself as the main structural spine; supported by it, the secondary struts, trusses and an 'inverted staircase' of concrete planes to hint at spatial separation, to modulate light and space; and then resting over these, the outer canopy of structural glazing, with clear thermal glass, louvered blinds for sunlight control, folding and sliding windows for natural ventilation. So just as Hadid gave beams to the world of deconstruction, so Coop Himmelblau gave their multi-layered 'frames', of concrete supporting steel supporting glazing bars, each twisted and distorted against the others. Not to mention 'plates' of inverted 'stairs' for shading. For Coop Himmelblau love to use light in their work; they see it as offering 'sculptural qualities'; indeed they are inordinately proud of a moving slit of light cast on a particular wall. As the sun moves, so this arrow of light moves too to illuminate the opposite wall. And in the evening when the client has control he becomes creator of converse effects; he beams artificial light from within his boardroom to the outside world with his complicated lighting system of halogen spots, lines of neon, sharp arrows of light and the glow of indirect lighting, which all add additional dimensions to the spatial qualities of his Rooftop.

Coop Himmelblau see their Rooftop also as Open Architecture. For now that the form is there it is useable in many different ways. If the lawyer moves out it can be converted, instantly, into apartments or put to some other quite different use.[11] Coop Himmelblau see their twisting and bending of forms, quite consciously, as destroying any 'fit' of form to function. Nor will they design furniture, for that would be far too constraining. The user takes possession, takes charge, takes 'a grip on the space', makes changes of whatever kind they see fit; this is seen as the essence of Open Architecture.

Frank Gehry too speaks of 'open' architecture. For him, he says,

the most important thing about the building is accessibility. The building had a body language that says 'come in' . . . The architecture doesn't get in the way of people coming in and out. It's inviting . . . You should see the entrance from the park and feel like coming in, taking your jacket off, I want the building to be like a party . . . very inviting.[12]

Which was not perhaps quite true of his own house in Santa Monica, or rather his wife's. She had bought a small timber-framed house which was not quite adequate for their needs. So he did a little remodelling and, more particularly, added various elements such as an entry porch, a kitchen and so on. Since it was their own, as Gehry says, he could experiment with materials, explore corru-

gated metal, plywood, chain link fencing and suchlike, not to mention the degrees to which they enclose space: plywood offers a solid visual boundary, chain link an open one and so on. Gehry wanted to make sure that people still saw the old house, hardly violated: 'some guy just wrapped it in new materials . . . '[13]

Gehry's 'wrappings' at ground level consist of corrugated metal extensions to north and west, forming a kitchen, a dining room, an entrance and back yards. These are under decks visually 'contained' by his chain-link screens and their slender framing. Gehry's manipulation of materials, full size, on the job, is about as pragmatic as design could ever be, but he also acknowledges his debt to various artist friends; the late Gordon Matta Clark, Claes Oldenburg and others. Not to mention the history of art. In describing the design of his kitchen window, for instance, he says:

I became interested in opposing the (existing) bay window with a different kind of geometric activity, something that was more active . . . I fantasised that when I closed the box (the old house) there were ghosts that would try to creep out, and this window was a Cubist ghost. I became fascinated by that and started making models of windows that looked like the ghost of Cubism was trying to crawl out.

As for his dining room, Gehry says he 'was interested in the corner window. How you turn the corner.' He thought of Duchamp's *Nude Descending a Staircase*, and tried to 'figure out' how he could rotate the corner 'so as you walked around it, it would rotate . . . that piece of glass slides beyond the corner. It works from the inside and outside to rotate the cube.'

After which in a series of spectacular projects Gehry began to emerge as an architect like no other. These include the Loyola Law School (1981-84), the California Aerospace Museum (1982-84), his Fish Restaurant in Kobé, Japan (1987) and his Guest House for the Wintons at Wayzata, Minneapolis (1983-84). This is next to a (somewhat undistinguished) Philip Johnson brick box of a house but the Wintons wanted a guest house that would not compete. Gehry's answer was 'architecture as sculpture' in which five quite different 'pavilions' are placed together, in quite a tight complex, somewhat like a sculpture by Morandi. Indeed Gehry says he was thinking of buildings as 'bottles' which may take their formal strength from standing next to one another. It is centred on a tall, almost square pyramid covered with lead and with light cascading in through a window in the point. The pyramid has a brick fireplace alcove with a large square brick flue, around which radiates a long garage/service wing, clad in panels of a dark brown Finn-Ply, a bedroom in cream Kasota stone which curves to a point on plan, and another bedroom wing with a mono-pitch roof and clad in black, painted metal panels. The main bedroom is a very pleasant space with its curved wall and curving ceiling coming to a point in one corner and, like all the other forms of the building, it fits its functions very well.

This is also true to a spectacular degree of Gehry's Vitra Museum at Weil-am-Rhein, in Germany just across the border from Basle in Switzerland. Vitra is a huge furniture factory and their museum is devoted to chairs. From this Gehry's museum derives its amazing forms, which amount to a series of 'light scoops'; a large cross-shaped central one with others grouped around it which, according to need, might cast a shaft of bright light onto a particular chair, suffuse a whole wall of chairs with a moderate glow, or entice one round a corner to see what is coming next. There's another pragmatism here, not so much of materials as of environmental control, a subtle manipulation of light by three-dimensional forms.

TERMINOLOGY

Certain of these buildings, and others, according to taste, have been described by various critics in different ways. In 1986 for instance Lorraine Farrelly identified a 'New Spirit' in architecture, of 'openness and honesty' with 'the thrusting, dynamic imagery of Constructivism and . . . Futurism's savage beauty.'[14] Above all she saw it as a Dadaesque 'state of mind' out of which 'Surrealism, *arte povera*, Pop Art, Action Painting, Conceptual Sculpture, Performance Art, 60s Happenings, the Situationists and punk, New Wave' were generated. This 'New' state of mind was 'a resurgent spirit of enquiry, a renewed interest in space and movement, in the use of real materials – steel, concrete, timber, stone, even plastic, appearing as itself – in a stripping-back towards the essentials of architecture and, most important, the dynamism of asymmetry, the very genesis of freedom.' She saw this 'Spirit' as acting against the 'small scale, the complex, the vernacular, the historical, the decorative, the popular' of Schumacher and others. And above all she saw it as a death blow to that which she loathed more than anything: Post-Modern Classicism. In these Pluralist days, of course, all these are still alive and well – although few people speak of Farrelly's 'New Spirit'. Indeed in 1991, Peter Cook and Rosie Llewelyn-Jones hijacked her term for work of other kinds – for by then the 'New' was something different.[15] Others overlapped with Farrelly and called work in her 'Spirit' by quite different names: 'Deconstruction', 'Deconstructivism' 'Violated Perfection' and so on.[16] I prefer 'Deconstruction' for reasons which I argued in my *Student Guide* to the subject in 1991.[17] Because the work looks, well, deconstructed!

But are they really serious, these architects? Aren't they just playing games? Self-indulgent? Setting out to shock, to irritate? Some are, no doubt, but in the process may hit on something epoch-making. It depends on your frame of reference. My first ever conference paper was on the subject of creativity and ever since I've seen design as a matter of having creative ideas, choosing the good ones and rejecting the bad ones.[18] These days I use Karl Popper's terms, 'conjectures' and 'refutations'.[19] A designer can conjecture and refute; or he can conjecture, and let the client refute, or indeed society in the mass, as it does with clothes, records, books, and all the other products of consumer culture. This book is evidence indeed that architecture in the early 90s is a field of vast creative ferment. Of a kind which certainly it wasn't when I gave my paper in 1966. Most architects had been brainwashed then by such pioneers of Modern thinking as Gropius,[20] by historian/critic/polemicists such as Giedion[21] and Pevsner,[22]

to design simple, rectangular buildings – as vertical slabs or horizontal sheds – always flat-roofed and probably flat-sided, in white-painted plaster, grey precast concrete panels, glass curtain walls with black steel frames and so on. They had to do such things to be taken seriously; to be thought 'socially responsible'. The days were over, said Gropius (1956) of the 'artistic gentleman architect' indulging his private fantasies. Pevsner had insisted too that to be relevant in the 20th century the architect must be 'cold', must design, not for particular clients but for anonymous users in the mass. There was no room for wilful self-indulgence. Others such as Mies were less concerned with social conscience. Their clients, on the whole, were the large multinationals, but Mies too joined battle with those who sought to be 'interesting' rather than 'good'. Mies himself quoted Thomas Aquinas to the effect that 'reason is the basis for all human work', from which it followed that design should be 'objective'.[23]

Hence the flatness of the roofs, the greyness of the slabs, the blackness of the frames around the windows; these were intended to express the suppression of self: 'social conscience', 'rational objectivity' and so on. The opposite, indeed, of a 'Free Spirit'. But the buildings which resulted, precast concrete high-rise flats, curtain-walled office slabs, steel-framed 'light-and-dry' prefabricated schools, have proved to be the most hated and least durable buildings ever made in history. Some of them have actually fallen down (Ronan Point). Others have been blown up (Pruitt Igoe) or are threatened even now with demolition (Marsham Street). Curtain-walled office blocks have been refurbished and reclad, such as those at London Wall 'humanised' by Terry Farrell. The prefabricated schools burned down in very large numbers – by arson or accident – whilst others again have been refurbished and re-clad by architects such as Ted Cullinan for the Hampshire County Council – the county, indeed, where this whole genre was challenged and killed off by Colin Stansfield Smith and his highly creative team.[24]

It's worth looking at what they found so depressing: not just the leaking flat roofs and the crumbling, over-glazed curtain walls, but the crass insensitivity of designs in which all the rooms were 'clamped' between floor and false ceiling with no modelling at all up into the third dimension. I call it SLEBS – Space Left Empty Between the Slabs – to be divided by partitions. This more than any other factor proves common to all classic Modern Movement forms: prefabricated schools, precast concrete slab apartment blocks, steel-framed curtain-walled office slabs and so on. Nor was this just the work of second-raters. It's there at the very core of Modern Movement thinking, in Le Corbusier's seminal *Five Points for a New Architecture*.[25] It is present in the Dom-i-no frame of concrete columns supporting horizontal concrete floor slabs, with hardly any penetration up and through: a piano-shaped hole in one floor of the Villa Stein and that's about all.

Unlike Mies, Gropius and the rest, Le Corbusier at least lived through this SLEBS phase and later, with the Jaoul's Petit Maison Weekend at Vaucresson (1937), St Baume (1948) Roq et Rob (1950), the Jaoul Houses and Ronchamp (1955) began to go 'sculptural' again, to think up into the

Frank Gehry, Wosk House, Beverly Hills

Frank Gehry, California Aerospace Museum, Santa Monica

Bernard Tschumi, Parc de la Villette folie, Paris

Bernard Tschumi, Parc de la Villette folie, Paris

third dimension. This is why Pevsner went onto the attack of 'late Le Corbusier and the structural acrobatics of the Brazilians' in 1960. He saw them as 'attempts to satisfy the craving of architects for individual expression, the craving of the public for the surprising and the fantastic, and for an escape out of reality into a fairy world.'[26] It's difficult to re-alise now how brave it was early in the 1970s, how foolhardy, to put pitched roofs on their new schools.

But it's the 'keep-'em-flat' doctrine that's always seemed to me antisocial. If the public actually craves a 'fairy world' who is Pevsner, who is any critic, any architect to deny them? What is being deconstructed more than anything else is that 'we know best' view which gave us the flatness, the greyness, the drabness. Deconstructed, literally, by this explosion of forms which often in themselves look deconstructed! Such buildings may or may not be related to Jacques Derrida and his complex philosophies. Some are, some aren't and whilst one can understand say, Frank Gehry's anger at being 'crammed . . . into a box' with other, very different architects and labelled 'Deconstructivist', his attitudes, and theirs, do have certain things in common. They'd all agree with his sentiment:

> I got very angry when other architects started mak-ing buildings that look like Greek temples. I thought it was a denial of the present. It's a rotten thing to do to our children. It's as if we're telling them there's nothing to do but look back. It's like there's no reason to be optimistic about the future. So I got angry.[27]

They share, as we've seen, attitudes to the brief as merely a springboard for their creative ideas; what's more the forms that all of them produce have certain things in common, including apparent fragmentations of one kind or another. They may well insist that their approaches are modern but they are not those of the Modern Movement. Clearly they reject flatness, of roof form, wall surface, internal SLEBS; flatness as a basis of thinking in any way. Such flatnesses indeed are the very subjects of deconstruction which is why the results, in almost every case, are highly legible visual symbols of things being broken up and fragmented. As Thomas Kuhn would say, a paradigm has shifted,[28] and at least one, for in this time of pluralism there are alternatives, competing paradigms such as Classical, vernacular and so on. But it is certainly the Modern Movement forms that are being deconstructed.

However, the architects' attitudes vary greatly to the philosophy of Deconstruction. It so happens that those I've reviewed so far were indeed selected as 'Deconstructivists' for the New York Exhibition of 1988,[29] but I've used other terms in describing their approaches to design which I find it useful to plot as follows:

MOST INTELLECTUAL	MOST INTUITIVE	MOST PRAGMATIC
	Coop Himmelblau	
Libeskind		Koolhaas
Tschumi		Hadid
Eisenman		Gehry

No attempt need be made to fit them into a single 'box', they all pursue their different lines: Eisenman his rare intellectual concepts, with or without Derrida; Coop Himmelblau their 'psychograms', Gehry his on-site prag-matics and so on. Gehry need not feel, should be disa-bused of any feeling, that anyone is trying to force him in a Derridean pigeon-hole.

In this broader sense then, deconstruction is still a useful term. A clear description of those fragmented, incomplete, interpenetrating architectural forms which have been emerging since the early 80s. By the side of which such catch-all names such as 'New Spirit' seem rather inadequate. They can be applied at any time, anywhere, to forms which look in any way new! 'Free Spirits' are a little bit different, in that the term indicates certain attitudes to work – just as once there was a 'New Free Style'.[30]

NEW SOCIAL USES

But surely, could it not be argued that the Free Spirits are antisocial, in that their attitude to the brief is often cavalier, and (whatever may be the truth about clothing, records, books and so on) people rarely have the opportunity to choose their architecture?

The answer to this depends on the building type. If you bought a house then presumably you chose it, but if you live in 'housing' then probably you didn't. It is social architecture which has led to such horrendous problems: people didn't choose 'their' concrete housing slabs, 'their' leaking prefabricated schools, 'their' solar over-heating steel and glass office towers and so on. It's in these building types that most problems have arisen and where cries, quite rightly, have gone up for more public participa-tion. But they do choose their parks, their museums, their night clubs, including those designed by our New Spirits! So what at first sight may seem antisocial, Pevsnerian indulgence at its worst, may well turn out to offer social possibilities well beyond those that may be conceived by any 'form follows function' attitude.

Take Bernard Tschumi's Parc de la Villette, which takes the form it does because he deconstructed his brief into 'folies' and the small buildings attached to them. But go to La Villette on a summer Sunday afternoon – as many tens of thousands do – and like any decent park it 'makes the spirit soar'. The spirits of tourists, no doubt, after trudging round the vast Museum of Science and Industry; but of many Parisians too, trapped in the city at a time when most of those who can have chosen to leave. They go there to picnic, play football, snooze in the sun, get as close as they dare to making love. Such things happen, of course, in any decent park, but Tschumi's folies offer something special: not just the bars and restaurants they contain, the galler-ies, the play school or whatever. They offer viewpoints from which one can be monarch of all one surveys, all the ramps, staircases and screens, the ultimate settings for games of 'cops and robbers'. Some of the gardens also invite skateboarding of a virtuosity matched by that found in few other environments. So Tschumi's flouting of the original brief has led, not to an architecture of social deprivation, but to one that serves society in huge masses and in hitherto undreamt-of ways, and matches the mood of the 1990s more precisely than any kind of 60s 'megastructure' ever could.

Or take Eisenman's Wexner Center. When photographs were first published in the magazines the – empty – Wexner looked like a centre *against* the Visual Arts rather than one for them, with its strange, apparently ill-lit and ill-proportioned spaces. It seemed to lack such elementary things as wall space for hanging paintings or sympathetic lighting – much as Richard Meier's museums do in Atlanta or Frankfurt. This is hardly surprising since, as Eisenman said, 'art has always been critical of life, that is what gave art its potency, its poetry . . .'[31] But architecture was supposed to *serve* art, to be a background for it. 'Absolutely not' said Eisenman: 'Architecture should challenge art and this notion that it should be a background.' And then in the Fall of 1990 the Wexner provided settings for the work of some 20 artists designed for, inspired by Eisenman's building. Tadeshi Kawamata, for instance, had a series of deconstructed bus shelters along East 15th Avenue, into and through the Wexner, and across the campus; Chris Burns placed polystyrene battlements onto Eisenman's plain-topped towers; Christian Marclay made a carillon of Eisenman's steel-gridded mall and Sol LeWitt terminated it with a white brick tower. Internally Malcolm Cochran and MICA TV made use of their dark spaces for cine and video projections. The more conventional spaces got more conventional art but each, in its way, had encouraged an artist, by its scale, proportions, height, quality of light and so on, to produce art of a kind he may never have made before. Now clearly no traditional gallery by Soane, Smirke, Wilkins or Schinkel could inspire such different kinds of art. Nor could newer ones by Wright, Kahn, Foster or Meier. Nor even Post-Modernist ones by Stirling, Venturi and so on, however splendid their spaces may be for displaying existing art. So the Wexner Center for the Visual Arts simply seems to do its job: it actively inspires, almost obliges creative artists to go further in their creativity; frees up, in other words, their spirits.

As for Gehry's Vitra Museum; no space ever, anywhere, has been fashioned with greater concern for the admission of daylight in fascinating, ever-changing variety, not even Kahn's Kimball Museum. There are shafts of light funnelled onto individual chairs; whole rooms glowing with strange luminosity; 'panels' of light projected onto panels of chairs. It's that 'funnelling' of light, of course, together with Gehry's circulation ramps, that determines the museum's extraordinary external forms; form follows light, circulation, in a way that no Modernist envisaged. Never envisaged because any kind of accurate 'fit' between forms and complex functions inevitably means breaking away from flat roofs, flat walls, internal SLEBS! It's Gehry's uniquely pragmatic approach to such things as light and circulation that leads to such apparently wilful terms which can only be described as 'deconstructed'. There simply is no way that Modern Movement SLEBS, Modern Movement 'transparency', could achieve, to this extent, what Le Corbusier described as the essence of architecture: the 'masterly, correct and magnificent play of masses brought together in light'.

TRANSCENDING THE BRIEF

Coop Himmelblau think the brief should be left open. They don't want to dictate what the client may or may not do. Eisenman and Tschumi want to go further than that; they want to take the brief and deconstruct it. Both of them describe elaborate procedures for such deconstruction, which I have discussed in detail elsewhere.[32] Eisenman's descriptions are more scattered than Tschumi's, not to say less coherent, and they require some explanation. As early as 1980 for instance, in his dialogue on House X, Eisenman had begun to question 'the role of man in Western culture since the Renaissance', in which our relations to the objects we make has been 'positivistic . . . a kind of conical unfolding from anthropocentric man as creator'.[33] One wonders how it could be otherwise – or why – but Eisenman sought to subvert it by 'an inversion of this unfolding', a rejection of any 'historical or narrative logic'. Rather than being formed of 'hierarchical relationships' which, since they are traditional, 'can be known', the objects we design, including buildings, will become 'fragmented, relativistic', not to mention 'autonomous', referring only to themselves and quite rejecting the world around them.

Eisenman's interest in such things was much extended by his entry to the Venice Biennale of 1985.[34] This required the creative re-use of two castles at Montecchio, outside Vicenza, associated in popular mythology with Shakespeare's *Romeo and Juliet*. Eisenman chose to leave the fabric of the castles alone, merely landscaping and connecting them by paths, one linear and direct, the other winding, both with architectural incidents evoking various elements of Shakespeare's play. Eisenman saw these as presenting 'binary oppositions' between 'love and conflict, strength and weakness, truth and untruth, life and death'.[35] These gave him themes for his programme, but by no means the necessary architectural forms. These he found by drawing parallels between the themes and the physical formation of Verona, the setting for *Romeo and Juliet*. Here he found his binary oppositions in the ancient Roman plan, with its *cardo* and *decumanus* dividing it into four sections, and the overlaid grid uniting them; and also with the River Adige whose S-shaped bend divides and unites two sections of the city, and with the legendary locations of incidents in the play, such as Juliet's house, with her balcony, and her tomb.

Eisenman worked these into his design by his processes of scaling, taking plans of Verona with the river, plans of the cemetery outside it, plans of Montecchio with the castles, plans of each castle separately and so on. He 'superposed' these in different colours, at different scales and at different angles to clarify his various binary oppositions. These drawings are printed as a boxed presentation on transparent film, as *Moving Arrows, Eros and Other Errors*;[36] plans of the city, the castles and the cemetery printed several times on the same transparency, at different scales and in different orientations. Eisenman looked for creative analogies in the various clashes and registrations between them. Thus by superposing these gorgeous transparencies Eisenman found elements for his design which took their meanings from each other rather than from some external context.

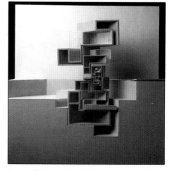

Peter Eisenman, Cannaregio project contextual object, Venice

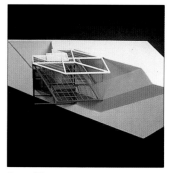

Peter Eisenman, House El Even Odd

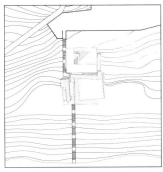

Peter Eisenman, Guardiola House,
Santa Maria del Mar

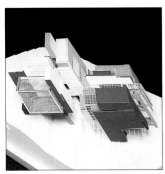

Peter Eisenman, House X

It was crucial for the concept of 'discontinuity' which Eisenman had used in Berlin that his site should be more than a 'here and now', a 'privileged presence'. It had a past, readable as a palimpsest, a present, certainly, but also a potential for the future, a 'quarry' for Eisenman of its 'immanence'. That is one aspect of his scaling, and 'recursivity' is another; his drawing of parallels between incidents in the play and the form of the city to give an actual programme. He could have used the binary oppositions which he found in both as sources for familiar architectural oppositions, such as function/form, structure/economics, inside/outside and so forth, but preferred instead to take the oppositions within the city plan and superpose them in his transparencies. Thus, his design for Juliet's castle includes versions of itself, a scaled-down plan of Verona with its grid, the river Adige and the cemetery, all realigned into a complex of superposed forms with multiple meanings.

Thus Eisenman achieves his third kind of scaling, 'self-similarity'. Most shortened accounts of the *Moving Arrows* text[37] omit this as unintelligible, and certainly there is much confusion. Yet given earlier applications, such as the Wexner armoury in its two versions, one can just about read something into 'self-similarity'. It means *analogic* repetition, not the 'geometric mimesis usually found in the aesthetic object'. But surely his grids are self-similar too? The point for Eisenman is that his building tells its own story without reference to things outside itself; a self-complete text rather than the mere representation of some evocative historic form. But it is hardly surprising that in his 1988 interview with Lynne Breslin Eisenman admits that in Romeo and Juliet, his theory of scaling was by no means properly articulated, that even in the *Moving Arrows* box 'we did not know what we were doing'.[38] The box is not a book, nor even a set of plans; it is another way for architecture to *be*, to have its own existence, as an 'artefact' quite different from an actual building.

Eisenman's definitions of discursivity, recursivity and self-similarity in *Moving Arrows* still remain rather impenetrable. So does his 'statement of position', his rationale for scaling on which so much of his later work is based. These hark back to hints in his dialogue on House X, and Eisenman says:

> For five centuries the human body's proportions have been a datum for architecture. But due to developments and changes in modern technology, philosophy, and psychoanalysis, the grand abstraction of man as a measure of all things, as an originary presence, can no longer be sustained, even as it persists in the architecture of today.[39]

He develops these ideas in more detail in later projects such as the Tokyo Opera House (1986), the University Art Museum at Long Beach in California[40] (1986 to the present), the Progressive Corporation in Cleveland, Ohio (1986), the Choral Work, a garden which he designed with Jacques Derrida for Tschumi's Parc de la Villette in Paris (1986 to the present) and the Guardiola House at Santa Maria del Mar on the Bay of Cadiz (1989). The Guardiola House is perhaps Eisenman's most extreme rejection of man 'as originary presence'. It is formed of three-dimensional 'els'

– cubes which are solid on three sides and open on the others, which can thus be seen as 'container and contained', defining, more or less, a 'place and non-place' which exists 'between the natural and the rational, between logic and chaos'. Nowhere has his brief been more 'destabilised' – and how radically different all this is to the approach of Coop Himmelblau, who see the human body as the actual, inevitable, physical generator of their designs, designs intended to stimulate human beings by the play of light on their forms.

Tschumi developed much of his 'anti-brief' thinking from his reading of French Post-Structuralism: Barthes, Foucault, Lacan and, of course, especially Derrida. He was also much influenced by the International Situationists in the late 1960s and gained from them the idea that 'events' are more important than 'functions'.[41] Like Coop Himmelblau Tschumi sees it as no longer valid to think that form follows function, in the simple-minded Modernist way. He drew from Foucault, he says, or rather Rajchman on Foucault, ideas of 'events' rather than 'functions', and for Tschumi an event is never fixed[42]; is by no means the beginning or end of anything. An event rather is a combination of space, action and movement which invites us constantly to rethink and reformulate our ideas; it is some kind of turning point which may lead us to question the actual physical setting in which we are performing it, may indeed suggest that it might be better in some other setting.

So things are constantly in a state of flux for Tschumi; his aim is to construct a 'heterotopia' – another term from Foucault – in which at any time we will be offered an infinity of choices stretching there before us, endlessly. The more complex, dislocated, fragmented and multiple the places on offer, the more we will be able to choose what it is that we, in that moment, actually want to do. On this basis Tschumi seeks a new direction for our times: no specific places for specific things. Instead of that he seeks a mutual 'contamination of all categories . . . constant substitutions . . . confusion of genres'. Nor does he see this as some unattainable ideal: Tschumi's heterotopia exists; here, now, available in the world's most exciting cities such as New York and Tokyo. The more bustling, the more crowded the city, the wider the range of choices it will offer. Tschumi loves the sheer confusion of such cities; the jostling juxtapositions of department stores, museums, health clubs, railway stations, putting-greens on roofs (in Tokyo at least) and so on – the antithesis to the Modern concept of 'zoning' in which such things were separated.

But Tschumi's aim goes further than simply recreating such confusion. He wishes to design conditions which force us to develop new kinds of society. Traditional cities were hierarchical, centred on the temple, the cathedral, palace, parliament or whatever. And so were the Modernists' cities with their strict zoning into places for working, places for living, and service locations. But Tschumi wants his cities to be non-hierarchical in form, non-traditional in their values. At first sight this savours of 'determinism', the architect's belief that by his planning he can force people to live in a certain way, which of course was the point of Le Corbusier's office towers, his housing slabs and so on. But since Tschumi's earnest desire is not to 'determine', to make 'determination' impossible, it does seem somewhat different in kind. Tschumi's aim is that we try to understand our current social, political and other circumstances, not to mention the processes by which the media promulgate them. Which these days of course are 'Pluralist'. Whilst Tschumi pursues that aim – which clearly is the purpose of his wider choices – he seems, like so many, not to have recognised that this is also the aim of so much recent literature by Harvey,[43] Jameson,[44] Rose[45] and many others, that such Pluralism is the essence of Post-Modern values. Of course one understands why for Tschumi, as for others, the architecture labelled 'Post-Modern' is some kind of anathema; why he hopes there will be no connection or association between his own work and that 'double coding' of Modernist SLEBS planning and facades with Classical detail – Quinlan Terry's Richmond River Front, Terry Farrell's Embankment Place – which we have come to know as 'Post-Modern'.

It's not such forms, it's the spirit that makes Post-Modernism; that Pluralist 'anything goes' which those theorists write about. And it's that Post-Modern spirit that Tschumi reflects in his aim for new cities that encourage new relationships between 'spaces' and 'events'. Of course like Eisenman, Coop Himmelblau and the others Tschumi challenges the traditional rules of architecture in 'Composition, Hierarchy and Order'.[46] For him, as for the others, there are no one-to-one, cause-and-effect relationships between 'form and function, structure and economics or (of course, architectural) form and program'. The point is to substitute for them 'new concepts of contiguity and superimposition', of 'permutation and substitution'.

In his project for the National Theatre of Japan, Tschumi started with music-like 'Notations' which helped him to deconstruct the traditional relationships between entrance lobbies, auditoria, stages, backstage facilities and so on into a series of 'bands' laid behind each other. By which, as he says, the 'deconstructed elements can be manipulated independently, according to conceptual, narrative, or programmatic concerns.' Tschumi took this 'banding' further in his design for Kansai International Airport, of which the most extraordinary elements are massively long 'wings' – totalling a mile in length – to either side of the central facilities, containing a 'band' of arrival and departure gates; a four-storey 'slab' containing hotel bedrooms, offices and so on; and another long, 12-metre wide block, the 'Wave', containing cinemas, exhibition spaces, swimming pools, golf courses, shooting galleries and so on. Access to these was by travelator following the curves of the Wave itself which, supported on the skew, was to stimulate the vertigo of early flying; beyond the Wave was another band of gates and connections. As Tschumi points out there would have been 'spectacular . . . disjunctions . . . stunning visual rifts' between his various bands; new kinds of modelled interior space indeed.

Tschumi's National Library for France was also an exercise in interactions: meeting points between circulation systems for the public, library staff, books, information systems and mechanical services. Also it seemed to Tschumi that the High (Electronic) Tech of library systems should be matched by the High (Electronic) Tech of circuit

training in the gym, so there was another circuit – a running track – on the roof, which determined a basically oval form enclosing the public facilities with book stacks and so on outside it. This approach gave, once again, dramatic internal spaces which could not have been achieved in other ways.

Like Tschumi, Lebbeus Woods has been fascinated since the middle 80s by the ways in which architecture might change people's lives, or rather, the things they might do if offered spaces which challenged them to live in new and different ways, encouraged them to challenge the status quo. Woods explores what he calls 'heterarchy', his vision of an urban life which frees individuals of the restrictions, the conventions imposed on them by the community.[47] Freed from such social constraints, might we begin to understand just what it is to be 'human'? For in Woods's view it is individuals, rather than communities or societies, that are 'the highest and most complete embodiment of the human'. Like Eisenman he sees recent developments in science and technology as liberating factors, not to mention new political freedoms. Given the ways in which it allows information to be accessed the electronic revolution has broken down traditional boundaries between global, national, regional and even local interests. Traditional hierarchies, government or commercial, can no longer hang onto their power; this too helps us regain our sense of 'human-as-individual'. We find our 'common, exalted basis' as humans through direct, sensory, sensual experience of kinds available only in architecture and the city. This lures Woods on in his search for a 'universcience', the basis for 'the architecture of a landscape suffused with the cool light of self-conscious intelligence and the radiance of transcendent love'.

So Woods has worked his way towards freedom for the individual, linked to others of his kind by electronic and other means in a series of projects. This concept seems to be a variation on the Archigram idea of 'module' or 'pod', but whilst Peter Cook's constructions were pristine in their engineering precision, Woods's seem to be decrepit; bashed, battered and rusting in metallic facets with forms which, in drawings at least, look much like Duchamp's *Nude Descending a Staircase*. So it was with his 'Geomagnetic Aeroliving Laboratories' of 1987; heavy, decaying metal 'airships' which were meant to be 'home laboratories or laboratories that are homes'.

Of course one understands that from 1961 to 1989 there was something Kafkaesque about living in divided Berlin. So it's hardly surprising that Woods should want to subvert the confronting political forces by burrowing underground to form a network of links from East to West, which erupted to the surface at the Alexanderplatz and elsewhere as towers; much like border-guards' towers overlooking the Wall, deconstructed into rusting metal frames and plates. These forms were earthbound as were Woods's Centricity Modules, but his Aerial Paris is based on quite opposite conditions. Instead of troglodytes, emerging surreptitiously to the light, his Parisians would be the 'aerial performers' of a flying 'circus', free in the skies over Paris. Housed in 'kinetic structures', they would form a Woodsian 'heterarchy' of 'gypsy experimenters'; experimenters, that

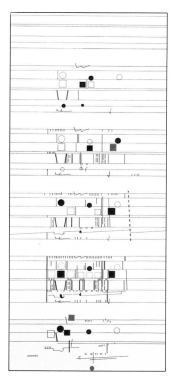

Bernard Tschumi, National Theatre of Japan, Tokyo, musical 'notation'

Lebbeus Woods, Zagreb Free Zone

is, in 'experience'. Woods intends this kind of freedom, slightly more constrained, for Zagreb and a united Berlin (for as the Wall was breached in 1989, Woods's Underground Berlin became redundant). So he developed two new and intriguing concepts, 'Freespaces' within a 'Free-Zone'. Woods saw his 'Freespaces' as hardly visible, snaking through existing structures; free from any predetermined purpose or meaning.

Woods was hoping to sow the seeds of an 'as yet unknown culture', of his free individuals joined to others only by electronic means, in speed-of-light interactions. These splendidly equipped computer hackers would have access to all the information hitherto restricted by institutions, governmental or commercial. So Woods's Free-Zone would be an 'electronically woven network' of Freespaces amounting, so he says, to 'a new urban pattern, a new way of living founded in the free-exchange of self-knowledge and the inhabitation of an entirely human Nature'. Of course as Berlin was opened up so it seemed 'ripe for development'. Big business moved in and tried to exercise its predictable corporate strategies, and the Government too sponsored conservation in the hope of making Berlin a tourist trap. Woods's purpose was to subvert these: his Free-Zone would be dangerous, subversive, a setting for anarchic events embedded in buildings at the heart of the city. Given their decaying, crumbling nature, the Freespaces would be quite unsuitable for conventional occupation: 'useless and meaningless', they would encourage anarchic views; anti-control or any form of determinism; anti- any institution, tolerated by the authorities only insofar as they remained hidden.

Whilst there was no chance that Woods's Berlin would ever be built his Free-Zone, Zagreb got very much nearer; a Freespace was commissioned for the Zagreb Museum as a Peter Cook-like module to be located and relocated by helicopter. But it looked as if Coop Himmelblau's Remodelling had taken a nose-dive off the Rooftop in Vienna, crashed and rusted. Unlike either of the Berlin Freespaces it is intended to be seen, visible and aggressive. And of course equipped with highly sophisticated electronic equipment so one can sit there, cooped-up physically, but 'free' mentally to tap the world's information sources: to make what use one can of the power such information brings. Indeed Woods's Freespaces represent in many ways the extreme of Martin Pawley's *Private Future*,[48] all-embracing 'pods' doing for all the senses what Walkmans do for the ears. Like Coop Himmelblau Woods insists that no uses are determined: uses are 'invented by those who claim Freespace as their own'. He positively exults in the 'difficulty of occupation' so 'the fainthearted' need not apply. There's an 'absence of discernible order' in which 'hierarchy is frustrated, heterarchy is unavoidable'. But since given even Zagreb's population there won't be enough Freespaces to go round, someone will have to decide who gets one!

So what is on offer here from Tschumi, Woods and the others is a ferment of creative ideas in opposition, often directly, to the more dismal aspects of 'socially responsible' architecture, indeed of 'social responsibility' itself. Take SLEBS, for instance, that unbearable flatness of so many Modern interiors. It never raised the spirits, not even in the Villa Savoye; indeed few things could be more lowering. So it's hardly surprising that many architects recently have concentrated on the three-dimensional modelling of interior space.

INTERIOR SPACE

Architects like Nigel Coates, Coop Himmelblau, Zaha Hadid, Philippe Starck and others seem to design in ways which have gone deliberately anti-SLEBS.[49] They may not use the term – that doesn't matter – but they do give us more to inhabit than the space between the slabs, the space between slab and false ceiling.

In Coop Himmelblau's Open House or their Rooftop Remodelling the inside is the outside in the sense that the glazing in which they are clad offers little in the way of visual separation between the two. Such division as there may be is hinted at by a mesh of glazing bars. Robert Venturi, of course, was perfectly clear that failure to separate the inside and outside was one of the great shortcomings of the Modern Movement; he saw it as precluding two things: the design of coherent interior spaces – internal 'sculpture' as it were – and the design of coherent external masses, sympathetic to the city. To which one might add the environmental problems, solar heat gain and so on, of so much Modern Movement overglazing. There is much to be said for his arguments, although Coop Himmelblau have very much more to offer than your usual, bleak and rather soulless Modern Movement glass box. And the Open House, after all, is conceived as a passive energy system.

But in later projects they seem to be offering more enclosure of the kind which Venturi sought.[50] Their Rehak House, designed for a steep, south-facing slope on an isthmus at Malibu, consists of two Hadid-like beams crossing each other to give an X-shape elevation so that one directs views downwards towards the sea and the other away from it towards the city. There are flying platforms, accessible rooftops and a tower which ties all the volumes together. And their Jasmac Bar for Sapporo, Japan is designed for a high, narrow and rather shallow site. Coop Himmelblau wanted to build moveable rooms, flying staircases and burning walls but these proved too much for the client. So the facade is a collage of deconstructed planes, fairly open to street, whereas the rear facade, a Rooftop Remodelling up-ended with an opaque membrane, curves up, round and over as the bars (for drinking) get smaller and more expensive. The flying staircase more or less survives with six such bars attached, ascending from the basement. The lower ones are substantially level but with sections of sloping floor, whereas the upper ones have completely sloping floors which must be especially disorientating for those in advanced states of inebriation. The topmost is a shaded glass cube.

Of all these internal spatial-adventurers Nigel Coates, perhaps, comes nearest to the idea of accepting vertical columns and horizontal ceilings. Even so, in his Caffè Bongo, Tokyo, having entered under an aircraft-as-portico – a wing with suspended engines – one finds a huge wing, internally, curving round the room, which divides it into two storeys. And in the Bohemia Jazz Club, also in Tokyo, there are similar devices with 'engines' planned as parts of the air-conditioning system. But he moves into three dimensions in Sapporo with his Arca di Noè Restaurant. Externally this is a Noah's Ark, surmounted by a robust Classical temple. But internally the posts of the SLEBS construction become such sculptural objects in their own right that the spaces they contain take on the quality we seek. And in his Glasgow Katharine Hamnett shop, or his Jigsaw in the King's Road, the walls and ceiling fuse together in a manner of which Gaudí would have been proud.

Philippe Starck, too, in his early work seemed to accept the 'realities' of straight up and down construction. But as Boissière says, he sees the bar or restaurant as the place where people are most likely to be themselves, human, convivial.[51] They make spectacular entrances, causing frissons of excitement almost akin to stage fright. They give themselves up to the pleasures of drink, gesticulate more wildly than usual, engage in games of seduction. They speak eloquently of the world and its affairs, so it's settings for such things that Starck provides, drawing on the trappings of theatre: foyers, grand staircases, balconies, stage, proscenium, wings, boxes, galleries and so on, in lavish materials such as marble, velvet and lead, whose rich colours and subtle lighting may conjure up comfort or unease, sexual excitement or metaphysical calm. Starck sees the toilets in particular as areas of extreme sophistication; places for convivial conversations, the transaction of business, voyeurism, exhibitionism. There is a perversion about them which, for Boissière, suggests they may be places where those 'acting out the loss of innocence of the metropolis might foregather'.[52]

Starck first began to display such ideas at the Café Costes in Paris with its two huge Rossi-like columns-as-cylinders supporting the balcony and framing the grand staircase. The roof too is Rossi-like in section, but glazed. Then increasingly Starck opted for glamour, the most obvious quality of his Manin Restaurant in Tokyo, where he disguised the Modernist concrete frame by painting it black and using velvet-padded walls and mahogany panelling to mould within it a space of great richness. Here too are sophisticated washrooms with white, semicircular basins reflected in blue glass. This sumptuousness extends to the Hotel Royalton in New York with its Baroque portico leading to a Rossi-columned lobby, its main circulation route marked by Brigitte Starck's dark blue carpet bordered with white birds and fish, extending into the rich, dark blue corridors, and there are sober colours too in the bedrooms with their mahogany panelling, grey-green carpets and walls. The Hotel Paramount, also in New York, has equally rich interiors with, in the lobby, red roses sprouting from the marble wall. Indeed the whole is full of Starck's amusing detail, such as the curvaceous chaise-longue of riveted bronze plates by Mark Newson, the mahogany, tree-like postcard stand, the angel-like 'protector' for a marble clad corner and so on. The Paramount's washrooms have deeply conical metal basins, within a robust steel table, whilst the toilet cubicles are patterned riotously in tiles, brick red, light blue, off-white, ochre, black and so on.

Glamorous as these may be, Starck's *tour de force* is undoubtedly the Teatriz Restaurant in Madrid which he sees as a 'balance . . . of fantasy, rigour, and sympathy' intended to 'give emotion whilst remaining friendly, make up fantasy whilst remaining rigorous, and create ambiguous places whilst remaining elegant'. There is a light entrance hall with tapering-barrel columns, and the restaurant itself has a painted, Surrealist floor based on a de Chirico painting. The Classical ceiling has long grey velvet drapes, forming almost a tent, whilst the approach to the bar from the restaurant is by way of a narrow proscenium with curtain. Beyond that is an elegant gold bar but once one passes through the proscenium this turns out to be at the bottom of an old stage tower with its original rough brick facing and stage mechanisms showing. The washrooms here have marble basins on equally Baroque supports. The toilet cubicles, however, are separate 'towers' in blue tile with matching metal doors.

But of all the New Spirits it is perhaps Zaha Hadid who provides the most spectacular interiors. For years there were those who predicted that whatever her skill as an artist, Hadid could never build. But of course she has proved them wrong, at Sapporo, Gröningen and elsewhere. Her restaurant at Sapporo, the Moonsoon, is a complex interior within a very simple building: a compressed and dynamic inside within a thoroughly static outside. The interior too has its contrasts between a formal restaurant and a lounge for relaxation. Hadid sees these as strange and synthetic worlds, diametrically opposed to each other as 'fire' and 'ice'.

So the icy ground floor is cool in its greys and greens, formed largely of glass and metal. It is traditional in Sapporo to make ice buildings in the winter, and the tables seem like sharp broken fragments of ice drifting at strange angles across a non-existent pond, whilst the huge ceiling grille, of concentric half-ovals, looks like nothing so much as the inside of a whale. Upstairs everything is different: Hadid describes 'a fire in brilliant reds, yellows and oranges. A bar which tears through the ceiling of the ground floor spirals up to the underside of the dome like a fiery tornado bursting a pressure vessel.' Elsewhere a 'plasma' of organic shapes allows sofa backs and trays to be 'plugged in' at any point so that eating and lounging may be combined in an infinity of arrangements.

Hadid's interiors are modelled from quite unfamiliar and rather abstract shapes, yet there are enough points of human reference, stairs, bars, seats and so on, to help us know what size we are in relation to the vastly intricate spaces. A sculptural form, Hadid's 'orange peel', swoops down from the ceiling to the bar where we can touch it, feel how big it is in relation to ourselves. And thus by entirely non-traditional means everything works together, space, form, lighting and so on, to give us a sense of enclosure, of being in a space designed as sculpture.

INDIVIDUAL BUILDINGS

Hadid clearly is concerned with design for the delight of the senses, as was Tschumi at La Villette, Gehry at Vitra and so on, unlike those Modernists, old and new, whose primary concern is purity of geometric form. Most of the

Nigel Coates, L'Arca di Noè, Sapporo

Zaha Hadid, Moonsoon Restaurant, Sapporo

Philippe Starck, Nani Nani, Tokyo

Arquitectonica, Miracle Center, Miami

New Spirits are sensualists in this way. Some, it is true, just seem to deal in funny shapes. One could say that of Starck as architect rather than interior designer. Indeed there are those who wish he wouldn't do buildings, that his talents should be reserved for small-scale objects of industrial design: lemon squeezers and toothbrushes, chairs and so on. It's hardly surprising that Starck employs no systematic process, that his work is entirely intuitive. Like Eisenman or Tschumi in their very different ways Starck likes to call everything into question, which he does with great humour and wit, not to mention wide-eyed naivety.

Starck's Nani Nani, in Tokyo, is a striking, oozing form: a great, green, narrow 1930s wireless set – almost about to tip over – with horizontal bands of windows wrapped around its curving ends. Starck sees it as a massive object, imposed upon the city for the sole purpose of 'unleashing stupefaction'. Indeed Starck declares that as far as buildings are concerned he only likes 'monsters'. For him the ideal city would be a 'conglomeration of out-of-scale objects, full of energy and vitality'. His Asahi Beer Building in Tokyo is also a Starck 'funny shape'; an inverted pyramid of polished black granite plunging into an illuminated plinth. The trapezoidal walls are punctured by tiny, glowing, circular openings and the whole is topped by a massive gold, pointed horizontal flame – or is it a tear? – whose bulbous 'base' barely seems to touch the roof on which it stands. For Starck the luminous base 'plays with energy', the pyramidal 'urn' with 'mystery' and the flame maintains his building 'as a place of passion'.

Arquitectonica too use funny shapes of that kind.[53] Their Center for Innovative Technology in Virginia contains offices and research laboratories for the Software Productivity Consortium with an exhibition hall, briefing and press rooms, classrooms, a fitness centre, dining facilities and so on. It has four storeys of parking and a landscaped roof deck out of which emerges an inverted pyramid of offices very much like Starck's Asahi. There are similar forces at work in their Shopping Center for Atlanta with 120,000 feet of shops, restaurants, cafés and night clubs contained within two storeys on a sloping site giving access from both sides. The central plaza has a reflecting pool, towers and bridges dominated by a geodesic sphere. And their sumptuous Banco di Credito in Lima is built around an open courtyard, echoing Spanish Colonial houses, with a four-storey SLEBS alternation of grey marble and blue glass standing on white piloti. But the sheer horizontality is interrupted by projecting bays, square and rectangular – abstracted Colonialism again – whilst the circular entrance hall penetrates up through the various layers to emerge as a cylinder projecting through the roof. Their Miracle Center for Miami consists of a plinth containing four storeys of parking over which are two storeys of mixed-use development: 230,000 square feet of shops, ten movie theatres and a health club. And hovering over this there is a nine-storey tower containing 98 apartments. But the most extraordinary features are the trapezoidal, decorative 'plates' of simulated black and white marble hovering in front of the plinth.

Rem Koolhaas and OMA also use distorted geometric forms. Their Netherlands Institute for Architecture and

Building, yet again, had an inverted pyramidal office tower over a podium which contained entrance, exhibition gallery and library. Their (built) National Dance Theatre for The Hague is a somewhat clumsy collage in which an inverted, truncated gold cone is surrounded by disparate geometric blocks: Modernist – with horizontal windows – and even Post-Modernist with unmatching diagonal cladding, sloping roofs, curtain walled areas and so on.

ENVIRONMENTAL DETERMINANTS

Whilst Starck, Koolhaas and others might design the same building for different sites, even for different cities – Arquitectonica, at least, will often anchor a building against a slope – others derive apparently wilful forms from developing much closer dialogues with the context into which they are building.

Günter Behnisch, for instance, produced perhaps the most complex deconstruction of (internal) building forms and frames – apart, conceivably, from Coop Himmelblau's – in the Hysolar Institute at Stuttgart, and followed this with others in the Library of the Catholic University at Eichstätt, the Secondary School at Schäfersfeld, his German National Bank at Frankfurt and State Clearing Bank at Stuttgart. But in his Extension to the German Postal Museum in Frankfurt he was far more concerned with fitting into an established context; building next to the existing museum. His site is so limited that he put two storeys of exhibition space under the garden of the existing villa and a new three-storey block along the west side, containing the entrance, information desk, a shop, a cafeteria and an auditorium. The two upper levels are for exhibitions, permanent and temporary, and the strict metal-clad rectilinearity is broken by a large, semicircular glazed lean-to, for vertical circulation but crucial also for admitting daylight into the lower levels. Its circular formation is reflected in the ramps, balconies and auditorium.

Jean Nouvel too was constrained by his site for the Institut du Monde Arabe in Paris where the Boulevard St Germain meets the river Seine. The northern side of his northern block, a nine-storey museum, follows this curve whilst his narrow southern block, a ten-storey library, is a strict rectangle and the visible structure is entirely metal and glass. So for example the lift shafts and the library staircase thrill those who are moved by such things. So does the southern wall of the library; an extremely clever play on Islamic forms in what looks like curtain-walling etched with patterns of tiling from the Alhambra. On closer inspection, however, it is apparent that far from being etched the glass is clear, with behind it an immensely complex arrangement of camera-like irises: 70-odd to each square panel with a large one in the centre and smaller ones clustered around it.

In principle they open and close according to the measured intensity of solar radiation, and indeed one sees them moving as clouds pass across the sun. As Nouvel says, 'The most difficult task was to explain to the client that this construction was not a simple curtain blind but a light-control mechanism, which is naturally much more expensive.'[54] He suggests that electrically controlled Venetian blinds would have been simpler, more efficient and much cheaper: 'But it would have been no fun at all.' Every schoolboy knows that once the sun's heat gets into such a greenhouse it warms up anything in its path, including Nouvel's irises, which then re-radiate the heat back into the building. And simple observation shows that the building's users find them inadequate, hence the improvised blinds, curtains and screens. But the important thing for Nouvel is that 'for the first time technology has been harnessed and money spent purely for pleasure . . . selling sensation instead of function.'

Odile Decq and Benoît Cornette had a better answer in outside screens. They stop the solar heat before it gets to the glass as, say, in their Banque Populaire at Rennes. So their curved glazed facade has a complex arrangement of screens on outriggers, forming an openwork diagonal mesh. Indeed it seems they are fascinated by screens, which they show in their *Model is the Message* in which low green screens define an intermittent corridor and high red ones, at right angles, and with large openings, define possibly useable spaces.

Hasegawa too uses screens, in profusion. At first sight she seems to have been turning to Gaudí in her search for ways of sculpting space. Her Nagoya Pavilion is a Gaudí-like translation – into perforated metal – of natural forms such as trees and the parabolic dome of his Palacio Guell multiplied many times over. The main facade of Shonandai Cultural Centre is a reworking too – again with perforated metal screens – of his Casa Battló whilst the courtyard has geometricised trees much like the Sagrada Familia. And Hasegawa's Tower of Wind and Light is a metallic, if smaller, Sagrada Familia spire. Hasegawa's domes savour somewhat of Disney World, or at least of EPCOT, but few interior spaces have used services to such effect for the sculpting of space as her (black) auditorium. Small wonder that Bognar describes the Centre as an assemblage of 'dispersed and collaged architectural elements . . . exposed to and animated by light, wind and sound',[55] suggesting also that they 'allude to natural formations . . . [and] become analogous to some fictive or symbolic landscapes buried in the Japanese collective memory'.

Morphosis draw even more from the landscape into which they are building, as they suggest in describing their Chiba Project, a golf club two hours out of downtown Tokyo: there they concerned themselves with interactions between the natural landscape and their architecture, between nature and the man-made, so as to break down distinctions between the two.[56] Like Tschumi at La Villette Morphosis attempt to engage all the senses as one moves around their building/landscape, perceiving their work 'as an instrument of measure, a sum of knowledge, capable of organising time and space'. This is at odds to Eisenman, who wants to exclude man as the 'measure' of all things.

Like Coop Himmelblau, Morphosis too draw on the human body since they see golf as a game of movement with the rhythm of walking from green to green, the arc of an arm in full swing, the nature and sequence of physical spaces in and around their buildings, the forms of which emerge from movement patterns: of automobiles, of drivers and pedestrians. The curved wall at the entry derives from a turning circle and beyond it lies a linear sequence of

volumes accommodating various functions. A second circular wall embraces the larger landscape facilitating movement between the golf course and the pavilion for dining and social events. Morphosis see their two curved walls as holding in place their more static inner spaces – essentially contemplative and introspective – whilst the social pavilion is exposed to the natural setting in all its vastness. Their muted colours suggest buildings growing out of the landscape, indeed Morphosis aspire to an environment which is more than just a 'truce' with nature, one which is a statement of 'man and nature', rather than just of 'man versus nature'.

The same attitude permeates the design by Morphosis for a Performing Arts Pavilion in the San Fernando Valley, Los Angeles. Here they look for correspondences between the wide geographic context, the actual site and their Pavilion which, in principle, is a response to the relentless uniformity of the Los Angeles suburban grid. What's more their site was within the Sepulvada Basin, a man-made landscape designed to prevent water from flooding the Valley. Which of course presented them with a conflict of nature and modern engineering; the landscape was neither natural nor beautiful, but it was necessary. So Morphosis took alignments from the suburban grid and the man-made landscape to produce three intersections which mark the distribution of people, of cars and of water. They see these intersections as 'figures' against the 'ground' of their Pavilion, emphasising sequences of movement; patrons' arrival by car, parking and movement through the landscape into their foyer and their theatres.

Their design is layered vertically since most of their Pavilion – a strange word in this context – is buried into the ground. One enters by a sunken piazza, a 'place of appropriate scale' as prelude to their vast sunken foyer, a complex space between their 1,800-seat theatre and their 500-seat, multi-use 'black box'. This gives access to the facilities one might expect, cloakrooms and so on, whilst staircases and ramps project into the foyer, like tentacles, from the auditoria – as one looks up between them one can see overhead intersecting paths, cars parked at higher levels and so on.

The auditoria, of course, rise towards the surface where a beam-shaped building accommodates the administration whilst masking the fly tower, bar and roof of the large theatre, supported by a bowstring truss. These are the only components of the Pavilion proper to emerge above the actual ground plane, and according to Morphosis they are conceived as (somewhat Constructivist) sculptural incidents in the landscape, making connections to other, smaller buildings in the surrounding park. The whole aim of digging down was to 'de-scale and fragment' their theatre complex so it would not stand out, pavilion-like, but would be integrated, literally, into the landscape. It is, they say, 'a building of the earth and makes a direct connection to the Greek or Roman Theatre (Delphi)'.

So the landscape overlays the building, extends the character of the architecture onto the site without extending the actual built forms. The park is still a field of reeds and wild grasses punctuated by those masses and voids against which is actually revealed the presence of build-

Itsuko Hasegawa, Nagoya Pavilion

Odile Decq and Benoît Cornette, Banque Populaire, Rennes

Frank Gehry, Vitra Design Museum, Weil am Rhein

ing. Within the landscape there is an outdoor amphitheatre, and landscape rooms for dining, for contemplation and recreation, intersected by the thrusting circulation beams of the theatre.

Unifying all this, however, is a pedestrian link at the highest level, some 30 feet wide and suspended from a bowstring truss. This, the most visible feature at surface level, connects a linear system of parking, some of it underground, whilst water channels, and indeed a lake, bring the landscape 'into the conceptual structure of the scheme'. The abstract grid of intersections, pedestrian walkways, water channels and so on, links to various man-made features providing conscious oppositions to the natural landscape. The Morphosis collaboration of artist and architect, architect and artist produced this sky structure, this sky-walk, to balance and challenge the architecture of the earth, and the sloping nature of the site allows an extension of the foyer/lobby arrangement to be continued as an observation platform from which one may perceive the overall order of the park and distant connections to the vast suburban horizon.

It's interesting that the other southern Californian, Frank Gehry, also seems increasingly concerned by the way in which his context and environmental factors might help determine his building forms. In the case of his Vitra Museum the basic determinant was natural lighting, whereas in his Disney Concert Hall for Los Angeles acoustic considerations are of paramount importance. Gehry's presentation at the Venice Biennale in 1991 was perhaps the most public demonstration of his methods in action. There were, first of all, his conceptual sketches: very fuzzy drawings indeed, somewhat like Felix Topolski portraits overlaid by so many networks of lines that one could see a person's face emerging in many guises. So it is with Gehry's notional drawings; many forms could have emerged from what he drew but in each case the actual form emerged from a multiplicity of models. Indeed, he says, in describing his design process – for the American Center in Paris – 'I had an idea', which of course he crystallised in sketches. And nothing fundamental changed, but: 'the way in which I work, starting with models which, little by little, I bring into focus, inevitably takes far too long. I spend a great deal of time on site discussing with the client and I meet a lot of people.' In the case of his Concert Hall Gehry displayed sets of 30 or so models each to show how various parts of his building developed including overall form, auditorium shape and so on but with many more creative variations for each.[57] The result, as it seems to be emerging, will be a veritable explosion of highly functional forms and spaces making Scharoun's Berlin Philharmonie look positively chaste.

Even though his neighbour in Los Angeles, the existing 1960s Music Pavilion, is by no means distinguished architecture, Gehry respected its presence: as he says, he couldn't stop its being there, its very presence was a fact. Indeed the Pavilion was built 'with a great deal of care, by people who thought that they were realising a work of considerable importance.' So of course to deny that would have been presumptuous. It's hardly surprising, therefore, that Gehry's contextual sensitivity extends to the Paris of the Rue de Bercy around his American Center. So he says of the adjacent buildings that, whatever their quality, he must accept their proximity and try to bring out whatever basic beauty they may have.

So it was an 'elementary courtesy' that Gehry construct something 'acceptable to France', taking account of context, scale and proportion, the wishes, the Frenchness of the French.[58] Gehry saw his building as 'An American in Paris' but he wanted to express the Americanness of America which he saw as a matter of cultural mixing, a 'blending' together of functions, circulation and so on, to present in many modes the 'American Way of Life'; by movies and theatre, language classes, food and drink, exhibitions, shopping, living – there are apartments – and by the sheer animation of people moving around, such as one finds in a John Portman hotel or indeed the Pompidou Centre. So there will be interactions between the spaces; restaurant, multi-purpose hall and so on. He wants to experiment with the very nature of the building itself, which Gehry sees as a grand, if complex 'unity', transparent enough for multiple activities to show. But Gehry is building in Paris, not Los Angeles, Malibu or Santa Monica, not far indeed from Notre Dame. So how should 'Paris' be expressed? By respecting the character of the city whilst inserting something new and different, expressive of American *joie de vivre*.

The site is one block from the River Seine, near the Gare de Lyon: a 170-foot frontage along the Rue de Bercy and a depth of 170 feet south of that, but with a corner splayed off in a 66-foot triangle facing a small park. There's street life in Paris of a kind one cannot find in California so Gehry's north and east facades, forming an L-shape, respect this Parisian form: 'simple, comfortable, polite to the street and the existing surroundings'. The facade to the Rue de Bercy is 'calm', broken, even, into two linked masses responding in scale to its neighbours; it even has store fronts like theirs. But the space contained by Gehry's L-shape faces the little Square de Bercy and the splayed-off corner of his site. Gehry found this 'major torture' but filled the space within his 'L' with a quarter-circle of building modelled with his characteristic exuberance. Halfway round for instance, there's a huge canopy; a Parisian 'mansard' slipped down to street level behind which is a sculpted tower of lift shafts and escape stairs. Beyond this again there's an atrium which starts square but gets progressively squeezed to a curved slot as it passes up six floors of the building and is glazed in its higher reaches. Left of this again is a two-storey restaurant with a blank-facaded cinema above it and over that again the building breaks out into a Vitra-like sculptural apartment which Gehry calls the 'pineapple'. There are sober, rectilinear apartments within the street corner, and right of the entrance there is a larger theatre; above this a language school, an exhibition hall, dance studios and workshops for associated artists with sculpted balconies and escape stairs along the eastern side. The theatre has a five-storey, glazed foyer with a full-height Frank Stella.

As he was conceiving the Center, says Gehry, he thought of buildings as 'bottles'. A single bottle just 'sits' there but when you put a cluster together they generate an 'energy' between them. Asked if he said 'bottles' or 'bodies', Gehry opined that it might be both! 'Bodies' reminded him of those Parisians who see his canopy as the skirt of a swirling ballerina. The Centre, he says, is like a ballet dancer: 'lifting her skirt, inviting people to come inside . . . the ballerina lifts her skirt . . . and, since I'm a dirty old man, that's the way you enter the building.'

The most extraordinary piece of 90s contextualism however, deriving culturally and physically from its context, will be Daniel Libeskind's Jewish Extension to the Berlin Museum. Like Coop Himmelblau, Eisenman, Tschumi and others Libeskind too questions the very nature of architecture: he sees most architects as founding their buildings in the 'realities' of physics: in materials, climate and so on.[59] But whilst buildings are made of bricks and glass there is rather more to them than that. To think of them only in such terms is like thinking of human beings as founded on 'fish and protozoa'. Of course they are, 'but there is a difference between foundation and *formation*.' It's 'formation' that interests Libeskind, something that 'has to do with desire'; much as Kahn used to speak of 'what the buildings wants to be'! For Libeskind it is 'immanence' rather than the 'concrete reality' of an object.

Libeskind has explored the 'non-physical' aspects of architecture in a number of ways, such as his Micromegas, including such exquisite drawings as his 'Arctic Flowers' in which a complexity of lines – some of them looking like architectural forms – implies an unfathomable multiplicity of dimensions. Then there were the three machines he crafted, with exquisite labour, for the Venice Biennale of 1985: the Reading Machine containing books, the Memory Machine which was a little 'theatre of architecture' and the Writing Machine, a kind of hand-cranked prototype computer. And of course there are his extraordinary word games in the manner of Gertrude Stein: 'Will to Power, Powe r willt o, Erw illtopow' and so on, not to mention his stream-of-consciousness essays in the manner of James Joyce such as 'Fishing from the Pavement'. Above all Libeskind's belief is that in his beam for Berlin 'the unsupportable supports the support . . . retrieving Utopia from the pit . . . '

Which might be a description of the way he approached the design of his Jewish Extension to the Berlin Museum.[60] Given the profundity of his theme, the unspeakable fate of the Jews at the hands of the Nazis in Berlin, their actual extermination in the Holocaust – Libeskind's mode of designing could not be more different from that of the Modernists. He thought of two intersecting lines; one zig-zag and the other straight. The zig-zag is built of solid, parallel walls supporting floors, whilst the straight one is a 'slot', a void of space passing through the floors of the zig-zag. The actual forms of Libeskind's zig-zag were devised in extraordinary ways: by looking for addresses of those Jews in Berlin who contributed so much to cultural history, all those writers, scientists, composers, artists and poets, including Arnold Schönberg and Ludwig Mies van der Rohe. Having found them Libeskind connected their addresses by straight lines across the city, and this gave him the elongated Star of David which provided the basis of his form.

Libeskind was interested too in Arnold Schönberg, the theorist of Twelve-Tone in which the composer, anxious to avoid the sense of hierarchy given by traditional key signatures, B flat, C sharp and so on, determines to write in no particular key. It is hardly surprising that over the years Schönberg found it increasingly difficult to 'centre' such music, to make it 'hang together'. But the unity he found lacking in the music itself could be replaced by setting words which had a compositional structure of their own. This process led Schönberg to an impasse in his masterwork, the opera *Moses and Aaron*, which he found himself unable to complete. Because, although he could write music for Aaron's populist 'revelations' of their God, he could not find music for the 'revealed and unimaginable truths' of Moses himself – and therefore left them as spoken words.

Given the fate of the Jews in Berlin, few of their possessions remain. So what exactly was there to be displayed? Libeskind obtained from the government in Bonn two large, leather-bound volumes giving the names of all those lost in the Holocaust, including the dates of their births, dates of transportation, presumed place of death and so on. And finally Libeskind gave 'shape' to the route through his Museum, presented a sequence of relevant experiences, by drawing on Walter Benjamin's essay 'One Way Street', his description of the urban apocalypse. Thus Libeskind offers a sequence of events, some 60 'stations of the star' as one moves along his zig-zag route. The crucial point for Libeskind is that the history of the Jews in Berlin is bound up, at one with, the history of Modernity itself.

This of course is an extreme example, where space itself is used for poetic, even religious purposes as an exhibit – the 'void' in essence is all that remains of Judaism in Berlin, and is for that reason the essence of Libeskind's concept, as he says:

> There is a Void in the building that is built as a space
> but the use of which is precisely its uselessness, ie it
> is not used as a normal museum in which to put
> normal museum objects.

MEDIA CENTRES

Gehry and Libeskind of course will be using various kinds of media to display the American Way of Life, or the fate of the Jews in Berlin, and it's hardly surprising that architects at the forefront of developments should be intrigued by the possibilities for design presented by the new media. Zamp Kelp and Haus Rucker for instance used video monitors to display jewellery in their 'Ornamenta 1: Built Fiction' exhibition at Pforzheim. The exhibits were very small, art in miniature, which could easily have got lost in conventional displays. There weren't enough rooms either so they penetrated the existing building and site with square blue pillars. They had solid outer skins, somewhat like the 'monolith' in Stanley Kubrick's *2001*, which had instant intelligence for those who touched it. Like Kubrick's, Haus Rucker saw their columns as appearing in different places at different times to deliver their portentous message: civilisation revalued through the culture of jewellery. Video monitors were mounted into the columns so the latter could

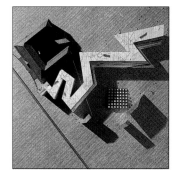

Daniel Libeskind, Jewish Extension to the Berlin Museum

Günther Zamp Kelp and Haus Rucker, 'Ornamenta 1' exhibition pieces

'reveal' themselves and their real or imaginary contents: apparently weightless jewellery gliding through space.[61]

Their Mekka Medial for the Gare d'Austerlitz in Paris was a multi-media installation with 40 cubic spaces in which events of various kinds could take place, opening downwards through the floor plane. Suspended above these was a yellow cube housing facilities for broadcasting and administration. The cube looked as though it were hovering – it had a single bee's wing and it was meant to 'focus' Western media much as the Ka'aba in Mecca focuses Islam. It could be manoeuvred over any of the open cubes to transmit to the rest of the world whatever was taking place there. Haus Rucker Company's Transformation Bunker is a Jewish Museum, serving for Cologne much the same purpose as Libeskind's for Berlin. In their case the museum is sited on the Körnerstrasse where atrocities against the Jews actually took place; there is a Rossi-like 'memory' to this place. Yet Haus Rucker wanted to evoke the feeling that in the surrounding streets normal life continued quite unscathed. So they designed a two-storey 'bunker' – a solid concrete structure – to contain cultural events and on its upper floor a documentation centre. Over this rose a three-storey, triangular-section steel frame housing a kindergarten, living units and over these again exhibition and action rooms. Then at the top in the narrow part of the frame, a platform affording views over the city. Most potent of all, however, was a blue pillar, rising out of the 'bunker'; much like those at Pforzheim but 30 metres high, housing Droese's *I have killed Anne Frank*.

Haus Rucker's Centre for Art and Media Technology at Karlsruhe was to be a 30-metre cube with a huge sliding door to the east and other facilities grouped within the thickness of the walls, floor and roof, and with gantries across the middle. The exterior would be varied to the building's different uses and even its appearance was to range from that of a solid cube to a much more delicate, even transparent one; Haus Rucker thought it should be difficult 'for the visitor to comprehend the whole'. Then their Exhibition Project for Seville was a large rectangular shed, double-skinned, steel-framed and open to the square which fronted it, but with a water curtain down its open end and a circular drum, hovering some eight metres above the square, with escalator access to changing displays, such as an Alpine panorama constructed of glass crystal.

Krueger and Kaplan's Art Park was less specifically a building. They designed it for a small 'canyon' at Lewistown, New York, formed by the demolition of an old railway tunnel. Its central feature was a large metallic 'thing', a tailless Manta Ray suspended within the canyon and equipped with infra-red sensors to detect approaching visitors from one end or the other of the canyon and to monitor their presence, location, movement or stillness within it.[62] To which the thing would respond in appropriate ways, with arousal, defensiveness, aggression, paranoia, boredom or confusion; it had 15 built-in patterns of 'behaviour', triggered by the humans below. Such responses were 'expressed' by fluids, still or swirling within the 'wings' of the thing, the shooting-out or withdrawal of power antennae, the flashing of fog lamps, rear lights from trucks and so on. If, having arrived, visitors simply stayed

passive, the thing would go dormant too, but if they kept milling around then it would become quite agitated. The point was to develop a new field; not so much Artificial Intelligence as 'Artificial Personality'; to give visitors the feeling that the thing was *watching*, contemplating them, that there was more to its behaviour than any simple, one-to-one, mechanical responses; that the thing had moods which affected its behaviour.

Diller and Scofidio too use video and other projections in their installations and performance art. In 1987, for instance, they built 'sets and body constructions' for Susan Mosakowski's *The Rotary Notary and his Hot Plate,* a re-enactment of Marcel Duchamp's 'Large Glass' *The Bride Stripped Bare by her Bachelors, Even* in the very museum (Philadelphia) where the original is displayed. The 'stage' was divided by a stretched rubber screen into 'front' and 'back'; behind the screen there was a bed and above this a large mirror, which, at 45 degrees to the horizontal, reflected the bed and whoever lay on it, apparently above the screen. So the 'bride' might occupy the space in front of the screen while the 'bachelor' lay on the bed behind it, with his disembodied head projecting through a hole giving a 'chain of commands' to his body. The screen/bed arrangement might be rotated through 180 degrees, bringing the bachelor to the front, but he and the bride would always be on opposite sides of the screen. At any one time there might be a real bride and a 'virtual' bachelor, or a real bachelor and a virtual bride. The bride wore an 'exoskeleton' and 'chastity armor', while the bachelor constructed a 'virtual suit' around himself, representing the figures of Duchamp's *Nine Malic Moulds*. There was also Duchamp's *Eyewitness* as a voyeur, and a *Juggler of Gravity*. The 'line of gravity' – Diller and Scofidio's screen – 'becomes a revised proscenium', dividing male and female, the actual and the illusory, 'physical and pataphysical'.

Fascinated too by architectural elements, Diller and Scofidio made their *Urban Suburban Rural Windows*, an installation for the Milan Triennale of 1986, with bracketed shelves and, above and below these, tiny model chairs projecting horizontally from the wall and reflected in diagonal mirrors. Their *Inside-Out: The Window on the Garden* was a series of self-reflecting mirrors of which the artists said:

> The window reconciles the original violation of the wall . . . The window is a legal limit that tempts the uninvited. The window is an apparatus that conspires with other machines to homogenise the weather.
> The window resists horizontal load and breeds dust.

Their *withDrawing Room: versions and subversions* of 1987 was a 'probe into the conventions of private life'. They took a house on Capp Street in San Francisco, a 'dwelling, studio and site', where, over two-month periods, artists-in-residence made installations which were opened to the public and then dismantled. After 15 installations the interior was 'covered by scars', as 'an ever-thickening palimpsest' under successive layers of paint.

The point for Diller and Scofidio was to 'address the issue of domesticity' and, by 'incisions, excisions, implants and inscriptions' to explore the role of architecture in sustaining domestic conventions. Their *withDrawingRoom* contained two 'domestic fields', one real and the other fictive. They saw these as existing between two 'skins'; that of the house and that of the human occupants. Private acts 'penetrated' into the public domain and public acts 'violated' the private domain. They could cut a section through the house, and any furniture in the way, 'to reveal structural information normally privileged by the sectional drawing'. Thus revealing 'archaeological strata' of the original house including the ground floor, the 'crawl space', even the earth beneath. A mirror in a lightwell was rotated to reflect that 'interstice as a laceration'. Then the main living space was opened through two storeys with an S-curved bridge at the upper level. Thus they could suspend, say, a dining table at a virtual upper level with chairs on brackets rotating about the plates. They saw this as a location for codes of behaviour to be played out 'between host and guests, relations of gender, behavioural; relations between the eater and the meal . . .' They gave the house an 'honorific' centre with diagonal walls dividing the ground floor, the centre of which 'pin-wheel' was marked by the hinge between two parts of a bed. One of these was fixed, the other could be united or rotated through 180 degrees, thus giving the occupants every conceivable relationship, from total unity to divorce.

All of this challenged – or so they say – the 'Property Line' (by their cutting through the house); 'Etiquette' (by their table, chairs and so on); 'Intimacy' ('gender, desire and denial', as represented by the bed); and the 'Narcissistic Impulse' (of conformity, health obsessions, paranoid hygiene and the corrosions of age, all represented by a mirror!) The point was to question those things we take for granted and in this 'environment of destabilisation', as Betsky says, to 'address rituals of property, etiquette, intimacy, and narcissism: progressively defining the self by . . . division and withdrawal, stripping away society to discover the body.' Their installation *Para-Site* at the Museum of Modern Art was equally disorientating; a larger version of *Urban Suburban* . . . with similar, horizontal chairs, tilted screens and video screens mounted on brackets.

Tschumi's fascination with electronics extended to the many computer drawings of the airport and library which he published and to his Video Gallery at Gröningen. There he and others – Coop Himmelblau, Eisenman, Hadid, Koolhaas – were asked to design pavilions for the display of videotapes showing rock music, pornography or whatever according to choice. Others may have thought such tapes ought to be seen in total darkness, or at least in total privacy, but Tschumi concerned himself with 'the immaterial representation of abstract systems (television and electronic images).' So his Glass Video Gallery is transparent: anyone can see who is watching what. It is a tilted, inclined, Libeskind-like beam built almost entirely of glass and containing a series of interlocking spaces, defined only by the structural 'glass fins' and their tiny metal clip connectors. Which makes for extraordinary, multiple reflections and the simultaneous viewing of many screens.

Tschumi's transparent walls and reflecting planes may well look unreal, whilst Diller and Scofidio may explore the Surreal. So does Hani Rashid, of Studio Asymptote, who

quotes Picabia as precedent.[63] Like all these other Surrealists he seems to be trying to find new ways of looking at familiar objects and like Lebbeus Woods he employs a tenuous understanding of recent science to help him in his quest. Above all he cites the 'optigraph', an instrument for surveying derived, so he says, from the Greek; '*optikos*; of seeing and *graphein*, to write.' He describes many versions of which one consists of a circular brass box containing an 'index' and a 'horizon glass' which enable one to lay out lines at right angles. So, by extension, Rashid suggests his 'optigraph' may be a telescope for copying landscapes – such as Peter Greenaway's architect used in *The Draughtsman's Contract* – an instrument for projecting pictures onto a screen (in a 'camera obscura'), an instrument for measuring the limits of vision and determining its imperfections, or as 'a measure of capacity, the turning of the mind to that which has already occupied it'. And of course Rashid can use his optigraph to distort the visual image in various ways; mirror reflection, inversion, changing the relative sizes of objects and so on.

So of course Rashid could describe fantastic distortions of objects, say, close to the Berlin Wall. Or the Pont Neuf in Paris, where Rashid saw an ever-changing record of light and activity in which the place was 'reignited from its colourful history'. This suggested further functions for the place, such as a 'fairground, bazaar, an employment exchange, bookstalls, a card factory, a dairy and "*cabinets d'aisance inodores*"'. New buildings, attached to the Pont Neuf, might 'move towards the Place Dauphine' and in them one might partake in many activities 'such as having a tooth pulled, watch a tight rope dancer, buy a Fragonard, pick up a new book or a first edition, arrange to go up in a balloon, take fencing lessons or attend a surgical demonstration.' Similarly when the optigraph was set up north of Notre Dame Rashid's 'reading' suggested that the government offices which occupy this quarter might be replaced by light industry, in 'wood, bronze, velvet, tin, cotton, paper and china'. Materials which might all be transformed into beautiful objects. And there would be 'aromatic dens' for producing strange kinds of furniture: 'the "Duchesse" for relaxation, the "Voyeuse" for watching, the "Chauffeuse" to facilitate undressing' and so on. All good Surrealist stuff, certainly, but one wonders why such a lively imagination needs a distorting device to trigger it.

Mark Fisher is concerned not so much with solid, permanent architecture as with massive projections; the projection, in his case, of a Rolling Stones tour of the United States, 'Steel Wheels', in September 1989. Fisher had to design a transportable set which could be erected, rapidly, at any available stadium in every one of 33 cities; dismantled, transported and re-erected again in another city. Mick Jagger chose Mark Fisher because he had set Pink Floyd's 'The Wall' up against the Berlin Wall as it was being demolished. Fisher's 'deconstructed tech' captured Jagger's mood in 1989 but as the latter said (1990): 'as far as technology's concerned, it's very 19th-century. I was a bit aware of that . . . The set is a glamorised version of the urban landscape . . . a lit version of something that you might see in an industrial city.'[64] Or for that matter the Pompidou Centre.

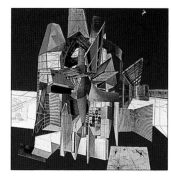

Studio Asymptote, 'Optigraph' project

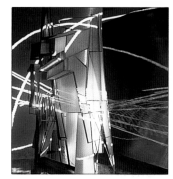

Studio Asymptote, 'Fringes and Uncharted Zones' project

Coop Himmelblau, Funder Factory, Carinthia

So what did Fisher design for Jagger? A 300-foot stage with, for sets, a 'deconstructed oil refinery'; a steel frame with eight-storey towers for the lights; endless banks of lights to give endless possibilities; spotlights, suffused glows, an infinity of flashing patterns; generators for producing billowing smoke, huge video screens projecting images of the musicians. And two 'giantesses' – inflatable balloons – with, at the climax of the show, a spectacular firework eruption. Mick Jagger himself saw the irony of presenting his Rolling Stones on such a crumbling High Tech stage. To which gleaming and not-so-gleaming metal he and the audience – although not, it seems, some of his crew – preferred the bourgeois comforts of good upholstery. As Jagger himself put it: 'no soft edges . . . no velvet, no nice sofas'. For Arcidi too there was a hidden symbolic agenda for to show such technology in such a decrepit state, 'heralds the obsolescence of modern industry'.[65] It was all very well in the 1960s for Archigram and others to see such technology as a 'social liberator', and perhaps even for Rogers to build such things as the Pompidou Centre or even Lloyds. But by the late 1980s to reduce such 'gleaming icons of a new urban order' to the 'desolate hulks' of an 'oil refinery' set with bits and pieces hanging off; this was an eloquent comment indeed on the obsolescence of such 'tech'. But Fisher's 'oil refinery' wasn't really the set. It was merely a support for the performance, lurking there in the shadows behind the bright lights. As the music changed, so the lighting was changed; where the music was harsh there could be sharp flashes of light and where it was romantic the lighting could be softened and subdued. Would that more such architecture could be 'switched off' in that way!

GROUPS OF BUILDINGS

Apart from individual buildings the New Spirits have also been designing groups of buildings on every scale from domestic to industrial, to the scale indeed of whole cities. The largest such domestic structure, probably, is Coop Himmelblau's studio complex for Anselm Kiefer, which in some ways derives from their Funder Factory: a long, low, white, Nick Grimshaw-like 'hangar' with a greatly deconstructed entrance corner and the splendid 'dancing chimneys' of its energy centre. So it's hardly surprising that the hangar form emerges in their Kiefer complex. Kiefer knew their work and their working methods, their usual materials, their ways of dealing with light – obviously important to a painter – and so on. And of course like other clients Kiefer was much involved in the early discussions, able, as they put it, 'to play in the team'. They weaned him away from certain preconceptions by their usual 'open' discussions and of course Coop Himmelblau found themselves with cryptic marks on paper, 'like charged particles'. They saw these as creating 'a field of energy', the configuration of an 'only momentary existence'. The marks could be connected by straight lines, opening up for Coop Himmelblau 'a multitude of possibilities'.

From this the design emerged as four not quite parallel hangars varying in length and width and bound together by catwalks at clashing angles which 'carry the emotion of the drawing'. The largest of them is white, like a small Funder Factory, with 'nave' and 'aisles' divided by columns and square 'light scoops' crashing diagonally into the roof. A transparent cube containing Kiefer's offices and studio also crashes in at the northeast corner – facing the view – and a rusting, Hadid-like beam emerges from it to the northwest at high level. South of this main hangar there is a longer, narrower one in corrugated metal with a curved roof, whilst the outer hangars are further Hadid-like beams. A fifth 'bar' crashes, more or less at right angles, into the northernmost of them. A much longer storage bridge, acting as the artist's 'memory', runs into, diagonally through and beyond the southernmost three of these beams and far to the northwest. Coop Himmelblau see this as a 'city'; a play on the German 'werkstatt' – a 'workshop' and 'stadt' – a 'city' – planned around 'conflict and promenade, condensation and long walks'. Indeed the Kiefer complex could be the beginnings of a town since the 'grids of uncovered structures' continue beyond the hangars and 'point to future extension'. Coop Himmelblau see such incompleteness as 'potential movement' and the buildings themselves are conceived as 'decaying tech'; rusting and disintegrating right from the beginning. Clearly, just like Mark Fisher's set, this constitutes an attack on Modernist mechanical perfection.

Gehry's Furniture Museum is of course adjacent to the Vitra Factory; outside the boundary fence but 'attached', visually, to Gehry's production 'hanger', which it faces by 'ears' or, rather, sculptural ramps. But that is only one of four large production sheds; those south and west of it are by Nick Grimshaw and further units are planned north of these. The west end of the Vitra complex consists of smaller buildings at clashing angles including the original factory shed, a curved entrance by Eva Jiricna, a showroom and walkway by Antonio Citterio. So it's hardly surprising that when Zaha Hadid was asked to design a bicycle shed, boundary walls and a fire station at the western end of the 500-metre 'drag' between Gehry's, Grimshaw's and the new production sheds she should try to rationalise not just emergency routes for the fire engines but the Vitra site as a whole, to use landscape to make it more coherent. Which might include a workers' club and a sports field. Hadid sees her landscape as a matter of 'choreographic notations inscribing into the ground the ritualised fire exercises'.

It's hard to know exactly what she means but one can see from the drawings that the scheme, as proposed, 'is not the delineation of the final project but proposes a dynamic pattern to allow the spaces to gradually develop'. That development, of course, will be constrained by the two new production sheds. As for the Fire Station itself, Hadid designs a series of 'layered screening walls', some containing Hong Kong Peak-like beams for shower and changing areas, a fitness centre and so on, behind which there is an outdoor fitness area with barbecue. And over the intersection of these beams Hadid places a third one, reached by a staircase between them. Naturally the beams diverge, in the deconstructed manner of Hong Kong, from the main spine wall which fronts the Fire Engine House itself, and is punctured for vehicular movements out and in, 'perpendicular to the linear flow of the walls'.

As for her Media Park, Zollhof 3, Hadid's problem was to help transform the old Harbour at Düsseldorf into an enterprise zone. Her design is based on the general docklands tradition of a protective wall, unwelcoming and solid towards the street but offering glimpses through. The other side of the wall will be open towards the landscape, stepping down, 'modulated' towards the water. One end of the wall is built up to form a five-storey hotel over a large triangular terrace; the roof a ground level mall of shops, galleries and showrooms, restaurants, a cinema; activities requiring public access from the street and opening back also towards the water. Next to the hotel a six-storey communications slab is built over the 'wall' with an attached 'black box' containing studios for broadcasting or recording, and beyond this again the upper accommodation is broken into nine clashing slabs crossing the 'wall' with double height spaces for executives facing onto the water. Below these too are deep spaces for media studios and between them a large conference space.

Bernard Tschumi too dealt with an 'edge condition', rather a different one, in his railway station design for the ancient Japanese city of Kyoto. As we've seen Tschumi views with great excitement cities such as Tokyo and New York; the very cities which others view with despair. For in his view they 'only appear chaotic; in reality they mark the appearance of a new urban structure, a new urbanity. The confrontations and combinations of elements may provide us with the event, the shock, that I hope will make the architecture of our cities a turning point in culture and society.'[66] One may agree with that; welcome such a prospect say for Kansai Airport whilst wondering if such urban density and vitality need be brought to the edge of the city which contains such oases of tranquillity as the Imperial Katsura Palace, the Ryoan-Ji Garden and so on. But as Tschumi says he intends for Kyoto Station a new hybrid mega-project of the 90s including a convention centre, a 600-room hotel, a ten-storey department store, 2,000 parking places, a cultural centre, a cultural plaza with an image theatre, sky restaurants, health clubs, wedding chapels, amusement arcades, a gourmet city, an Emperor's waiting room and so on.

Tschumi's design emerges from a 'skyframe', a 250-metre long, open-framework, Hadid-like 'bar' one storey up across the station's entrance front from which are to project, vertically, seven 'transparent' steel and glass towers. Each of these is aligned with a Kyoto city block: one for the cultural centre, two for the hotel and so on. There are openings between them at ground level to keep access open through the station and over the railway tracks. For Tschumi, of course, this is a splendid opportunity for the 'cross-programming' of elements which, combined, could aspire to the symbolic: the image theatre, the sky lounge, the wedding chapel, the athletics club, the amusement arcade, the gourmet city, the museum all 'staged' into his 'skyframe', his 'programmatic extractor'. His seven glass towers, 15 by 5.4 metre slabs, are from 62 to 83 metres high with ultra fast elevators and they contain video viewing rooms, video bars, sky lounges, museum displays, small restaurants, private dining rooms, kimono exhibition spaces, wedding waiting rooms, exercise and weight-lifting spaces, small amusement halls and, in their upper reaches, aviaries, teahouses, greenhouses, banner displays and observatories. Tschumi sees his 'skyframe' as 'a new spatial artefact' affording 'a new programmatic mix' and indeed it promises excitement of a rather special kind. But perhaps for somewhere other than Kyoto?

Bernard Tschumi, Kyoto Railway Station

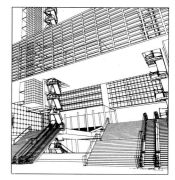

Bernard Tschumi, Kyoto Railway Station

URBANISM

Of course there is a strong feeling that whilst much of this work is exciting, its very exuberance may give it – as Starck suggests – the quality of a 'monster' in the city. One Guggenheim hardly destroys Fifth Avenue but a plethora of such selfish forms is bound to destroy any sense of urban enclosure along streets, around squares or whatever. So it's interesting to see how the Free Spirits tackle problems of urbanism. OMA have produced an urban renewal scheme for the Bijlermeer in Amsterdam and a larger urban strategy for Lille where, says Koolhaas, their combination of 'flexibility of form with a firm integration of road, rail and commerce might just do the trick'.[67] But their office towers for Lille are skittish permutations on Modernist towers, more or less vertical, with room-deep slabs attached in overlapping layers, tapering in elevation, section, or both and clad in contrasting materials: 'a world of amusement, and variety.' Coop Himmelblau have attempted to regulate the development of urban sprawl between Pierre de Pevry, Lieusaint and Moissy Cramayel in their scheme for Melun-Senart which links them. They envisage what looks like a deconstructed infrastructure carefully designed to link the three small towns to control the apparently random results of urban forces at work between them: density, complexity and height. They further plan a green belt and business park, an urban entertainment and sports centre but, most particularly, beams of 'urban lofts' to be built along their 'lines of force' for conversion into apartments by their users. And in the third phase of their development Coop Himmelblau propose an intensely developed 'downtown and interchange'.

There is perhaps less of such urban excitement in Tschumi's planned extension to one of the finest historic cities in Europe, that is Chartres, west of Paris. Tschumi's development of some 459 acres on the outskirts is to contain offices, housing and leisure facilities. The brief came to him in four sections: a masterplan for the extension of Chartres towards Paris; some 300,000 square metres of office development; 150 houses, and such leisure facilities as an indoor sports hall, meeting halls, restaurants, a 250-acre park, sports grounds and a golf course. Tschumi planned a meandering strip of offices-contained-by-landscape – somewhat similar to OMA's Parc de la Villette – parallel to the western edge of his site and crossed by an east/west linear park. This contains a long rectangular pool, tennis courts, oval buildings for meetings, a restaurant for office workers, and a club house for squash and tennis. Then south/east of the intersection Tschumi placed a large golf course with housing along its eastern edge.

But whilst there has been, and is, much development around Paris, the focus for a new urban spirit these days, not surprisingly, is Berlin.[68] We have seen already Lebbeus

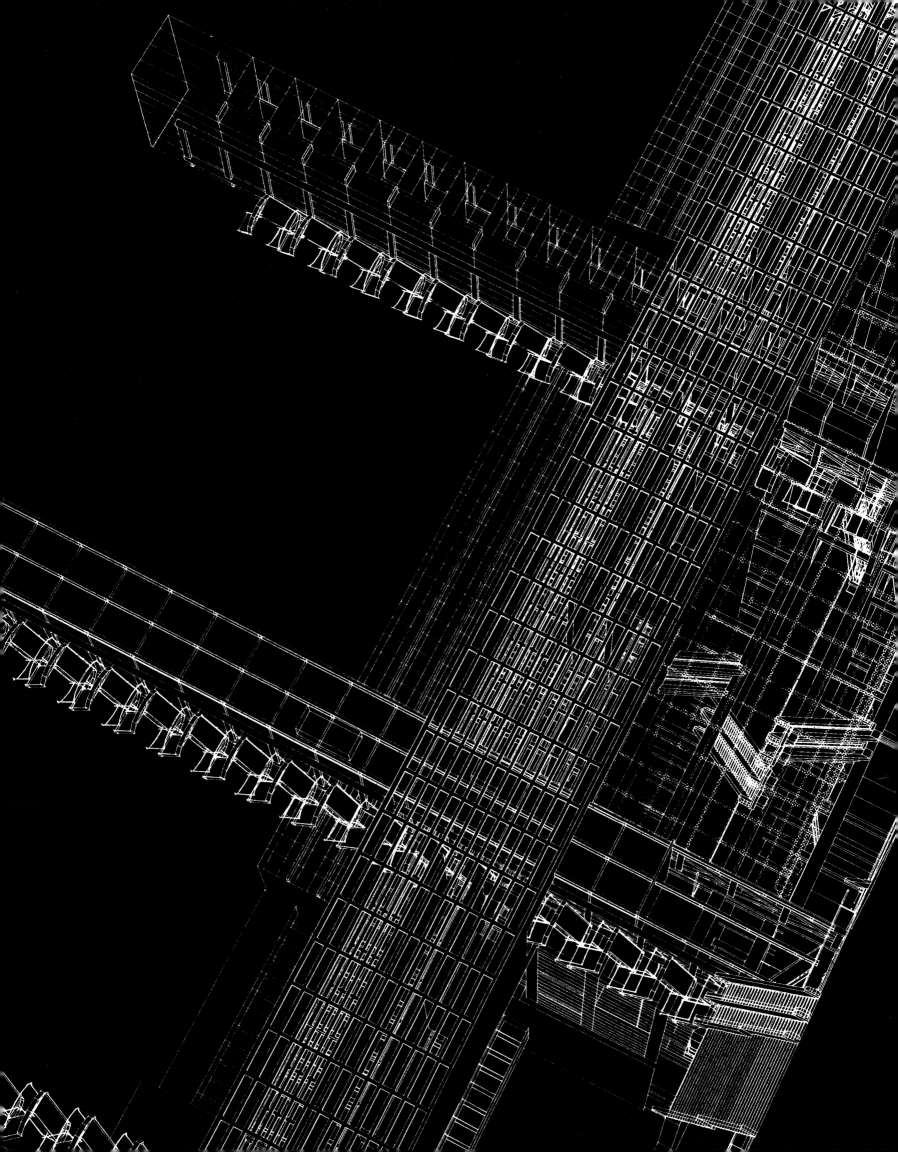

Woods's scheme for linking divided Berlin, East and West, by his subversive underground scheme, and his equally subversive scheme for a united Berlin threading into and through the buildings. And of course since World War II there have been demonstrations, every ten years or so, of what was then the New Architecture. Most of these can be seen around the Tiergarten, Berlin's vast urban park. Immediately to the north of its western end, for instance, lies the Hansaviertel, built for the Interbau (Internationale Bauaustellung, or international building exhibition) of 1957 and consisting mostly of high-rise housing by some 50 international architects, including such figures as Aalto, Gropius, Jakobsen, Niemeyer, Vago, van den Broek and Bakema. Le Corbusier's Unité d'Habitation was built further west at Charlottenberg.

Then in August 1961 the East German government built the Wall which ran northwards some 750 metres east of the Tiergarten along the line of the outer Medieval wall, enclosing, along that line, the old centre of the city, the Stadtmitte. The Reichstag lay just west of the wall, with south of that the Brandenburg Gate and south of that again the much eroded Potsdamer Platz. At which point the Wall turned eastwards again between Hitler's bunker – site of his demolished Reichschancellory – and, in the grounds of the Martin Gropius Bau, the site of his demolished Gestapo headquarters. The West responded, in the 1960s, with the Kulturforum just west of the Potsdamer Platz and south of the Tiergarten, with Scharoun's Hall for the Berlin Philharmonic, Gutbrod's Arts and Crafts Museum, Stirling's Science Centre, Mies's National Gallery and Scharoun's National Library. The Kulturforum is matched along the Tiergarten at the southwest corner by a large projection, the Berlin Zoo, with just to the west of this the Zoo International Station. The southern edge of the Zoo is marked by the Budapester Strasse from which, at the Europa Centre, the Kurfürstendamm emerges, that glitzy commercial showcase for the Western way of life, and runs southwest for some three kilometres.

And then of course 30 years later, the Interbau demonstrated Post-Modern attitudes to housing with a large array of projects by Ungers, Grumbach, Gregotti, Rob Krier, Hollein, Rossi, and others along the southern edge of the Tiergarten, of which Libeskind's beam was to have been the final project, some 250 metres south of Scharoun's National Library.

There are clusters of IBA buildings elsewhere, especially south of the Stadtmitte around Friedrichstrasse; the central spine of Philip Gehrlach's Baroque extension to Berlin which runs north from the Mehringplatz. Here are IBA blocks by Herzberger and Rossi, Rob Krier's early scheme for the Ritterstrasse and his highly coherent one for the Schinkelplatz designed around five corner-connected courts. The largest development of all is some 250 metres northeast of the Mehringplatz, adjacent to the Berlin Museum, with vast terraces and gardens by Kollhoff and Ovaska, Frowein and Spangenberg, Heielscher and Mügge within which are set individual 'villas' by Demblin, Isozaki, Kreis and the Schaads. As one proceeds north up Friedrichstrasse one encounters the housing blocks by Eisenman, and OMA's just south of the former Checkpoint

Charlie, where the Wall ran west along Zimmerstrasse. Beyond these one encounters Leipziger Strasse, the Unter den Linden and the Friedrichstrasse Station; for so long the point of entry to East Berlin for those who chose to travel by train.

Let's take the Friedrichstrasse as our major south/north axis and consider the major streets which cross it. The Leipziger Strasse starts east of the Kulturforum, indeed east of the Potsdamer Platz in Lening's once-octagonal Leipziger Platz. There used to be gates by Schinkel between the two plätze, small Doric temples on the line of the Medieval wall, but these were destroyed in the War. Indeed demolition of the Potsdamer Platz started before that in the 1930s, for the building of a Runder Platz on Hitler's vast north-south axis, added to which wartime bombing, the Wall and traffic planning have rendered it incoherent as any kind of *platz*. When the East Germans built the Wall they cleared behind it a ten-metre 'death strip' and beyond that again a 'no-go area' of 100 metres, which, now the Wall has gone, leaves a jagged wound where East and West were so decisively divided for so long. The Leipziger Platz, immediately to the east of Potsdamer Platz, is also a shadow of its former elegant self so it is hardly surprising that it is this segment of Berlin in particular which has become a focus of schemes to symbolise reunification and renewal.

The most prominent sites around the Potsdamer Platz have been snapped up by Sony, ABB and Daimler-Benz who commissioned Richard Rogers to design office towers which, at different heights, were to be staggered around a star-shaped *platz*, an *etoile* like the Place Charles de Gaulle in Paris. But somewhat wary of such blatantly commercial exploitation, the Berlin Senate organised a competition with notable entries by Ungers, Alsop and Störmer, Foster Associates and Libeskind. Alsop and Störmer, for instance, reinstate the Leipziger Platz in its original, octagonal form to be available for public spectacle. They concentrate their scheme on circulation – one storey above ground level – radiating from the Potsdamer Platz station. Their fan-formation of buildings is perhaps a 20th-century updating of Lening's Baroque Mehringplatz, but at their outermost ends, Alsop and Störmer's buildings shoot vertically into the air as brightly coloured towers. Ground level is freed for leisure use – as an extension of the Tiergarten – with brightly coloured hard landscape containing shallow, brightly coloured canals which will freeze in winter for skating. Cars, both for circulation and parking, are relegated to an underground position and so is the servicing of buildings.

But whilst a plethora of towers around the Potsdamer Platz might act as urban markers they would do nothing much to integrate the Kulturforum into the rest of Berlin. So the winners were Hilmer and Sattler who, perhaps more than other entrants, respected the Senate's wish to rebuild a European city, with buildings with constant street facades, rather than to build an American city of towers. This of course was an extension of IBS thinking, which has been seen as an 'opting out', a 'loss of opportunity' and so on – but their aim was to design not so much a visual focus of the kind which towers would have provided, as a 'genera-

Peter Eisenman, Friedrichstrasse IBA Housing, Berlin

Bernard Tschumi, Kyoto Railway Station

33

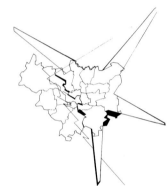

Zaha Hadid, Berlin Tomorrow project, 'The Dead Zone'

tor' of urban functions, a 'focus' in that sense, a 'natural stop', and for Berliners a 'natural meeting place'. Baker suggests (1991) that this really should have been a 'media communication zone' with research institutes, mediatheques, publishers and so on.[69] There might be to the east, symbolising public concerns, the offices of an open university and to the west, symbolising private enterprise, offices for the various media. And uniting them, facilities for conferences and lectures. It was a matter of 'uniting Scharoun and Schinkel', with invitations to Rogers, Piano, Koolhaas, Campi, Isozaki, Meier and Moneo to design within it.

Scharoun's major buildings, of course, lay westwards in the Kulturforum whereas to find Karl Friedrich Schinkel's we have to go eastwards again. But first northwards to the Brandenburg Gate which marked the westernmost end, towards the Tiergarten, of Berlin's great boulevard the Unter den Linden. It is lined with undistinguished postwar embassies and ministries to the point where it crosses Friedrichstrasse. Beyond that the buildings become increasingly distinguished with, lining the north side the German National Library, the Humboldt University, Schinkel's Neue Wache – his little memorial temple – and the old Arsenal. The Bebelplatz lies south of the Unter den Linden surrounded by the Old Library, the domed, much restored St Hedwig's Cathedral and Knobelsdorf's State Opera; beyond which again there lies Dietrich's Opera Café connected by an arch to Nering's Palais Unter den Linden. As late as 1700, Berlin's original Wall – the Medieval fortification – crossed the Unter den Linden where Schinkel's Neue Wache now stands and one block beyond that, after the Arsenal, the River Schleusen crosses the Unter den Linden which is linked by Schinkel's Bridge to the Marx Engels Platz. This vast parade ground was formed in the 1940s by demolishing the old Royal Palace and paving over its ornamental garden, the Lustgarten, the name of which has now been restored. It is bounded to the north by that purest of all Neo-Classical buildings, Schinkel's Altes Museum, flanked by Raschdorff's vast Neo-Baroque Cathedral, built around 1900 and beyond these Berlin's amazing collection of museums – if only for their exhibits – on Museum Island. The southern edge of the Lustgarten, where the old Royal Palace used to stand, is closed by the postwar East German National Council and southeast of this again lies the (much reconstructed) historic heart of Berlin surrounding the Nikolaikirche.

Beyond the Lustgarten the line of the Unter den Linden swings north of east as Karl Liebknecht Strasse to the Alexanderplatz, site for one of Mies's Glass Tower designs but marked currently by the 230-metre Telecommunications Tower, the most conspicuous urban marker of what was East Berlin. So it's within this immensely complex context that further proposals for Berlin must be reviewed. Of course things changed in November 1989 when the Wall was opened from East to West; changed even more in 1990 as it was demolished. It is hardly surprising that as Lebbeus Woods remarked, commercial interests should move in quickly: bankers, developers, international hotel chains, businesses and so on. For there where the Wall had been, and its 'no-man's land', there was space 'ripe for development' central in what had been one of the world's

great cities. They wanted to build, and fast. So Vittorio Magnago Lampugnani, Director of Frankfurt's German Architecture Museum, persuaded the *Frankfurter Allgemeine Zeitung* to sponsor the 'Berlin Tomorrow' exhibition, not just for new buildings in Berlin but for new urban strategies also to unite the so-recently divided city.[70] Of 25 architects invited 17 responded; so did Lebbeus Woods although he was not invited! The area selected for the proposals was roughly a diamond shape some two and a half kilometres in each direction between the Brandenburg Gate and the Alexanderplatz, between the Mehringplatz and the Lustgarten – or the nearby Friedrichstrasse Station.

The southern point of this 'diamond', south Friedrichstrasse, lay in what was the West – that is south of Checkpoint Charlie – and so did the westernmost tip at the Brandenburg Gate: along that stretch of the Wall, from the Potsdamer Platz to the Reichstag, facing the Kulturforum and the Tiergarten, which for most of us seemed to represent the most truly symbolic split between East and West. Here if anywhere, the fundamental decision has to be made as to whether to leave an 'open wound' or insert 'stitches' to urge the process of healing. Coop Himmelblau see the Wall's demolition as more than just the breaking of a barrier within Berlin.[71] They see it as the start of a 'healing' process across the whole of Europe from East to West. And Berlin, as they say, by way of the Zoo Station, is a major link in the 'chain' of a railway line from Paris to Moscow. Coop Himmelblau therefore bridge the railway line at Zoo Station, continuing along Hardenburgstrasse which at Budapester Strasse crosses a line they detect of 'innercity energy' zipping along the Kurfürstendamm. From this they generate their concept of a 'Berlin Crossing', or rather of two 'Berlin Crossings'; this first at the southwest corner of the Tiergarten, and another at the southeast corner, where the line of the Leipziger Strasse crosses the Potsdamer Platz. Coop Himmelblau's 'crossings' for Berlin, of course, are very much like those they envisage for Melun-Senart, as 'centres of energy'.

Their actual buildings are concentrated along the Leipziger Strasse where existing buildings are integrated into the multi-functional blocks of 'Parasite City' as 'infrastructural measures in the form of architectural cores of crystallisation (which) span a field of complex urban forces, setting the process of urban change in motion.' Here and elsewhere in such places as the parallel Kochstrasse, the Mehringplatz, the Potsdamer Platz itself, around the Brandenburg Gate and eastwards of Leipzigstrasse at Fischeringel – close to the Alexanderplatz – the towering 'containers' of their 'Developer City' also help trigger change. For crossings create points and points create crossings.

Whilst Coop Himmelblau have no hesitation in crossing the line of the Wall Norman Foster wants this and the 'noman's land' to be retained as an urban park, to provide space within the city, much as the demolition of the Medieval wall provided space around Vienna's Ringstrasse. But Berlin already had built on, obliterated the line of its Medieval wall, and any open space to the west of the Brandenburg Gate would simply extend the Tiergarten by 750 metres or so. So Foster concentrates his proposals along the now undivided Friedrichstrasse with infill to the many 'frayed' sites along its length and the highest concentration of all where Friedrichstrasse crosses Zimmerstrasse. Foster 'bridges' the wall-space anyway, but north/south at Checkpoint Charlie rather than east/west at the Brandenburg Gate.

Zaha Hadid was asked to consider the Alexanderplatz but since she saw its East German redevelopment – with its radio tower – as one of the few attempts to 'go beyond 19th-century urbanism' she adopted there a policy of 'non-intervention'.[72] But she also looked with interest at the 'border zone', the line of the Wall, and like Foster she suggested, 'this site must be preserved to prevent it from being covered by homogeneous commercial development.' Indeed to re-establish the traditional block 'over this ribbon of non-territory would erase all memory'. But Hadid sees two zones as offering possible sites; the Wall zone where it bisects the city either side of the centre, and the former perimeter fence. This 'dead zone' should be retrievable 'as a field across the city' available for reinterpretation with new programmes to some public purpose. More than the others, however, Hadid looks at strategies for the city as a whole. She draws a star-shaped plan to show how new corridor cities may be projected into the landscape around Berlin to accommodate imminent explosion of population. And then she lays new geometries over the dead zone; sometimes rectilinear yet slightly out of synch with the existing order. Others are random and somewhat overscaled.

Hadid seems to offer the grandest plans for Berlin, whereas John Hejduk is suspicious of super/master/grand planning of the kind which he believes has destroyed so many significant places. They usually destroy, not just the physical forms, but the very soul of a place. So Hejduk produced a modest entry indeed: a single fragment from his project for 'Berlin at Night', which fragment is a house and studio for a printer in Potsdam. This, the largest-scale intervention Hejduk is prepared to make, is itself broken down into a series of modest pavilions, some like Leon Krier's 'houses as columns' built up to three storeys high with mono-pitch roofs. They contain the printer's shop, his living space, his kitchen/dining space, his bedroom and his bathroom all linked by curving corridors. Modest indeed compared to Coop Himmelblau's factory-like studio for Anselm Kiefer.

Having proposed his aborted beam for Berlin and his once-badly-threatened Jewish Extension to the museum, Daniel Libeskind of course is concerned with visions of its *cultural* future. It's a matter of faith in the city itself – and of that cultural future, rather than things to do with short-term gains, with the cynical manipulation of economic and political variables. It's a matter of exploration too rather than exploitation; of invention rather than calculation. So Libeskind thinks it important to 'substantiate' the image of the historic centre around the Nikolaikirche – to revitalise the historic thoroughfare east/west, the Unter den Linden and its extensions in both directions, which had been split in the 19th century, long before the Wall, and that there is a further need to break down barriers. Berlin needs a new architecture; it's by no means good enough for the city to live on its architectural capital. One has to probe the

depths of the spirit of Berlin, the wellsprings of its character; intellectual and social, to open up an architectural vision. As of course Libeskind had begun to do with the processes behind the design of his Jewish Museum. So his actual design is a complex of buildings which he calls Über der Unter den Linden, formed of parallel plates interlocking, looking indeed much like blocks of his museum zig-zag. He draws them running westwards from the direction of Alexanderplatz towards Schinkel's Altes Museum after which, along the Unter den Linden, Libeskind's buildings give way to trees.

Jean Nouvel too thinks of Berlin as requiring 'a thoughtful approach'.[73] He sees it as a matter of travelling a 'slow path so that radical mistakes are not committed in the name of progress'. It may be, for instance, that instant political decisions will cause major and irrevocable changes to traffic patterns. So it seems to Nouvel that the area of the Wall should be redesigned as a symbol of new hope and optimism; that new political institutions should be ranged along the Unter den Linden and beyond, all the way from the Brandenburg Gate to Alexanderplatz. With perhaps a 'cultural promenade' from the Kultur Forum to Museum Island. And Friedrichstrasse would become a major business and commercial axis; an easterly alternative, perhaps, to the Kurfürstendamm.

So, says Nouvel, 'light it up, colour it, enlarge it, deepen your visions.' In the spirit of caution which Nouvel advocates gaps in frontages to the Friedrichstrasse should not all be filled at once. One should use the anomalies and surprises they offer to positive effect. 'Surprises' in his sense are views over and along, perspectives of spires and domes at the ends of streets, whilst the 'anomalies' along Friedrichstrasse are empty lots, blank walls, squares still in building, the S-bahn (railway) bridges and of course the remains of Checkpoint Charlie. So Nouvel's propositions are to make public spaces on both sides of the street: 'to express the ground forcefully by way of dotting, painting, informing, lighting, bordering, lining'; to light up every empty block with narrow buildings-as-billboards 'so that Friedrichstrasse will be bathed with light, colours, and logos of the firms which occupy it . . .' He wants to animate the bridges of the Friedrichstrasse Station and Checkpoint Charlie with 'digitalised light-news and electronic billboards; to create in the perspectives between buildings additional emerging objects, totems, new symbols for public buildings and corporate firms.'

As for the area of the Wall itself, Nouvel wishes to create a meeting line crossed by a series of streets, historic and long closed or even planned anew. He wants a 'sinuous space' with a golf green – a cross between a golf course and a computer grid. There should be walkways for families, tracks for joggers, for cyclists, for young lovers; lively spaces for shoppers, meditators, peeping toms: 'all the good and bad crazies of the metropolis'. There should also be shops and bars, restaurants, night clubs, flower shops, book shops, candy stores and bike stores; all the disparate images of life. There should be housing and office building on the way, offering great views and with all these vibrant locations for life, Berlin as a city will dare to look at itself again.

John Hejduk, Berlin Tomorrow project, 'The Potsdam Printer's House/Studio'

Jean Nouvel, Berlin Tomorrow project, 'The Meeting Line'

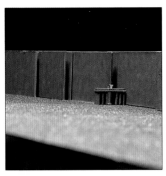

Daniel Libeskind, Berlin Tomorrow project, 'Über den Linden'

Bernard Tschumi, Berlin Tomorrow project, 'Eastern Blocks'

The Venturis, by contrast, think of connections further west. They propose a new boulevard, immediately south of the Tiergarten, Kurfürstendamm to the Brandenburg Gate, hence along the Unter den Linden, across the Lustgarten and ultimately to the Alexanderplatz. And to reinforce the link at the point where, perhaps, separation had been at its most visible, most symbolic, they propose an enormous staircase-like arch construction literally over Brandenburg Gate. Again by contrast Bernard Tschumi doesn't really want West Berlin to expand eastwards over the former Wall. He would prefer, rather, that the block structure of East Berlin expands, in the form of bridges, westwards over the line of the Wall, literally into the Tiergarten. His blocks would start at Otto Grotewohlstrasse (the line of the Wall east of the Brandenburg Gate) run between Leipziger Strasse and Mittelstrasse (which is one block north of the Unter den Linden) to continue, as bridges, over the traces of the Wall. 'Such a block structure', says Tschumi, 'would turn into a set of platforms and bridges that would act as the generator of new urban spectacles: fairs, theatres, exhibitions, political rallies, funerals.'[74]

So it is that in very different ways these New Spirits see themselves as solving the most urgent of current urban problems. The liveliest of them, Coop Himmelblau, Nouvel and Tschumi, see urban vitality of the kind represented by the Kurfürstendamm – Berlin's answer to, say, Fremont in Las Vegas – laid over what had been drab, grey, dreary East Berlin. Just as in individual buildings, so in their Urbanism there is an openness, a mingling, a changeability of functions, a lightness, a brightness, a razzmatazz as remote as could be from the earnest zoning, the flatness of

the roofs, the greyness of the slabs, the blackness of the framing round the windows that symbolised 'Modern' in the 60s. It was the flatness and greyness of the slabs around Mehringplatz that enabled Kleihues to set the IBA in motion. IBA moved away, commendably, and now the chances are there for these New Spirits to go further. Not just in Berlin but in other cities too, and there's no reason to suppose that results worldwide will be any less exciting, engaging to human response, solving of social purposes that what has been built already by Coates, Eisenman, Gehry, Hadid, Tschumi and the others.

But there's more than sheer excitement to what they offer, strange forms different for the sake of being different. There is, as we have seen, thinking embracing every scale from bathroom fittings (Starck) to interiors (Coates, Coop Himmelblau, Hadid and the others) to buildings (most of them) to groups of buildings (Coop Himmelblau, Hadid, Tschumi) to sections of cities (most of them) and to strategies for whole cities (Coop Himmelblau, Hadid, Tschumi and Woods). Then there are approaches to the social brief by which what at first seems antisocial turns out to serve new social purposes (Eisenman, Tschumi, possibly Woods), approaches to human psychology and physiology (Coop Himmelblau, Gehry, Tschumi) and approaches centring in ecological awareness of the site (Hasegawa, Morphosis). All in all these architects offer richness of a kind quite alien to those who dealt in the bland uniformities of an International Style, who worked with 'flatness' of every conceivable kind, who deplored any architect's self-expression. A paradigm is changing very quickly and we will all be much enriched by that.

NOTES

1 Tschumi, B, *The Manhattan Transcripts*, Academy Editions, London, 1981.

2 Eisenman, P, 'The City of Architectural Excavation', *AD* 1-2, January 1983.

3 Eisenman, P, 'Cannaregio', *Idea as Model*, IAUS Catalogue 3, Rizzoli, New York, 1981.

4 Eisenman, P, 'The beginning of the End and the Beginning Again: Some Notes on the Idea of Scaling', *Space Design*, March 1986.

5 Eisenman, P, 'The City of Architectural Excavation', *AD* 1-2, January 1983.

6 Prix, W, 'On the Edge', *Deconstruction III, AD* 87, 1990.

7 *Ibid.*

8 Popper, K, *The Open Society and its Enemies*, Routledge and Kegan Paul, London, 1945.

9 Krier, R, *Architectural Composition*, Academy Editions, London, 1988.

10 Prix, W, 'On the Edge', *Deconstruction III, AD* 87, 1990.

11 Prix, W, 'An *Architectural Design* Interview', *New Museums, AD* 94, 1991.

12 Gehry, F, 'The American Center in Paris', *The New Modern Aesthetic, AD* 86, 1990.

13 Gehry, F, 'Gehry House 1977-1979, Santa Monica, California', *The Architecture of Frank Gehry*, Rizzoli, New York, 1986.

14 Farrelly, EM, 'The New Spirit in Architecture', *The Architectural Review*, August 1986.

15 Cook, P and R Llewellyn-Jones, *New Spirit in Architecture*, Rizzoli, New York, 1991.

16 Norris, C and A Benjamin, *What Is Deconstruction?*, Academy Editions, London, 1989; Papadakis, A, C Cooke and A Benjamin, *Deconstruction Omnibus Volume*, Academy Editions, London, 1989; Johnson, P, and M Wigley, *Deconstructivist Architecture*, Museum of Modern Art, New York, 1988; and Betsky, A, *Violated Perfection: Architecture and the Fragmentation of the Modern*, Rizzoli, New York, 1990.

17 Broadbent, G, *Deconstruction: A Student Guide*, Academy Editions, London, 1991.

18 Broadbent, G, 'Creativity', in SA Gregory, *The Design Method*, Butterworths, London, 1967.

19 Popper, K, *Conjectures and Refutations: The Growth of Scientific Knowledge*, Routledge and Kegan Paul, London, 1963.

20 Gropius, W, *The Scope of Total Architecture*, Allen and Unwin, London, 1956.

21 Giedion, S, *Space, Time and Architecture*, Harvard University Press, Cambridge, Massachusetts, 1941.

22 Pevsner, N, *Pioneers of the Modern Movement*, Faber and Faber, London, 1936.

23 Mies van der Rohe, L, interview with Graham Shankland, BBC Third Programme, August 1960.

24 Weston, R, *Schools of Thought*, Hampshire County Council, Winchester, 1991.

25 Le Corbusier, 'Les cinq points d'une architecture nouvelle', 1926. Reprinted in Boesiger, W and O Stonorow (eds), *Le Corbusier and P Jenneret, Oeuvres Complètes Vol I*, Les Editions d'Architecture, Zurich, 1929.

26 Pevsner, N, *Pioneers of the Modern Movement*, Penguin Books, Harmondsworth, 1960.

27 Gehry, F, 'The American Center in Paris', *The New Modern Aesthetic, AD* 86, 1990.

28 Kuhn, T, *The Structure of Scientific Revolutions*, University of Chicago Press, Chicago, 1962.

29 Johnson, P, and M Wigley, *Deconstructivist Architecture*, Museum of Modern Art, New York, 1988.

30 Service, A, *Edwardian Architecture: A Handbook of Building Design in*

Britain 1890-1914, Thames and Hudson, London, 1977.

31 Eisenman, P, 'Strong Form, Weak Form', in P Noever (ed) *Architecture in Transition: Between Deconstruction and the New Modernism*, Prestel, Munich, 1991.

32 Broadbent, G, *Deconstruction: A Student Guide*, Academy Editions, London, 1991.

33 Eisenman, P, 'Transformations, Decompositions and Critiques: House X', *A+U*, January 1980.

34 Eisenman, P, and others, 'Castelli di Giulietta e Romeo', *Terza Mostra Internazionale di Architettura* (catalogue), Biennale di Venezia, Electra Editrice, Milan, 1985.

35 Eisenman, P, *Moving Arrows, Eros and Other Errors: An Architecture of Absence*, Third International Architectural Biennale, Venice, 1985. Box 3, Architectural Association, 1986.

36 *Ibid.*

37 Eisenman, P, 'In Terra Firma: In Trails of Grotextes', *Recente Projecten: Peter Eisenman: Recent Projects*, A Graafland (ed), and Eisenman, P, 'Peter Eisenman', *A+U*, August 1988.

38 Breslin, L, 'An interview with Peter Eisenman', *Form, Being, Absence: Architecture and Philosophy*, Spring 1988.

39 Eisenman, P, *Moving Arrows, Eros and Other Errors: An Architecture of Absence*, Third International Architectural Biennale, Venice, 1985. Box 3, Architectural Association, 1986.

40 Eisenman, P, 'University Campus, Long Beach, California', *Lotus* 50, 1986.

41 Tschumi, B, 'The Architecture of the Event', *Modern Pluralism; Just Exactly What Is Going On? AD* 95, 1992.

42 Tschumi, B, 'Event Architecture', in Noever, P (ed), *Architecture in Transition: Between Deconstruction and the New Modernism*, Prestel, Munich, 1991.

43 Harvey, J, *The Condition of Postmodernity*, Blackwell, London, 1989.

44 Jameson, F, *Postmodernism, or the Cultural Logic of Late Capitalism*, Verso, London, 1991.

45 Rose, M, *The Post Modern and the Post-Traditional: A Critical Analysis*, Cambridge University Press, Cambridge, 1991.

46 Tschumi, B, *Cinégrame Folie, le Parc de la Villete*, Champ-Villon, Paris, and Princeton University Press, Princeton, New Jersey, 1987.

47 Woods, L, 'Heterarchies of Urban Form and Architecture', *AD* 96, 1992.

48 Pawley, M, *The Private Future: Causes and Consequences of Community Collapse in the West*, Thames and Hudson, London, 1974.

49 Fawcett, A (ed), *Art Random: Zaha Hadid, Nigel Coates: New British Interiors*, Kyoto Shoin, Kyoto, 1991.

50 Venturi, R, *Complexity and Contradiction in Architecture*, Museum of Modern Art, New York, 1966.

51 Boissière, O, 'Starck, a Spirit of the Times', *Starck*, Taschen Verlag, Cologne, 1991.

52 *Ibid.*

53 Dunlop, B (ed), *Arquitectonica*, American Institute of Architects Press, Washington DC, 1991. Arquitectonica, 'Recent Projects', *Deconstruction III*, *AD* 87.

54 Nouvel, J, 'Projects, Competitions, Buildings, 1980-1990', in Noever, P (ed), *Architecture in Transition: Between Deconstruction and New Modernism*, Prestel, Munich, 1991.

55 Hasegawa, I, 'Architecture as Another Nature', *Aspects of Modern Architecture, AD* 90, 1991.

56 Morphosis, 'The Chiba Project, Tokyo', and 'Performing Arts Pavilion, Los Angeles', *Modern Pluralism; Just Exactly What Is Going On?, AD* 95 1992.

57 Gehry, F, 'Walt Disney Concert Hall, Los Angeles', in Elemond Editori Associati, *Biennale Veneziana: Quinta Mostra Internazionale di Architettura*, Electa, Milan, 1991.

58 Gehry, F, 'The American Center in Paris', *The New Modern Aesthetic*, *AD* 86, 1990.

59 Libeskind, D, *Countersign*, Academy Editions, London, 1991.

60 Libeskind, D, 'Between the Lines', *New Architecture: The New Moderns and The Super Moderns, AD* 84, 1990.

61 Haus Rucker Co, 'Recent Projects by Zamp Kelp', *A New Spirit in Architecture, AD* 69, 1991.

62 K/K Research and Development, 'Art Park, Lewiston, New York', *Modern Pluralism; Just Exactly What Is Going On? AD* 95, 1992.

63 Rashid, H, 'Optigraphs and Other Writings', *A New Spirit in Architecture, AD* 89, 1991.

64 Fisher, M, 'It's Only Rock 'n' Roll', and M Jagger and A Papadakis, 'An Interview', *New Architecture: The New Moderns and The Super Moderns, AD*, 1990.

65 Arcidi, P, 'Timely Adjustments: Retrofit Technology', *The New Moderns and The Super Moderns, AD*, 1990.

66 Tschumi, B, 'The Architecture of the Event', *AD* 62, Jan-Feb 1992.

67 Koolhaas, R, 'Parc Citroën, Cevennes; Urban Renewal Project for the Bijlermeer, Amsterdam; Urbanisation of the Central Space, Melun-Sénant: all in *L'Architecture d'Aujourd'hui*, April 1989.

68 Balfour, A, *Berlin: The Politics of Order, 1737-1989*, Rizzoli, New York, 1991.

69 Baker, N, 'Mending Spirit', *Building Design*, November 8, 1991.

70 Lampugnani, VM, 'Berlin Tomorrow', *AD* 92, Academy Editions, London, 1991.

71 Coop Himmelblau, 'Crossing Points', in Lampugnani, VM (ed), *Berlin Tomorrow, AD* 92, 1991.

72 Hadid, Z, 'The Dead Zone', in Lampugnani, VM (ed), *Berlin Tomorrow, AD* 92, 1991.

73 Nouvel, J, 'The Meeting Line' in Lampugnani, VM (ed), *Berlin Tomorrow, AD* 92, 1991.

74 Tschumi, B, 'Eastern Blocks', in Lampugnani, VM (ed), *Berlin Tomorrow, AD*

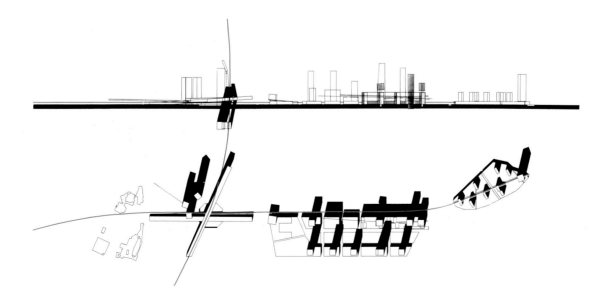

Coop Himmelblau, Berlin Tomorrow project, 'Crossing Points'

WILL ALSOP

HAMBURG FERRY TERMINAL

The ferry terminal on the River Elbe in Hamburg was the winner of a prestigious competition set by the Planning Department of Hamburg City and the ferry company DFDS. The commission was won in April 1989 in conjunction with Alsop and Störmer's German associates, Medium. The site is on an existing spit on the river joined to the mainland by a land reclamation project.

The brief contained three main elements: a new ferry terminal building providing all the amenities expected of modern international terminals; office accommodation of the ferry company DFDS Seaways; and a comprehensive plan for parking and queuing of passenger cars and freight containers.

In the original winning design the office and terminal space were accommodated within the same building, but the revised scheme has divided the areas into two structures, separated by a strip of water to emphasise the act of passing through customs control into Germany.

The form of the main building – the terminal itself – is dramatically curved, echoing the forms of ships and nautical structures nearby. The first design was entirely steel, which has since been modified to steel and concrete and most recently to an entirely precast concrete structure. It is raised on legs to prevent damage to the services platform in the event of flooding and to allow vehicle circulation beneath.

The underside of the platform has a polished aluminium skin, while the roof is a membrane of translucent plastics. Travellers can look out onto the water from the front south elevation through inclined curtain wall glazing. The concrete-framed raised office building is clad in natural-finish zinc on the walls and roof. It is connected by a glazed bridge to the plant areas beneath, which are enclosed by glass walls.

The 2,500-square-metre terminal complex is the first part of a three phase project: phase two will consist of an expansion of the first; phase three will add a further 5,000 square metres to incorporate a new cruiser terminal. Both in form and function the entire project is extremely fluid – a beautifully curved design structure repeated over a length of 500 metres and altered to accommodate a range of varying uses.

See opposite above

CARDIFF BAY VISITOR CENTRE

This project embodies an approach which after a lengthy gestation still resolutely defies categorisation. Now that it has been followed by a succession of major commissions across Europe, the Visitor Centre can be seen as a low-cost, low-tech introduction to the firm's singular line in architectural modernism.

The Centre is a temporary structure: granted two years' planning permission, its function is to house a series of exhibitions explaining the Cardiff Bay Development Corporation's scheme, which includes the building of a barrage across the bay, creating a huge freshwater lake.

The Visitor Centre reflects a number of the practice's recurring preoccupations: the unmistakable 'ovaloid' shape, which makes no obvious concessions to any conventional building style; a deceptive simplicity in the structure and materials used; the raising off the ground of the whole form, enabling it to be viewed from all angles, and generally, an unsentimental response to the client's needs and available resources.

From the outside, the structure appears as an almost uninterrupted flattened tube open and glazed at both ends to allow views of the bay and the docklands area. This effect has been achieved through the combining of a number of interlocking elements. Oval steel ribs support marine plywood panels, forming the basic structure, which rests on galvanised steel brackets attached to track-like steel foundations. The whole 'roll' has then been covered in a weatherproof PVC-coated fabric skin, secured underneath like the flysheet of a tent. Decorative abstract shapes cut out of the plywood panelling dapple the interior in diffused light.

The Visitor Centre has been described as appearing to have landed from outer space or the future, on the shore of the bay – an appropriate metaphor for a structure which deliberately avoids conceding to predictable expectations of architecture, past or present.

In spite of its simplicity and modest budget, it has much in common with the larger projects that increasingly preoccupy Alsop and Störmer's growing practice. It is energy-efficient, offers palpable pleasure to its users, fulfils a social function, demands attention and – quite literally as it happens – is transparently open-ended.

See opposite below

ARQUITECTONICA

MIRACLE CENTER, MIAMI

This is a block-long mixed-use complex on an urban site in the Coral Gables area of Miami. The seven-storey project includes 230,000 square feet of shops, a cinema, restaurants, and a health club on three levels. Above the retail area there are three levels of parking for 1,000 cars and an 18-storey, 100,000-square-foot tower containing 98 residential apartments. Hung askew from the stone-blue facade (painted stucco on concrete) are huge trapezoid panels, with a black on white stylised 'marbled' effect.

See opposite and below

SHOPPING COMPLEX, ATLANTA, GEORGIA

This 120,000-square-foot shopping complex is located in a revitalised area of downtown Atlanta. A group of two-storey buildings takes advantage of the sloping site, allowing primary access at both levels to restaurants, cafes, night clubs and speciality stores. The complex focuses on a central plaza and reflecting pool.

See page 42 above

CENTER FOR INNOVATIVE TECHNOLOGY, FAIRFAX AND LOUDOUN COUNTIES, VIRGINIA

This is a master plan and first phase construction for a 650,000-square-foot office and research complex. It includes the headquarters for the Commonwealth of this Center, the headquarters for the Software Productivity Consortium and a common facility of an exhibition hall, auditorium, briefing and press rooms, classrooms, fitness centre and dining facilities. The buildings sit atop a four-storey parking garage with a landscaped roof deck.

See page 42 below

BANQUE DE LUXEMBOURG

This is the new headquarters for the Bank of Luxembourg, a corner building on the Boulevard Royale in the business centre of the city, situated just where the boulevard makes a sharp turn, thus setting up the axial relationship of the building to the rest of the street. Most of the building's 200,000 square feet of space is in eight underground levels used for parking and safes. The six storeys above ground are for the executive offices, conference centres, public banking lobby and boardroom.

The approval dictated a building envelope consisting of a rectangular prism with setbacks in floor plan at the four corners and in section off the top floor and mechanical penthouse. Within those parameters the project was conceptualised into three architectural volumes: a central core clad in polished black granite and matching dark tinted glass, to emerge from the middle of the composition as a 'shadow', becoming evident at base, southern end, and top; a second rectangular volume, intersecting the core and suspended off the ground, clad in beige/grey Chassagne stone and matching amber-tinted glass. The volume appears to be cantilevered in the front, but is supported by a series of elliptical grey granite columns at the rear and a monumental, 43-ton, rough-hewn granite block at the front; and a third volume in the form of a segment of a reverse cone, emerging from the other two and reaching out towards the plaza and the corner. This volume is clad entirely in lightly tinted glass, supported by radiating stainless steel mullions in a vertical pattern. Within it are housed the more ceremonial and public spaces of the building.

See page 43

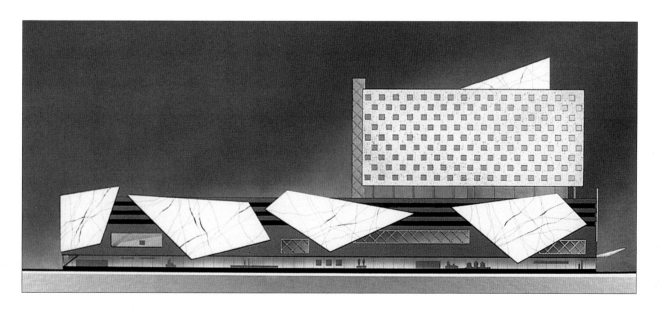

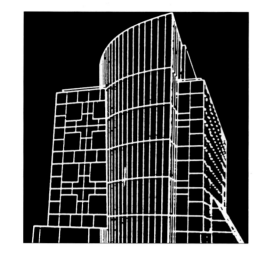

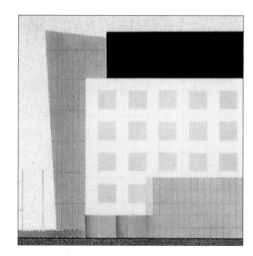

GÜNTER BEHNISCH

POSTAL MUSEUM, FRANKFURT

The German Postal Museum is the third such institution in Frankfurt, having been preceded by the Imperial and Federal Museums. Due to the convenient location of the Imperial Museum, and the public preoccupation with technological progress at the time, the museum was a great success, with attendance figures that were impressive even by today's standards. Following the war, the collection was stored in various warehouses in and around Frankfurt, and a portion of it was exhibited in a villa on the Schaumainkai that was designated as the Federal Postal Museum in 1956. While there was some initial enthusiasm for a strategy of integrating the dissipated collection with that of a new postal museum in Bonn, the idea was abandoned when the Frankfurt city council announced its plans for a 'Museumsufer' or riverside promenade of museums along the Schaumainkai. Günter Behnisch and Partners were the eventual winners of a competition for the new headquarters of the collection, which was to be brought together and updated for the first time in 50 years.

The decision to locate this facility on the same site as the villa that had served as the Federal Postal Museum had the advantage of providing both symbolic and physical continuity, but the restricted size of the plot made planning an annex very difficult. Provision for any future expansion, which experience has shown to be a necessary requirement in museum design, was also a potential problem, due to the lack of space. In addition, the old mansion was in great need of restoration if it was to retain any active role in the new institution. As Thomas Werner, the Director of the new museum, has said, the architect's idea of placing a portion of the exhibition area underground has meant that 'the plant-covered roof of the main exhibition floor takes up the character of the old garden, and the clear division of the old and new building parts towards the outside avoided the problems usually arising when old and new buildings are linked directly with one another. A truncated glass cone at the back of the garden connects the different storeys of the new building in a kind of patio and provides the inside of the building with a unique transparency, at the same time allowing daylight into the underground exhibition floor. The motif of the semicircle is repeated in some other parts of the building, such as where the building was constructed around the root boles of the existing trees. These semicircular elements are intended to form a contrast to the otherwise linear new building.'

The museum has five floors, of which two are underground. The first of these is used as the main exhibition floor, and the architect has established a connection between it and a corresponding level in the existing villa, which has not only expanded the available exhibition space, but also ensured that the older building will continue to be utilised. The second underground level is used as a car park, once again to maximise space usage, as well as providing much-needed storage space.

The entire ground floor, which has been liberated by this design strategy, has been turned over to entrance requirements with an information desk, museum shop, cafeteria and auditorium located there. Two upper levels are reserved for permanent and temporary exhibitions, and security of the temporary displays of postage stamps was an important factor in the location and design of those areas. An amateur radio station has been installed on the roof, continuing the Museum's commitment to technological implementation and display. The attitude taken towards exhibitions has best been summed up by the Museum Director:

'The concept of the exhibition was designed by a group of experts from the various branches of the Deutsche Bundespost on the basis of a design drawn up by the Düsseldorf Institute for Social Psychology. The result is a museum which not only intends to impart the technical aspects of postal and telecommunications history to visitors but which regards the history of communications as an integral part of the development of individuals, societies and nations. The architect has intentionally set out to contrast the new building with the old, in terms of materials and space planning, believing that this has allowed much more design freedom and is more in keeping with the forward-looking, technology-based image that the Deutsche Bundespost seeks to convey. Such contrast has also allowed a more decentralised organisation of exhibitions, using the open, three-dimensional spaces that have resulted to best advantage.'

Great care was taken to save as many trees as possible on the site, which has provided a park-like setting for the museum. Achieving this was not easy, because construction of underground parking and exhibition areas required special replanting techniques. Fortunately, this task was made more straightforward as many of the largest trees were located near the edge of the property.

Rather than responding to fixed exhibition requirements, Günter Behnisch has provided an architectural solution that encourages flexibility and change. As he has said, 'It is our experience that achievement in art is greater and ultimately better and more varied if relatively difficult problems have had to be overcome . . . and the creation of an exhibition is probably no different.'

The freshness of his own approach to the seemingly impossible quandaries presented in this particular case has provided additional support for this theory.

See opposite and pages 46-49

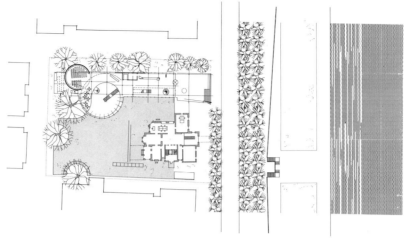

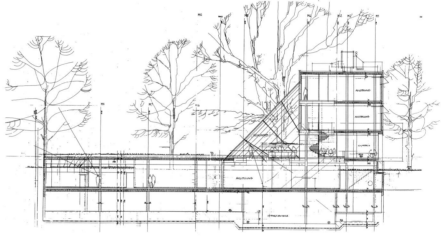

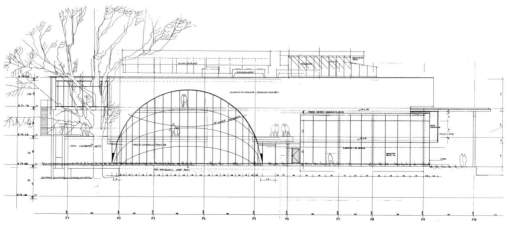

NIGEL COATES

NOAH'S ARK, HOKKAIDO

Noah's Ark (L'Arca di Noè), a restaurant and bar on the Japanese island of Hokkaido, was Coates's first completed building, the architect having previously concentrated on interiors.

Patrons Jasmac required a flagship building, something dramatic to set off their other hotel and leisure enterprises. Coates's answer is Noah's Ark run aground on Mount Fuji, a building with the feel of pure rich and delightful folly, but which also succeeds perfectly in fulfilling its functional requirements, turning to imaginative advantage what could have been the restrictions of its narrow triangular site.

Seen from the riverside, the ship shape is most apparent, while from the other side the prow emerges from a massive amorphous wedge of rock, formed by a process of spraying concrete over nets developed on-site. Above, the first floor and roof structures are Etruscan in style. Inside, artful plasterwork creates an impression of perished timber, and space is defined by a ship's gangway leading from the door at the 'prow' to the first floor restaurant, where it intersects dramatically with a second and very different spiral staircase, leading to the 'stern' entrance. Works of art and sculptures proliferate, including a magnificent chandelier by Tom Dixon.

See opposite

BOHEMIA JAZZ CLUB, TOKYO

This split-level basement club is one of three Coates interiors for the building, the others being a menswear shop and a hairdresser's.

Formally the main event is the cutaway upper floor, clad in aircraft aluminium and looping around the side of the building, providing seats with a view and an aerial platform for visiting musicians. Beneath this, alcoves are formed from inverted fins in the same material, with salvaged aircraft seats placed cosily in each alcove.

Above the seats hang conga drums, perfect in situ, made from silver jet-engine housings. Colours and patterns are bright and varied, splashes and stripes, oranges and purples thrown together with quieter pale creams and browns in a pleasingly unco-ordinated way.

Entered from above via a spiral staircase, the club has a good dynamic flow and an intimate, secluded feel, something like the 'grubby little boîte, or a Soho clipjoint of the 1950s' Coates had in mind.

See page 52

CAFFÈ BONGO, TOKYO

This building, perhaps the architect's best known, is immediately eye-catching even by the standards of the part of Shibuya in which it stands, largely on account of there being an aircraft wing jammed into the front of it, supported by a chipped Corinthian column.

These startling external elements set the tone for the collision of styles to be found within – narrative architecture with a vengeance, although it would be hard to say just which narrative: tarnished male nude statues gaze down from their podia, set high on a curving, segmented, aluminium aircraft-wing balcony, supported from the floor by tilting Victorian cast-iron columns shipped in from England, and an array of bright modern fixtures and fittings, high-tech lighting and video screens embedded in floor level cracks, are mixed in with Classical mouldings and columns. Surfaces of the walls and floor, crumbling in places, are bejewelled with inset pieces of junk, modern and old, including nuts and bolts, an electric fan, a saw and a phone receiver, almost as if this had been some kind of modern Pompeii. Tables and chairs are in Coates's neo-50s style, a steel spiral staircase leads up to the balcony, and the bar is curved like the prow of a ship; a slightly eerie, steely blue light predominates, adding something of the feel of a film set.

See pages 53-55

WOLF PRIX, COOP HIMMELBLAU
ON THE EDGE

The most apt question of our time is: how can we think, plan and build in a world that becomes more fucked up every day? Should we be afraid of these problems and suppress them? As we, Coop Himmelblau, are Viennese, we have a close connection to Freud who taught us that suppression requires a tremendous amount of energy. We would like to spend this energy on projects.

The safe and sound world of architecture no longer exists. It will never exist again. 'Open Architecture' means consciousness and an open mind. In fact, architectural history through the 20th century and into the 90s can be interpreted as a path from a closed to an open space. Ideally, we would like to build structures without objectives in order to release them for free use. As a result, there are no enclosed spaces in our buildings; they just interlace and open up. Complexity is our goal. Architecture, as it was proposed in the 19th century, is over. We have to go for a complexity that mirrors the diversity of world society. Interlaced and open buildings have no divisions: they challenge the user to take over space.

Many people say, 'Oh, your architecture is so aggressive. Why do you slant the pieces? Why do you break it? Why do you twist it?' The simplest explanation is: if you slant a piece of architecture, then you break the function so that very interesting spatial effects can be created.

At the beginning of every lecture, I make a point of showing a slide of our team. This is because team co-operation is one of the most important factors in the work of Coop Himmelblau. My friend and partner, Helmut Swiczinsky, and I have worked closely together on all the projects.

In 1975, we started to try to express our ideas on what we call 'Open Structures' – a reference to Karl Popper's book *Open Society* – by designing loft buildings. At the time, everyone was drawing beautiful little houses with columns, gables and tympanums. This wrong aesthetic angered us so we started to pierce and penetrate buildings with arrows.

Our project for a school in Stuttgart, Germany, was our first attempt at twisting part of a building. This particular scheme created an unusual interwound, interlacing space and, although it was never built, we are still very eager to create space for kids.

The *Blazing Wing* was a happening that we did in 1980. We set alight a courtyard in the middle of a city. As you can imagine, we had to get a lot of permits to do it. In fact, no one at this time knew how to set fire to a 15-metre-high, steel, constructed wing. Although we protected the walls with a water curtain, 21 windows broke because the fire was so hot.

In our 1982 project for a 50-flat apartment complex in Vienna, one of our main goals was to create an open system – a landscape – and keep it free for the use of the occupants. We proposed to begin by building a shell from which people would be able to choose the flat they wanted. In addition, we suggested that the flats should be built economically so that the largest apartments possible could be constructed; the flats would have been at least 2,000-feet long and five-metres high. We calculated that our construction would cost half as much as a normal social housing project; however, no one in Vienna, at this time, dared to go ahead and build it because it would have proved that building expenses for social housing in Vienna are far too high.

So here is just another example of the way we are working in Vienna!

It is only possible to create interwoven spatial systems by getting rid of circumstantial pressure. In order to get complexity in architecture you have to get rid of several things: first, you have to get rid of architectural, historical laws; second, you have to stop thinking about clients; third, you have stop thinking too much about the money you're making; and, finally, you have to stop thinking about cost.

The German word for design – *Entwurf* – is very precise. It shows that it is a very subconscious and dynamic procedure. In the last couple of years, without knowing where it would lead, we have condensed the moment of conception. We often talk about a project for a long time, without considering the tangible consequences; suddenly, during a drawing, there is a model. This is why team work is so important: while one of us is drawing, the other is converting the drawing into three dimensions by doing the model. If you look at the drawing, it is neither a work-sheet drawing nor a detail, but a multi-faceted ground plan.

This very subconscious procedure allows us to think and to draw very quickly. At the moment of conception we are able to avoid having to think about everything that should be considered afterwards, for example: how can we convince the client? How can we convince the building firm? It makes us very free.

Have you ever seen a leaping whale? I saw one in San Francisco and it was fantastic. I would like to compare this way of drawing with a leaping, champing whale. I was in a boat and the water was very calm but I could feel that there was something moving under the surface. All of a sudden the animal emerged and jumped 15-metres high. You have to imagine it: a 30-tonne, floating, flying object. In our creative procedure, we try to capture this very instance when the animal is moving from water to air. Sometimes we draw with our eyes closed in order to get this moment very quickly down on paper. It does not matter whether we are drawing on the table or on the floor. We are just trying to catch this feeling. You have to be a whale hunter. Success is not guaranteed, but that, too, is Open Architecture.

We have noticed that we complement verbal descriptions with hand and body motions. In art the method is referred to as action painting. It has been popular in Vienna, where there are a lot of artists trying to avoid circumstantial pressure in order to get a feeling – a *psychogram* of space. For example, during the city planning competition for a city outside of Paris, body language was the first drawing. The energy lines of the head were translated into the model. In between the energy lines, a city was created.

Perhaps a better example is a theatre. There are two concepts: one of the inner shape and one of the outer shape. If you look at a traditional proscenium theatre, the inner concept is the only part of the building visible to the audience. In a competition three years ago, we tried to create a multi-functional stage at Ronacher, from the basement to the roof, so that the whole volume of the theatre could be seen. The major decision for the project was whether we should follow the building codes and do a subterranean programme or ignore the codes and set up a whole new concept for a new theatre.

The site was that of an old theatre so that the brief of the competition veered towards renovation. Since a lot of Viennese architects are rather Po-Mo, we had to decide whether we should diverge from the norm and paint our windows black, or win the competition – so, we won it.

Body language and architecture – how they play together! One particular object we did in the late 60s contains a space that translates your heartbeat into light and sound. Another of our sculptures translates a facial movement – the expression of the moon – into colour and sound.

Creating sculptures and environments for museums or galleries was an important part of realising our design procedure. But it did not happen from one day to the next; it only came through practice and through being totally uncompromising. The first project we did in this way was an environment for a German museum. The drawing was done very quickly on March 5th, 1982. When Helmut and I saw the model of it we said, 'Come on, this is so ugly we have to build it!'

The key project for our open design procedure has been the Open House. The house is very complicated and is therefore like the disabled child whom we love very much. We spent a lot of time talking to the client because he was not sure what he really wanted. But this discussion was for defining emotional, rather than functional, needs. The house existed not as a building but as a *feeling*. The form and the details were not important; what was important was the lighting, the height, the weight and even the view. In order not to be led astray, not even by the graphics, I closed my eyes and used my hands as a graph of the feelings that arose. We did not call it an architectural drawing, but rather a psychogram of the house.

The next step in a project's development from that of drawing and model is the transformation into details and construction. It is in this phase that these seemingly arbitrary forms make sense. For instance, a slanted box allows us to create a double shell construction that can be used as a passive energy system because of its versatile, insulating capacity. The client may be convinced that he wants to use the house as it was intended: he moves into it and inhabits it, then he decides where he wants to sleep, where he wants to live and where he wants to read. The client may or may not choose to do this – that, also, is Open Architecture.

Although it is not immediately important, construction becomes crucial at the second or third step. In order to build this suspended, floating feeling, you have to know about more than just columns and beams. In fact, our structural engineer isthe only real deconstructionist in our group; only he knows how to calculate by separating every part and then can put it back together again.

Anyway, this first client of ours was from our home town Vienna. The project, however, was publicised by being printed on the cover of a book. We got a call that resulted in a commission to build the same house in Los Angeles. I am sorry to say this, but we did not win the race against time: our American client was very old and he died before we could start building it. Everything was finished so we bought back all the plans, even the land. Now we are trying to sell the house as a package and it will be sold at an auction at Sothebys. I have heard that Kim Basinger is very interested in it.

Our first sketch of the roof-top remodelling in Vienna shows every element and concept that we like to emphasise in a building in the later stages. This project is a kind of corner solution. In Vienna, when people build on corners, they all try to put up little towers, lovely cube-shaped constructions. Needless to say, we did not do this! We decided that our glass, cupola-topped scheme should be a way of playing with closed and open panels. This is the way we normally resolve a corner solution! Another important element is context. For us, context is not a matter of building in proportion to neighbouring structures. Instead, we broke up and crossed over the old roof with a transversal flashlight which came from the street and effectively created new space. Another prominent aspect of any project is the view, both the inside and the outside view. The inside and the outside have a relationship. You have to know that the area in which we built this conversion is heavily protected as a landmark; therefore, we were not allowed to change anything about the roof-top. So, how did we deal with this? We went to the mayor of Vienna and said, 'Look, we are not only architects, we are artists too. Please look at the model: this is a piece of art. How can the building commission chuck away a piece of art?' And he said, 'You are right.'

Our brief, in this case, was to build an office with a meeting room. We constructed a balcony in order to provide access from the roof garden to the meeting space. As I have already stated, a flash-light came in from the street, crossed the whole project and broke up the old roof. It was not, however, aggressive. We are not destructive; we only destroy in order to create new inside and outside spaces.

When we showed the construction model of the roof-top conversion, at the MoMA show, a lot of American colleagues came to us and told us that they enjoyed the project, but they did not believe it could be built. This really amused us as it was under construction at the time.

There are a great deal of advantages in dealing with a client once a building is under construction. The view of the first sketch of the roof conversion was the strongest from the inside to the outside so that the structural glazing pieces, which make up the cupola, are arched to the outside. The client however complained about this. He asked us to cover it. So we said 'OK, we can cover it and hide it but it will cost money.' So he of course said, 'OK, leave it!'

We love to use the sculptural quality of light in our work. The slit of light created by a light beam penetrating a wall is one of the best examples of this. When the sun shines, an arrow of light illuminates the wall opposite. In the evening, however, the client can become the creator as he makes an artificial light beam from the inside out.

Another strategy, characteristic of our work, is to be very economical on the parts of a building that we have to execute (such as the side wings of an office) in order to save money for the parts that we want to emphasise.

I will give you an example of yet another way we design. We were once commissioned to enlarge a staircase. The owner of the house, however, was not satisfied with what we had drawn up; he said that the staircase must have windows. We did not like having these windows, these light-slits, so we crossed them and built a correction of the first sketch. It took us two years to convince everyone to build it. I still do not believe that the client could imagine what this project would look like, but now he is going around like Alice in Wonderland. He is so proud of it. We were proud of it too when we first saw it built – it was like a diamond glowing on a roof-top.

We do not always design with our eyes closed; sometimes we work the other way around. We built a factory at about the same time that we did the staircase. Our first sketch was a white box, with no details. We both added and cut away some important parts before sticking them back together in a very strange way. It was a very economical structure to build; there is no detailed production hall. We thought we would let a factory do what a factory should do – produce things. As it is not a creative environment, it is a very economic structure.

Indeed, the factory is a white box with little more than three details. Since a freeway passes to the side of it, we called this facade the 100-Mile Power Facade. On the other side, there is a very small street going past it so we decided to design everything on this as on a 30-Mile Power Facade. The facades meet on a glazed corner, at a glass edge, indicating that there is a special room for presentation within. Let's call it a lobby! Overall, however, the factory, from both inside and outside, looks like a multi-functional space – empty.

Our project *Dancing Chimneys II* was quite different as it posed a builder's question. It made us ask ourselves: why do stacks always stand very straight? We did not, however, build the answer; we really built the question. We call it *Dancing Chimneys II* because from every angle it looks very different and, in addition, if you run around the energy centre extremely fast you can see the chimneys dancing. But you have to be very fast!

We have a project on our tables, right now, that explains very precisely what we mean by twisted and slanted building parts. Originally, it was a competition – which we won – to design an addition to an existing hotel. The hotel has a huge park and lake, so we agreed to open the park and twist the whole building complex into it. By twisting or slanting just one level of the four-storey high building, we can gain another level that we can use for, let's say, a sauna. The problem is that we cannot set stilts into the lake because you cannot touch nature in Vienna; you have to build around trees instead of through them. Our solution allows us to create a building that cantilevers about 100 feet. It would have been much easier to have stilts, however, if it had been permitted. I have to admit this is just an excuse because cantilevers allow us to define the energy lines, cut off from the air, that create space.

Another scheme that we are presently working on also uses cantilevers. It is for an office building in Vienna. Part of the structure twists in order to incorporate both nature and a recreation area into the building. The cantilevers have two other advantages: first, a lot of money and room can be saved on staircases because there are ramps which go from the basement to the top of the building; second, such a concept is very convincing for the client. Actually, by twisting and slanting things you gain a lot of special spatial situations.

Architecture needs at least three standing points to be stable. In the last two or three years we have been working on the third leg. We really want to get rid of it. In our first trial with this, there were two legs and the third leg was, of course, not a standing leg but more of an attention leg. In the chair that we designed the third leg was a very thin spiral. The first time we almost got rid of it completely was in our 40-foot tower for Osaka Expo. This seemingly third leg does not support anything because it ends in a needle-point. So we replaced the third leg with a very thin tension rod which makes the structure stable.

By getting rid of the third leg, the other two legs are ready to move. It has become very important for us to create moveable things, not only spaces but parts too. For instance, an office project we did is closed, not by a normal door but by a five-metre long and three-metre high glass wall with a sliding door. If it is five-metres long, where do you go?

We have also started to move around small parts in our projects. For instance, we designed a kitchen that has both vertical and horizontal movement in its bar table. It is complex: if you move this bar everything else moves too. It is very disturbing, but it is fun to cook because you are forced to be creative!

Our sports stadium in Vienna has a removable roof as well as a moveable bridge that is a skating area. There is an ice bar as well so that in the summer you can skate from the sporting rink to the bar. The elevator and the bridge also go up and down.

In the Japanese bar that we designed the main parts, too, are moveable. The bar not only moves on the inside but it actually breaks through the exterior roof. You know how these Japanese sites are all the same, very refined, very small. You have to go upward to make a door. There are six bars ascending from the basement and they all have very different slanted floors. You can actually rent the most expensive champagne bar. The more you pay in one of the bars, the higher you are elevated. I am sure there is only one position because everyone wants to be on top.

So, moveable parts are at the forefront of our latest projects. When we talked to our Japanese client for the first time, he was very concerned about Open Architecture. He thought that we did not need to use glass for the roof-top. The Japanese like their bars closed with no windows. So we designed a closed space; the only open space is in the roof where there is an overview of the city.

The way we got this project was very funny. I got a call from Tokyo and was asked, 'Do you want to build a bar in Tokyo?' I said, 'A bar, a restaurant, OK, why not?' So, I met the client. He had a bunch of publications about Himmelblau in his hand and said, 'I want you to make a bar for us and it should look like this, this and this; and this is the building you should build within it.' I looked at this building and said, 'How can we do that to a Post-Modern building? I don't know if the architects would be very pleased if we started penetrating their walls.' And he looked at me and said, 'OK, what do you want to build?' I said, 'We want to build buildings with moveable rooms and flying staircases and burning walls and things like that.' And he said very seriously, 'We will do that.' I said, 'Oh, God, I know, I know.' He then took out his filofax. It was no calendar, but packed with city maps. On every city map there were red pointers. He showed me, 'This is Sydney, this is Toronto, this is New York. This is my property.' And we ended up in Fukuoka where he said, 'Here, you will build.' I said, 'Yeah, why not? Of course.' And snap – a photographer came and there was the contract.

When we came to prepare this project for Fukuoka, I could not go to Tokyo so we made a video in Los Angeles. Consequently, we got a letter and the client said that this project was too good for Fukuoka, he had a better site in Sapporo. He sent me over to look at the site. It was perfect. We are now in the process of moving this project to Sapporo.

We have a second office in Los Angeles where we have had a commission to do a shopping centre. It is a combination of a bar, two restaurants, two bookstores and several boutiques. It is on a corner of Melrose Street. Melrose, in LA, is the only street where people walk rather than drive. So we decided, since it was a very special site, to place the bar on the corner and make the bar out of moveable platforms. It is the same game as the Japanese project: the more you pay, the higher you are. I am curious to see how the three bars will compete – who pays more and so forth. For us it is the first time since the Open House project, done in Europe, that we have really had to think how to build in Los Angeles. We are used to the Viennese tradition of having to do detailing thoroughly. In California, we are having to deal with splitting up boxes because building boxes in Los Angeles is a game – the boxes should last five years. We have tried to make the box more complex than it is.

Another project we have is for the Groningen follies. Several of our friends, including Zaha Hadid and Bernard Tschumi, were also invited to participate in this video exhibition. We all had to choose two programmes. We chose the rock 'n' roll and the sex programmes; then, we had to design a folly that would provide the space in which 40 people could watch the videos. We have placed our folly in the river so that it is only accessible by bridge.

I think the last lecture I did here in London was three years ago at the Architectural Association. When I showed my last slide, at the end, I said that I would be back if the project was built. Well, I came back! I will handle my next two projects in the same way. They are an office building for LA and a hotel tower for Vienna. The latter is not just a hotel, it is a hybrid building with an infrastructural programme: the lobby and apartments are on the top with the hotel in between. I promise, if this is built, I will be back to give you another lecture.

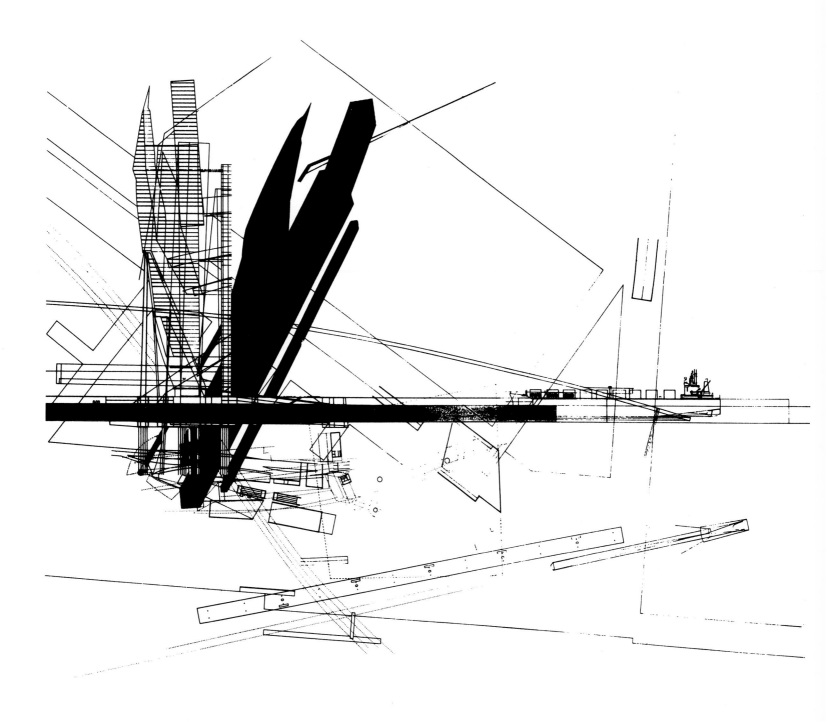

COOP HIMMELBLAU

OPEN HOUSE, MALIBU

Created from an explosion-like sketch drawn with eyes closed. Undistracted concentration, the hand as a seismograph of those feelings created by space.

It was not the details which were important at the moment, but the rays of light and shadow, brightness and darkness, height and width, whiteness and vaulting, the view and the air.

The house – slanted body and vaulted skin – is 2,050 square feet. The entry, a stairway.

The current of energy in the sketch is translated into statics and construction. The building itself – resting on three points and taut – almost floats. The construction of the taut elements makes a double-glazed skin possible.

Protection of the building brings about a double-shelled construction, suitable for its passive energy concept, as well as ever-possible alteration. There is no predetermined division of a living area. That could or could not result after the completion of the house – that, too, is Open Architecture.

See opposite and pages 66-67

JASMAC BAR BUILDING

A four-storey restaurant building with five different bars. The Champagne Bar is in a special room which can move up and down through the roof.

See page 68

REHAK HOUSE, MALIBU

The building site is very inconveniently divided. An isthmus juts through it, creating a northern plateau and a southern slope. We decided to design the building in accordance with the precipitous southern slope. The first sketch and the first model depict the concept. Two arms – we call them the city-view arm and the ocean-view arm – are affixed to the slope in the shape of an 'x'. Flying platforms, accessible rooftops and a tower all tie the volume together.

See page 69

OSAKA FOLLY

The creation of a society of plenty and charm for the 21st-century was the theme for the International Garden and Greenery Exposition at Osaka: based on the proposal of Arata Isozaki, one of the Expo's general producers, 13 follies were designed by a dynamic selection of invited architects. The architects were allocated similar budgets and the basic formula for size was a 7.5 metre cube.

Follies, to us, are prospective studies of future buildings; elements of the sculptures can and will appear within our upcoming projects.

The Expo folly in Osaka is therefore only seemingly a 25-metre-high tower within an observation platform. The elements of the tower – the head, body and construction – are, in fact, outlined elements of a six-storey building made out of steel and glass.

See pages 70 - 71

EUROPE SQUARE CENTRE

Monofunctional structures are no longer adequate for the architecture and the urban development of the coming millennium. Urban planning of the future will reflect the complexity of our intellectual and material life like a mirror. Not only the media, but also the architecture represents therefore the future of our urban culture.

A city is only then a city when you feel complexity and tension in the city, high and low, compression and emptiness, loud and quiet, heat and cold, softness and hardness, confusion and clarity – established in possible structures (Coop Himmelblau, 1987).

The Europe Square Centre, located on the western edge of the heart of the town St Polten, creates both in structure and form the ideal counterweight to the planned government centre. Both of these, thought of as centres of gravity, will form crystallisation points which will encourage further developments.

To take this demand into account the Europe Square Centre will be developed in three construction phases (A, B and C). The urban landscape context of the first phase creates a space sequence and a differentiated continuity of open and closed, public and private plazas, streets and galleries.

The basic idea in construction phase A is to open the Centre towards the Europe Square. The two office towers emphasise the entrance. The sunken plaza, covered with a glass roof, is a public square which also promotes a feeling of privacy.

The multifunctional programme of the centre is the basis for the complexity of the architectural design.

See pages 72 -75

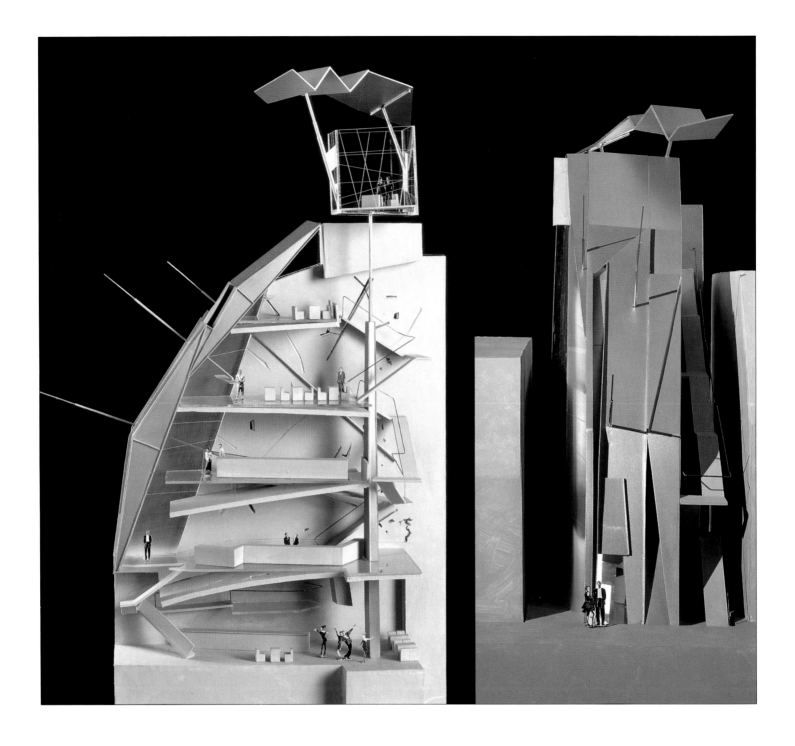

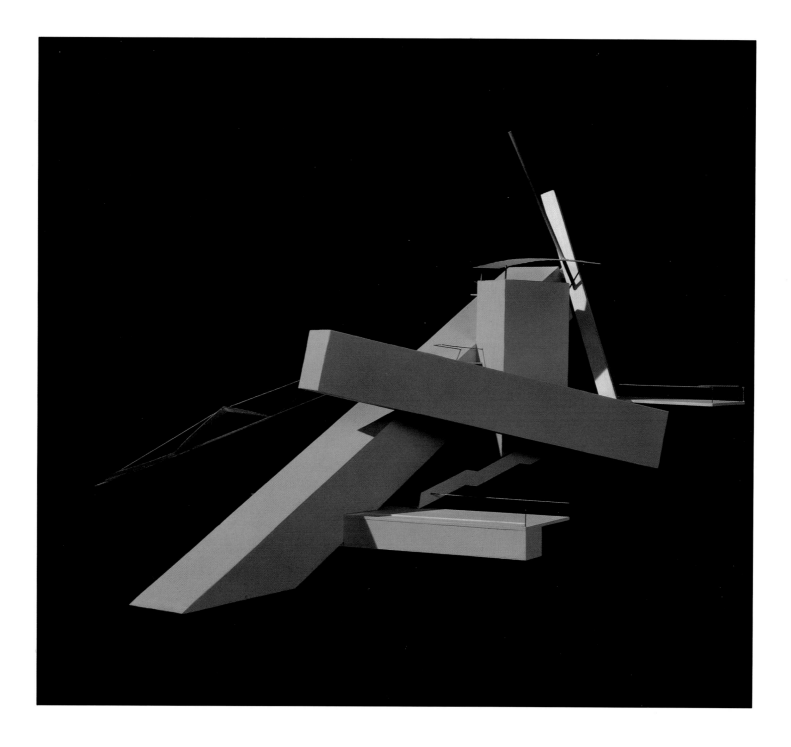

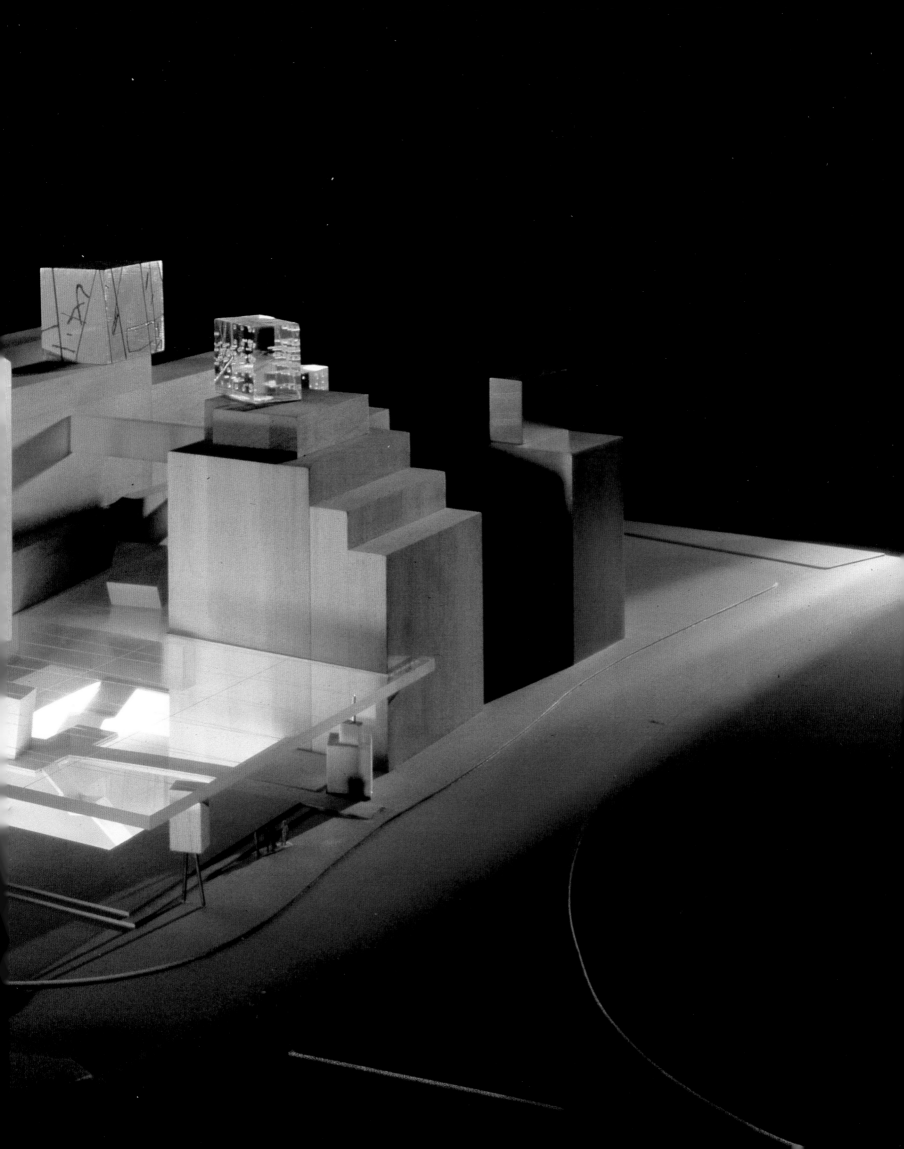

DILLER & SCOFIDIO

PARA-SITE
An Installation in the Projects Room, Museum of Modern Art, New York

Is it possible to assume a critical position towards an institution (the museum) while consenting to occupy it, or, can the target and the weapon be the same? Can architecture, positioned within the museum context, retain its power as architecture without being exiled into art?

The biological parasite is an organism living in or on another organism. 'The parasite changes hostility into hospitality, exchanges outside for inside.' As a physical site, the museum is regarded as an indifferent topography for opportunistic constructions. Favouring features most immediate for physical and electrical sustenance, the guest structures select from a taxonomy of physical relations to their host, which include suspending from, wedging between, cantilevering off, compressing against and suctioning onto.

The sycophantic parasite frequents the tables of the rich and earns welcome by flattery. 'The parasite pays in parables. The word is made flesh.' As a cultural site, the museum is regarded as an authority that constructs narratives – determined by the dominant point of view, by the rigid categories of Modernist aesthetics, by chronologies based on the paradigm of the textbook, etc. The installation pays with fetishised detailing of 'high design' to gain the museum's welcome of our rude violations beyond the 'designated site' of the Projects Room. Targeting MOMA's and, by extension, Modernism's privileging of vision as the master sense, purified and sequestered from the social domain, the project undertakes broader issues of visuality. It offers the entertainment value of voyeurism to a public unwittingly lured into a closer inspection of vision . . . socially constructed, gendered, scopophylic, paranoid, and in the service of control and dominance.

The technological parasite creates static-like interference in an information circuit. 'The system is cancelled when the parasited one makes noise in feedback.' The museum is regarded as an encoded field of exchanges between bodies, building and artefacts; all irreducible museological units. The guest structures, through physical and optical interventions, interrupt direct circuits in that field to torque it.

Situated between 'inscription' and 'prescription', this architecture of 'description' is concerned with neither past nor future, only the hyper-present. Though description is commonly understood to be recapitulation, passive and uncritical, we employ it actively, as intervention. By articulating the culturally loaded spaces of and between surfaces and foregrounding their relations, those relations are inevitably disrupted.

Location 1: The main entrance, the first legitimising frame of the institution. Substituting for the honorific grand entrance of the historic museum are four valves for non-stop exchanges of bodies. The lobby ceiling hosts four spider cameras, clinging face down, one centred over each revolving door.

Four side-by-side monitors, structurally wedged between the wall and ceiling of the Projects Room, receive input from the cameras to survey the reconstructed plan view through the entry wall.

The fictive viewer is rotated 180 degrees; the actual ceiling is the fictive floor plane. The monitors are optical hinges shared by fictive and actual viewers.

Location 2: The main stair, the sectional departure from street level. Substituting for the ceremonial grand stair of the historic museum is a mechanical stair; like the revolving door, another apparatus for the expedient transport of consumers through retail space. An existing column hosts two cameras cantilevered into the lobby, one aimed at the ascending escalator, the other at the descending.

Within the Projects Room, two receiving monitors are cantilevered from that column. The movement of the mechanical stairs provides a constant stream of bodies vertically scanned by the fixed frames of the TV screens.

The eyes of the fictive viewer and actual viewer coincide at the apex of the cantilever. The side-by-side monitors reconstruct the halved images of the escalator. However, binocular vision is cut by a blade into two monocular views.

Location 3: The rear doors open out to the Sculpture Garden, a domesticated outdoors. A camera from within the room is aimed outside onto a convex mirror that sees the doors. The mirror clamps and sucks onto the exterior glass wall.

The Projects Room hosts a tripodal structure wedged between two walls, bearing a receiving monitor displaying the movement of bodies between the lobby and garden.

The fictive observer is rotated 90 degrees; the wall is the fictive floor. Meanwhile, the horizontal median cuts the fictive construction in half. A mirror, rotated to 45 degrees above the construction, reflects sectional information, upright, turning the floor into the fictive wall and the wall studs into fictive floor joists.

See opposite and pages 78-79

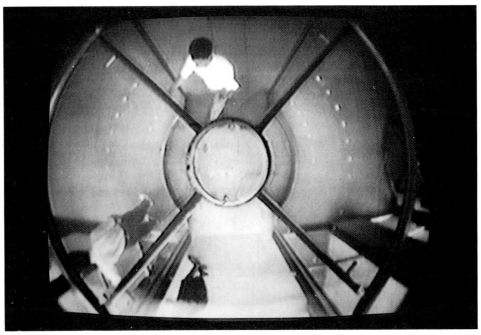

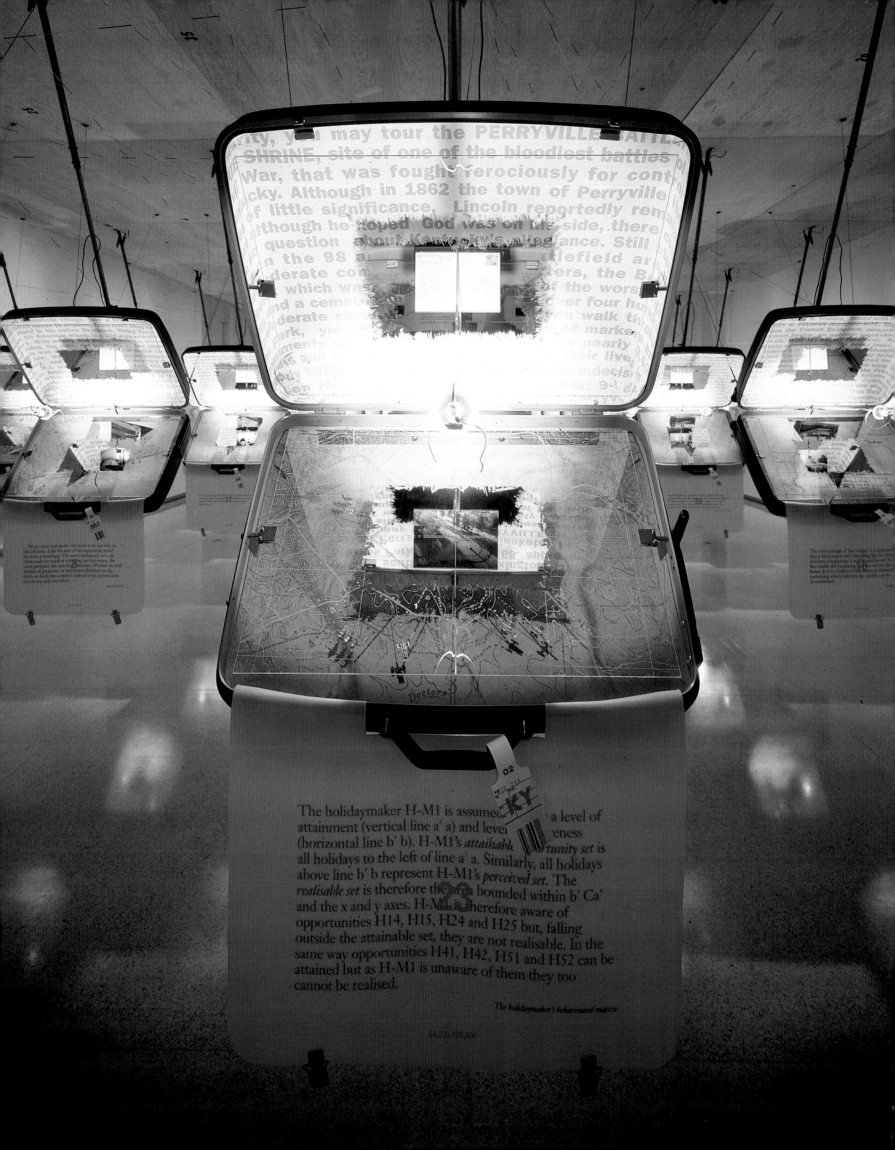

...ity, you may tour the PERRYVILLE BATTLE SHRINE, site of one of the bloodiest battles of... War, that was fought ferociously for cont... ...cky. Although in 1862 the town of Perryville... ...f little significance, Lincoln reportedly rema... ...lthough he hoped God was on his side, there... ...question about Kentucky's allegiance. Still... ...n the 98 a... ...ttlefield ar... ...derate con... ...ers, the B... ...which was... ...of the wors... ...nd a cemete... ...over four hu... ...derate casu... ...you walk th... ...park, you... ...of marke... ...ments t... ...nearly... ...s and... ...their live... ...uy little... ...he indecis... ...en Ha...

The holidaymaker H-M1 is assumed... a level of attainment (vertical line a' a) and level... ...eness (horizontal line b' b). H-M1's *attainab*... *...rtunity set* is all holidays to the left of line a' a. Similarly, all holidays above line b' b represent H-M1's *perceived set*. The *realisable set* is therefore the area bounded within b' Ca' and the x and y axes. H-M1 is therefore aware of opportunities H14, H15, H24 and H25 but, falling outside the attainable set, they are not realisable. In the same way opportunities H41, H42, H51 and H52 can be attained but as H-M1 is unaware of them they too cannot be realised.

The holidaymaker's behavioural matrix

$4,200,000,000

TOURISMS, suitCASE STUDIES, 1991
An installation at the Walker Art Center, Minneapolis

The old English word 'travel' was originally the same as 'travail' (meaning trouble, work, or torment) which in turn comes from the popular Latin tripalium *(a three-staked instrument of torture).*

Daniel Boorstin

In distinguishing travel from the mediated and consoling experience of commercial tourism, Patrick Fermor predicts that in killing the thing that it loves, tourism will become so hellish that it will start to resemble a quest for a new kind of strenuousness and perhaps return full circle to the idea of 'travel'.

In a time of rapid cultural assimilation in which mobility is replaced by the 'absolute speed' of telecommunications, travel curiously remains a highly valued activity. However, in today's travel/tourism, relations between bodies, geographies, histories, and technologies have reconfigured.

In the conversion of *site* into *sight*, the sightseer must pay for his optical pleasure. His desire for authenticity, for example, in the case of the historic site, to stand on the very spot the general fell, to occupy the actual room in which the celebrity slept, to see the original manuscript later drafted into law, is fulfilled through a construction of site/sight representations in which historic time may be petrified, re-enacted, or completely fictionalised. Some constructions of tourism overtly act as time machines thrusting us backwards and forwards through the present.

The tourist's accountability towards the authentic experience resides in the souvenir and the snapshot, both irreducible pieces of portable evidence of the sight having been seen. As the ultimate authenticating agent, the camera collapses physical distance into the space between prescribed photo opportunities. Within that shallow space, tourism displaces the *unsightly* into a visual blind zone while freely transplanting attractions from donor sites into the reconstructed visual field. Onto this altered geography, tourism disperses the location of origin, the home,

as a way of domesticating travel. 'You'll feel right at home' is the reassuring advertising slogan of Caravan Tours.

Contemporary travel/tourism parallels our new sensibility engendered by tele-technologies. It engages in a highly structured yet delirious free play of space and time in which our stability is simultaneously assured and thwarted.

As a travelling exhibition, the show's mobility parallels its theme. The exhibition travels in 50 identical Samsonite suitcases, the suitcase being the irreducible, portable unit of the home. In addition to transporting the contents of the exhibition, the suitcases double as display cases for the exhibition of their contents. Further, the exhibition accepts its own role as attraction, implicating the museum as a complicitous agent in the tourist trade.

Beds and Battlefields: Two types of attractions feed on the tourist's desire for authenticity and his abiding interest in the legacy of heroism. The *vacated* bed of the popular figure and the *vacated* landscape of the soldier are both imbued with 'presence' – presence, however, of a kind which accepts the replacement of immediacy with a system of representations.

The bed is the most private site of the body's inscription onto the domestic field. The tourist/voyeur, only permitted to peer through the door frame, confirming the official postcard view, is privileged to an enshrinement of the ordinary. Each artefact placed inside the sanitised field of vision is a marker that plays a precise narrative role in the embodiment of that public figure.

The battlefield, an otherwise undifferentiated ground, becomes an ideologically encoded landscape through the commemorative and hortatory function of the marker. As the marker inscribes the war onto material soil, it becomes the *sight*. Directed by a system of markers, the tourist/strategist participates in a re-enactment of the battle, tracing the tragic space of conflict by foot or by car.

The construction of 'aura' by the institution of tourism puts into motion a complex exchange of referentiality between the *sight* and its *supplements*, in which the tourist, craving unmediated vision, may no longer need to distinguish one from the other.

See opposite and below

GÜNTHER DOMENIG

STONEHOUSE, STEINDORF, CARINTHIA

As the Stonehouse takes shape, appearing like a bank of earth breaking out of a rockface, it seems more and more the translation of a mountainous landscape into architecture. The house was the subject of an exhibition at the Austrian Museum of Applied Arts in Vienna. About 12 years ago (1979-80), Domenig's first act of intervention in this site was the building of a wooden landing-stage, a complicated construction which oscillates between water and land, an object to climb up or jump from. But he has been thinking about the place for more than 20 years, trying to work out how to define a piece of family land closely linked with the story of his childhood, and how to mark it with a personal sign of individual rebellion and anti-conformity. His first attempt was a project in the form of a sketch showing a hill that had been broken up into pieces and shorn clean through. This is what started it all, the metamorphosis of an idea, the transformation of a story into a built work. Already you can see what the architect can no longer find words to describe but can only feel: personal references set in concrete, to be sure, but also a point of juncture between the vernacular building of Carinthia and the Code of the Universe, translated into the language of architecture.

The next step was the concept of a mound of earth breaking out of a rockface. This phase produced elaborate drawings invoking Domenig's memories of the configurations of the rock outcrops in Mölltal, where he spent many years as a child: 'I can't break free of my memories. I went back to Mölltal after 35 years or so and hid myself away in a mountain inn, where I made a conscious study of these configurations, sketching, absorbing the archetypal architectural elements they contain. This was the source of the series of sketches I call *Broken Architecture*.' This phase was, like all the ones that followed it, short-lived, sketchy, a continually fluctuating combination of helplessness and extreme competence, conveying both the perpetual desire to discover the immediate and new, and the will to make a rebellion, or simply a metaphorical sign.

This gave rise to the eruption of the forms, the penetration of the hollows, the paths leading up and down, the emergency exit appearing like a ravine cutting deep below the water table and ending in a spiral. Below the water level you feel the sudden drop in temperature – the coldness of the deep, but also the melancholy of the builder. The helix, the crypt, the catacomb, the coffin-cum-rocket, the glass cylinder that protects the ground-water like a tabernacle – all create a mystical chapel for the architect, a protective chamber, a place where he can retreat from the insults and degradations levelled at someone who is not prepared to appease the society in which he lives. His memories, his background and his family give him the strength to continue his struggle.

There's a way which leads out of this almost alarming, funereal, melancholy place into the bright sunlight. It takes you to the highest point of the house, from where you can see the building's geometrically powerful, highly imaginative forms cut like a knife through the artificial landscape created by the camping ground and swimming pool.

Perhaps this abstract fantasy expressed in concrete, this sally to the borders of a glittering, fictive world, has caused Domenig to betray his inner autonomy, his personal memories, his past, his relationship to his (artistic) friends, even his own beliefs in architecture.

Judging by the painstaking attention given to every important detail, this building is a long-term, open-ended project. Construction has been going on since spring 1986, but in the summer months Domenig has to observe a strict building ban imposed by the local authority during the height of the tourist season. As time passes, Domenig appears increasingly concerned that in the end this house, which was planned and developed for this place, and could stand nowhere else, will not be accepted by the locals, who are gradually becoming uneasy and have started to say that it is wrong for Domenig to have been building for so long and still not have an end in sight. A miner who had been observing the construction work right from the start through his telescope recently asked Domenig if he hadn't in fact got the direction of the building wrong. And local government officials have said they want to have a word with him about the project.

Domenig also clearly believes his project will be seen as a one-off, that he cannot influence the way others build in the region of his cool and somewhat intimidating work with its 'squint cube' for socialising, 'wedge' for eating and 'piggyback' for sleeping in. But for him there is no turning back. He continues, like a man obsessed, to work on translating and realising his thoughts into a building. From the beginning he has had to be patient: it took seven years, for example, just to get planning permission.

The power of the forms, the atmospherically rich moments, the fantasies, the strange familiarity of what is unknown in this building, which alters almost daily, are both the source of the architect's strength and the things which drain him. The Stonehouse is what fate has dealt to an architect who now must live with having the unknown as a concrete image before his eyes.

See opposite and pages 84-87

DIE VERZWEIGUNG

G Domening 80

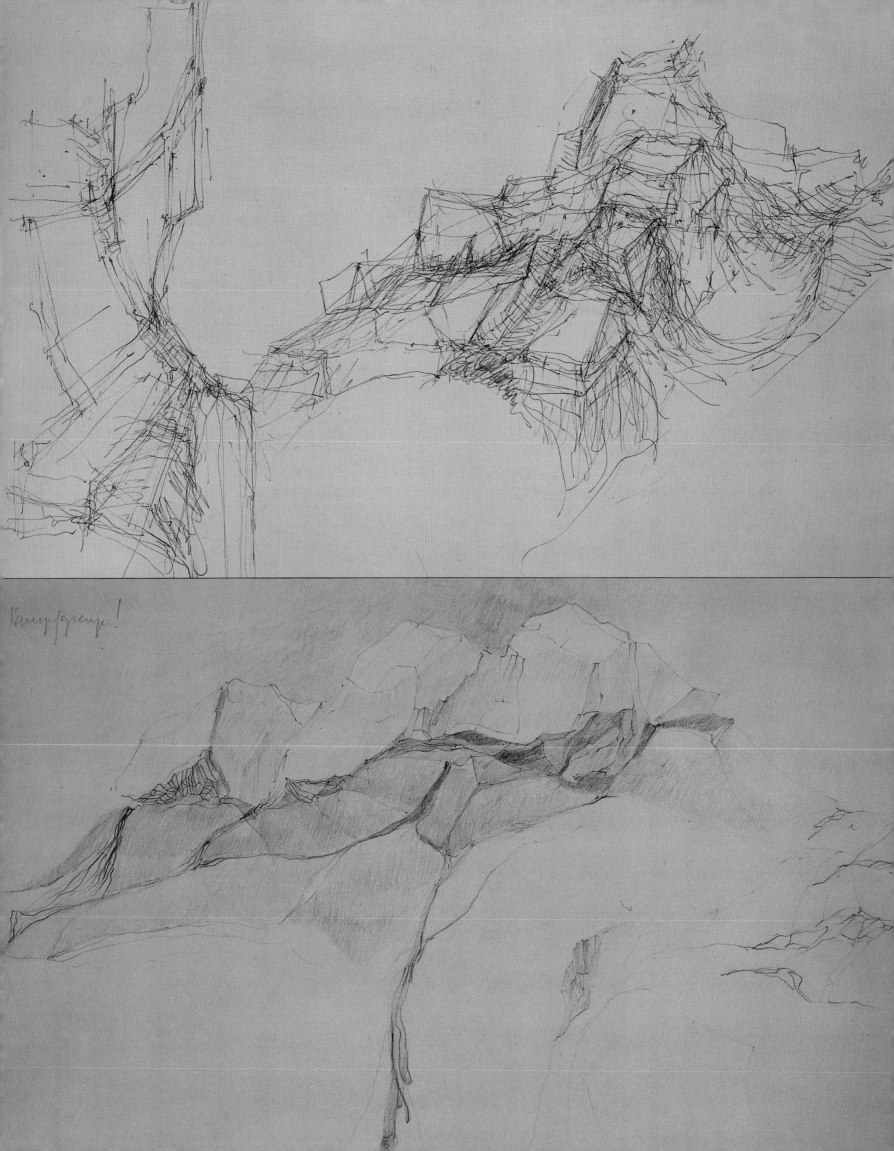

Kampfgrenze!

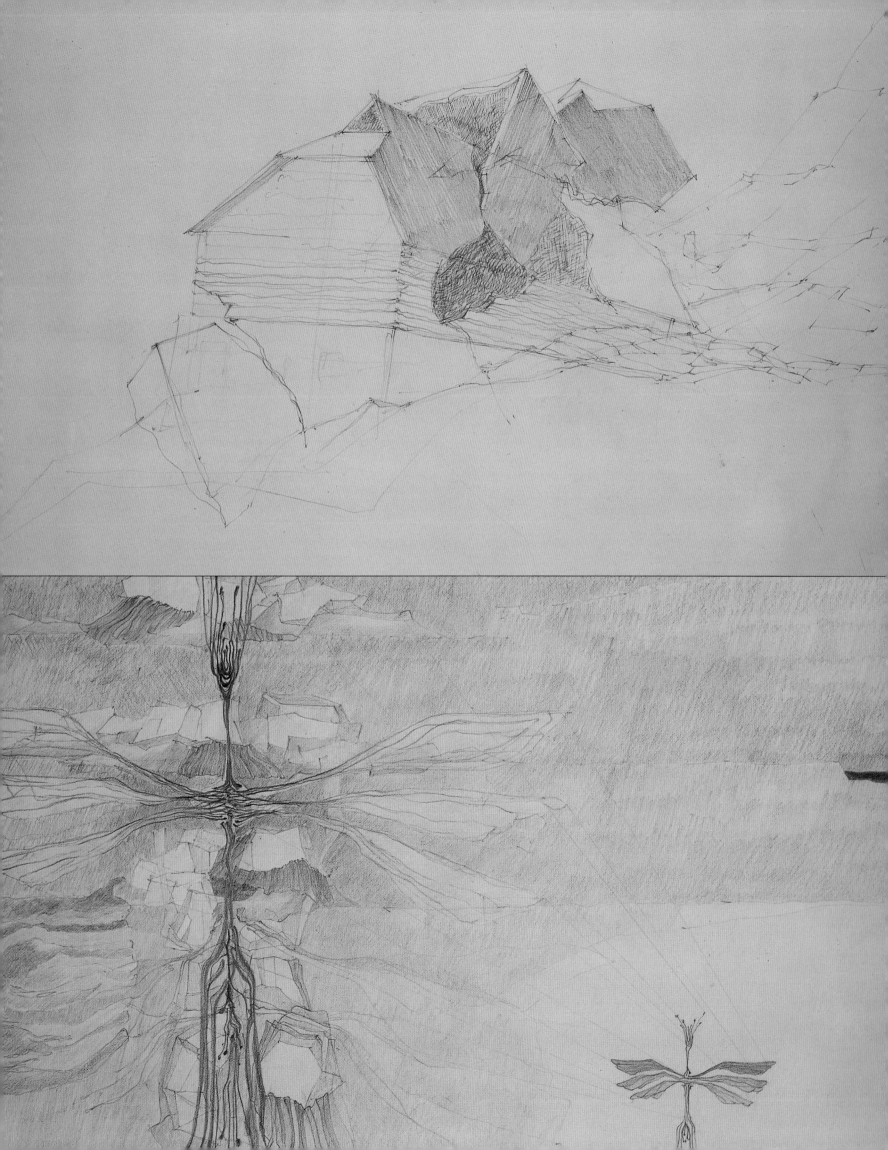

PETER EISENMAN
VISIONS UNFOLDING
Architecture in the Age of Electronic Media

During the 50 years since the Second World War, a paradigm shift has taken place that should have profoundly affected architecture: this was the shift from the mechanical paradigm to the electronic one. This change can be understood by comparing the impact of the role of the human subject on such primary modes of reproduction as the photograph and the fax; the photograph within the mechanical paradigm, the fax within the electronic one.

In photographic reproduction the subject maintains a controlled interaction with the object. A photograph can be developed with more or less contrast, texture or clarity. The photograph can remain in the control of human vision. The human subject thus retains its function as interpreter, as discursive function. With the fax, the subject is no longer called upon to interpret, for reproduction takes place without any control or adjustment. The fax also challenges the concept of originality. While in a photograph the original reproduction still retains a privileged value, in facsimile transmission the original remains intact but with no differentiating value since it is no longer sent. The mutual devaluation of both original and copy is not the only transformation affected by the electronic paradigm. The entire nature of what we know as the reality of our world has been called into question by the invasion of media into everyday life. For reality always demanded that our vision be interpretive.

How have these developments affected architecture? Since architecture has traditionally housed value as well as fact, one would imagine that architecture would have been greatly transformed. But this is not the case, for architecture seems little changed at all. This in itself ought to warrant investigation, since architecture has traditionally been a bastion of what is considered to be the real. Metaphors such as house and home, bricks and mortar, foundations and shelter attest to architecture's role in defining what we consider to be real. A change in the everyday concepts of reality should have had some effect on architecture. It did not because the mechanical paradigm was the *sine qua non* of architecture; architecture was the visible manifestation of the overcoming of natural forces such as gravity and weather by mechanical means. Architecture not only overcame gravity, it was also the monument to that overcoming; it interpreted the value society placed on its vision.

The electronic paradigm directs a powerful challenge to architecture because it defines reality in terms of media and simulation; it values appearance over existence, what can be seen over what is. Not the seen as we formerly knew it, but rather a seeing that can no longer interpret. Media introduce fundamental ambiguities into how and what we see. Architecture has resisted this question because, since the importation and absorption of perspective by architectural space in the 15th century, architecture has been dominated by the mechanics of vision. Thus architecture assumes sight to be pre-eminent and also in some way natural to its own processes, not as a thing to be questioned. It is precisely this traditional concept of sight that the electronic paradigm questions.

Sight is traditionally understood in terms of vision. When I use the term 'vision' I mean that particular characteristic of sight which attaches seeing to thinking, the eye to the mind. In architecture, vision refers to a particular category of perception linked to monocular perspectival vision. The monocular vision of the subject in architecture allows for all projections of space to be resolved on a single planimetric surface. It is therefore not surprising that perspective, with its ability to define and reproduce the perception of depth on a two-dimensional surface, should find architecture a waiting and wanting vehicle. Nor is it surprising that architecture soon began to conform itself to this monocular, rationalising vision – in its own body. Whatever the style, space was constituted as an understandable construct, organised around spatial elements such as axes, places, symmetries, etc. Perspective is even more virulent in architecture than in painting because of the imperious demands of the eye *and* the body to orient itself in architectural space through processes of rational perspectival ordering. It was thus not without cause that Brunelleschi's invention of one-point perspective should correspond to a time when there was a paradigm shift from the theological and theocentric to the anthropomorphic and anthropocentric views of the world. Perspective became the vehicle by which anthropocentric vision crystallised itself in the architecture that followed this shift.

From time to time architecture has attempted to overcome its rationalising vision. If one takes for example the church of San Vitale in Ravenna one can explain the solitary column almost blocking the entry or the incomplete groin vaulting as an attempt to signal a change from a Pagan to a Christian architecture. Piranesi created similar effects with his architectural projections. Piranesi diffracted the monocular subject by creating perspectival visions with multiple vanishing points so that there was no way of correlating what was seen into a unified whole. Equally, Cubism attempted to deflect the relationship between a monocular subject and the object. The subject could no longer put the painting into some meaningful structure through the use of perspective. Cubism used a non-monocular perspectival condition: it flattened objects to the edges, it upturned objects, it undermined the stability of the picture plane. Architecture attempted similar dislocations through Constructivism and its own, albeit normalising, version of Cubism – the International Style. But this work only looked cubistic and modern, the subject remained rooted in a profound anthropocentric stability, comfortably upright and in place on a flat, tabular ground. There was no shift in the relationship between the subject and the object. While the object looked different it failed to displace the viewing subject. Though the buildings were sometimes conceptualised, by axonometric or isometric projection rather than by perspective, no consistent deflection of the subject was carried out. Yet Modernist sculpture did in many cases effect such a displacement of the subject. These dislocations were fundamental to Minimalism: the early work of Robert Morris, Michael Heizer and Robert Smithson. This historical project, however, was never taken up in architecture. Why did architecture resist developments that were taking place in other disciplines? And further, why has the issue of vision never been properly problematised in architecture?

It might be said that architecture never adequately thought through the problem of vision because it remained within the concept of the subject and the four walls. Architecture, unlike any other discipline, concretised vision. The hierarchy inherent in all architectural space begins as a structure for the mind's eye. It is perhaps the idea of interiority as a hierarchy between inside and outside that causes architecture to conceptualise itself ever more comfortably and conservatively in vision. The interiority of architecture defined a hierarchy of vision articulated by inside and outside. The fact that one is actually both inside and outside with architecture, unlike painting or music, required vision to conceptualise itself in this way. As long as architecture refuses to take up the problem of vision, it will remain within a Renaissance or Classical view of its discourse.

Now what would it mean for architecture to take up the problem of vision? Vision can be defined as essentially a way of organising space and elements in space. It is a way of looking at, and defines a relationship between a subject and an object. Traditional architecture is structured so that any position occupied by a subject provides a means for understanding that position in relation to a particular spatial typology, such as a rotunda, a transept crossing, an axis, an entry. Any number of these typological conditionals deploy architecture as a screen for looking at.

The idea of a 'looking back' begins to displace the anthropocentric subject. Looking back does not require the object to become a subject, that is to anthropomorphise the object. Looking back concerns the possibility of detaching the subject from the rationalisation of space. In other words to allow the subject to have a vision of space that no longer can be put together in the normalising, classicising or traditional construct of vision; an other space, where in fact the space 'looks back' at the subject. A possible first step in conceptualising this other space, would be to detach what one sees from what one knows – the eye from the mind. A second step would be to inscribe space in such a way as to endow it with the possibility of looking back at the subject. All architecture can be said to be already inscribed. Windows, doors, beams and columns are a kind of inscription. These make architecture known, they reinforce vision. Since no space is uninscribed, we do not see a window without relating it to an idea of window, this kind of inscription seems not only natural but also necessary to architecture. In order to have a looking back, it is necessary to rethink the idea of inscription. In the Baroque and Rococo such an inscription was in the plaster decoration that began to obscure the traditional form of functional inscription. This kind of 'decorative' description was thought too excessive when undefined by function. Architecture tends to resist this form of excess in a way which is unique amongst the arts, precisely because of the power and pervasive nature of functional inscription. The anomalous column at San Vitale inscribes space in a way that was at the time foreign to the eye. To dislocate vision might require an inscription which is the result of an outside text which is neither overly determined by design expression or function. But how could such an inscription of an outside text translate into space?

Suppose for a moment that architecture could be conceptualised as a Moebius strip, with an unbroken continuity between interior and exterior. What would this mean for vision? Gilles Deleuze has proposed just such a possible continuity with his idea of the fold. For Deleuze, folded space articulates a new relationship between vertical and horizontal, figure and ground, inside and out – all structures articulated by traditional vision. Unlike the space of classical vision, the idea of folded space denies framing in favour of a temporal modulation. The fold no longer privileges planimetric projection; instead there is a variable curvature. Deleuze's idea of folding is more radical than origami, because it contains no narrative, linear sequence; rather, in terms of traditional vision it contains a quality of the unseen.

Folding changes the traditional space of vision. That is, it can be considered to be effective; it functions, it shelters, it is meaningful, it frames, it is aesthetic. Folding also constitutes a move from effective to affective space. Folding is not another subject expressionism, a promiscuity, but rather unfolds in space alongside of its functioning and its meaning in space – it has what might be called an excessive condition or affect. Folding is a type of affective space which concerns those aspects that are not associated with the affective, that are more than reason, meaning and function.

In order to change the relationship of perspectival projection to three-dimensional space it is necessary to change the relationship between project drawing and real space. This would mean that one would no longer be able to draw with any level of meaningfulness the space that is being projected. For example, when it is no longer possible to draw a line that stands for some scale relationship to another line in space, it has nothing to do with reason, of the connection of the mind to the eye. The deflection from that line in space means that there no longer exists a one-to-one scale correspondence.

My folded projects are a primitive beginning. In them the subject understands that he or she can no longer conceptualise experience in space in the same way that he or she did in the gridded space. They attempt to provide this dislocation of the subject from effective space; an idea of presentness. Once the environment becomes affective, inscribed with another logic or an ur-logic, one which is no longer translatable into the vision of the mind, then reason becomes detached from vision. While we can still understand space in terms of its function, structure and aesthetic – we are still within the 'four walls' – somehow reason becomes detached from the affective condition of the environment itself. This begins to produce an environment that 'looks back' – that is, the environment seems to have an order that we can perceive even though it does not seem to mean anything. It does not seek to be understood in the traditional way of architecture yet it possess some sense of 'aura', an ur-logic which is the sense of something outside of our vision. Yet one that is not another subjective expression. Folding is only one of perhaps many strategies for dislocating vision – dislocating the hierarchy of interior and exterior that pre-empts vision.

Architecture will continue to stand up, to deal with gravity, to have 'four walls'. But these four walls no longer need to be expressive of the mechanical paradigm. Rather they could deal with the possibility of these other discourses, the other affective senses of sound, touch and of that light lying within the darkness.

PETER EISENMAN

WEXNER CENTER, COLUMBUS, OHIO

The purpose of the Visual Arts Center is to provide for avant-garde and experimental arts; it is not meant to be a repository for traditional art. The building will contain permanent, temporary and experimental exhibition galleries, performance space, a 'Black Box Theater', a fine arts and graphics library, a film centre, studio spaces, administrative space, a café, a bookstore, music practice rooms, a choral hall, exhibition storage and preparation areas. The contract was awarded as the result of a limited international competition.

The initial phase of work at the Wexner Center was to develop a programme and a master site plan. In the great 19th-century tradition, the Center is a fusion of landscape and the language of building. This new building is a minimal intervention between two existing and adjacent campus buildings. The central circulation spine of the new building resolves the two existing geometries of the city and the campus.

Instead of selecting any of the obvious building sites on the campus, a new site was created, locating the building between several proposed sites and existing buildings. It also refers to past contexts with the exposure of the foundations of the armoury formerly on the site and the remaking of some of its elements. It has been described as 'a non-building – an archaeological earthwork whose essential elements are scaffolding and landscaping'.

The scaffolding consists of two intersecting three-dimensional gridded corridors which link the hall and auditorium already positioned on the site with the new galleries and arts facilities that are being constructed. One arm of the scaffolding aligns the street grid of the City of Columbus with the campus grid, which is 12.5 degrees askew, so the project both physically and symbolically links the university campus with the wider context of the city beyond, art with the community. But it does not do so in a holistic, unifying way, because the building itself is fractured and incomplete-looking. Instead of symbolising its function as shelter, or as a shelter for art, it acts as a symbol of art as process and idea, of the ever-changing nature of art and society.

See opposite and pages 94 - 95

KOIZUMI SANGYO OFFICE BUILDING, TOKYO

This building, serving to showcase light fittings for the Koizumi Sangyo Corporation, was designed in collaboration with K Architects, Kojiro Kitayama's plain and elegant eight-storey glass office block providing the context for Eisenman's abstract theory-inspired superimpositions.

Eisenman here continues to apply post-deconstructivist concepts as in his Chora-L work with Jacques Derrida and elsewhere, developing latent, potential, or 'other' orders, spaces 'between' which defy rigorous definition but always imply other spaces, shapes bearing traces of other shapes and the transformations worked upon them.

Throughout the building's interior the architect's favoured three-dimensional 'L'-shaped geometries are again to the fore, combining to form sophisticated asymmetrical sequences in three different scales, keyed in to three different graduated tones of green and pink. Externally, two 35-foot cubic exhibition spaces, positioned at opposite corners of the block (upper southeast and lower northwest) describe building-size 'L'-shapes around themselves. As a result of the complex design processes at play all parts of the building are thematically interlinked with all others, but no two spaces in the building are exactly the same.

See pages 96 - 99

COLLEGE OF DESIGN, ARCHITECTURE, ART AND PLANNING, UNIVERSITY OF CINCINNATI

The DAAP building could be described in terms of a freeze-frame from a motion picture, with complex sequences arrested at a certain moment; the juxtapositioning of its elements, and in particular the dynamic interaction between two rival orders (one precisely variegated, rigid and hard, the other curvaceous, softer, continuous) indicates the geological and physical processes – wave formations, shifting plate tectonics – which provided models for the building's design. These processes inform the structures with a sense of time, movement, perhaps even life; seen from above the segmented forms are reminiscent of some huge armadillo, which if the film restarted would shake its tail and lumber off.

See pages 100 - 103

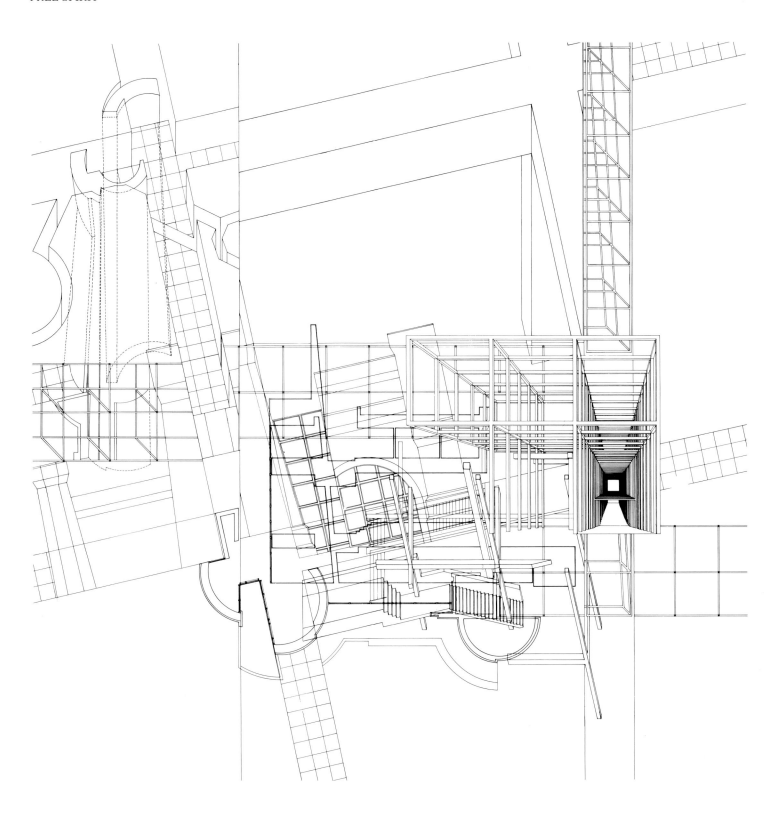

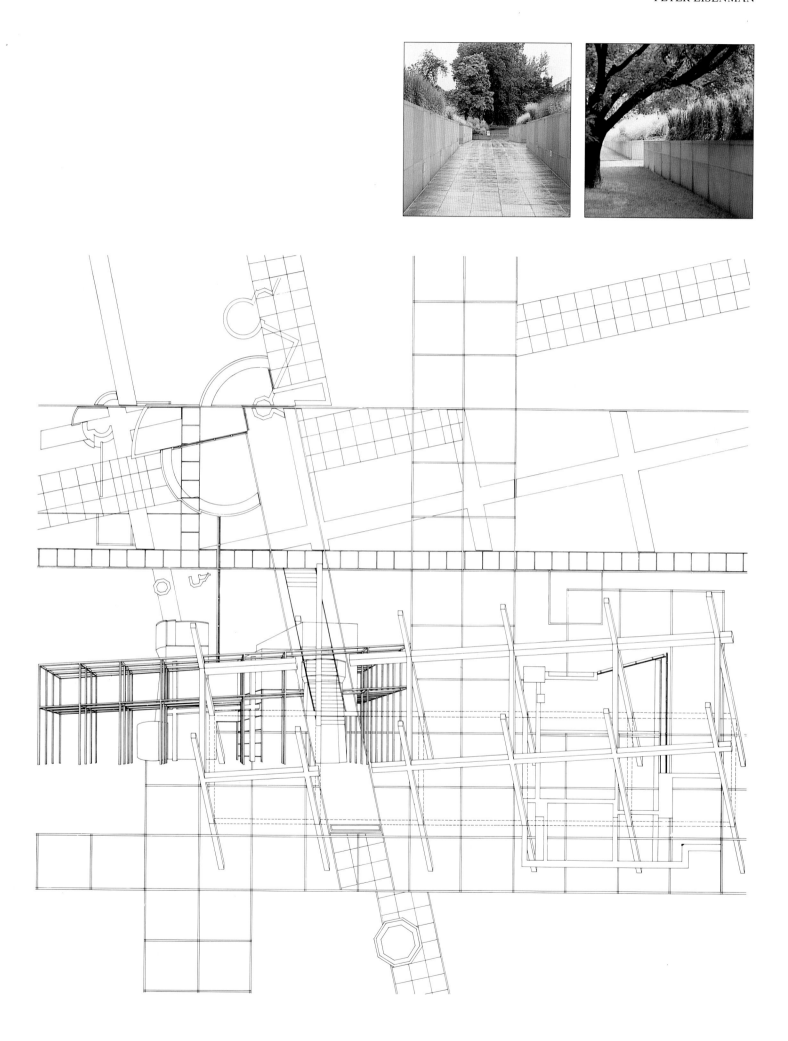

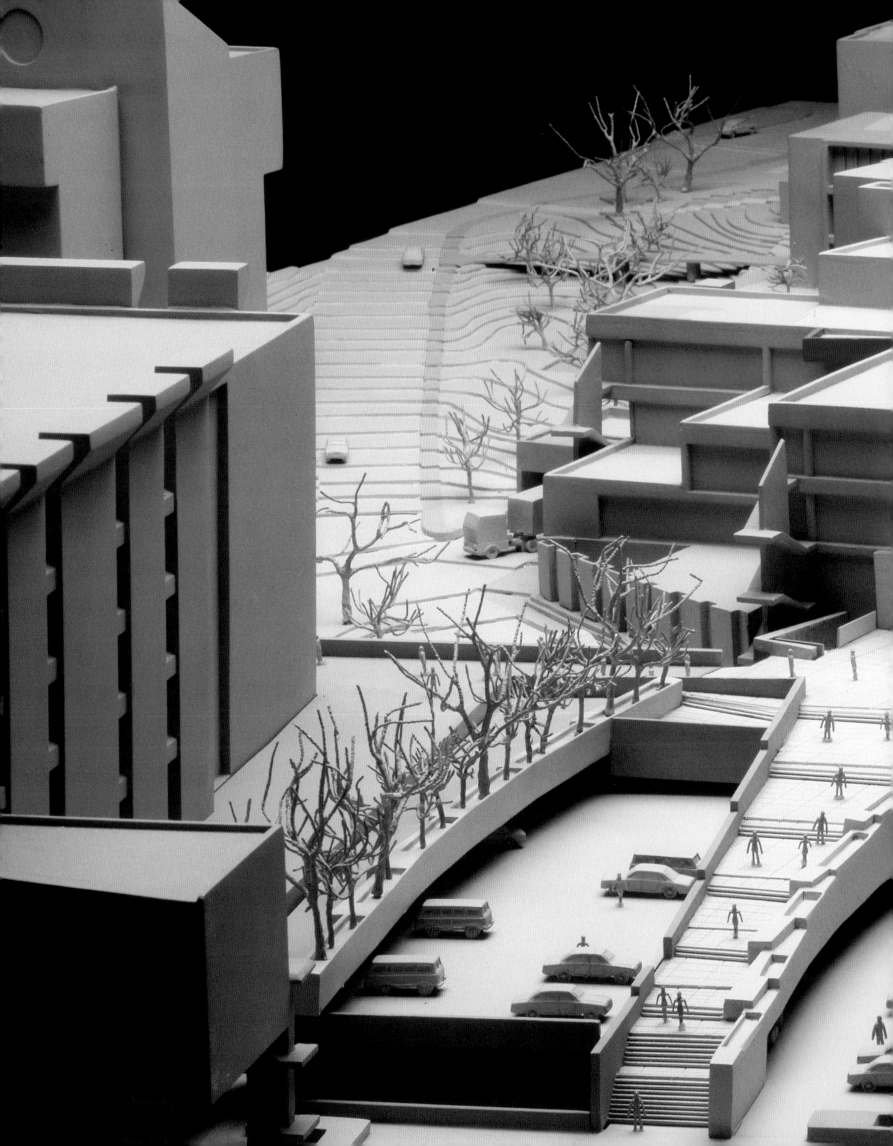

MARK FISHER

STEEL WHEELS

As a high-brow pursuit, Pop architecture has a problem. Popular culture is ephemeral, but most architecture is designed to be permanent. The high-brow dredging of popular culture to make Pop Art is OK for paintings. They can be hidden when they go out of fashion, and then rehung from time to time as historical curiosities. For architecture the only escape from old fashion is demolition. Long-life buildings are anathema to Pop architecture.

In the late 50s Reyner Banham contradicted Sir Hugh Casson, demonstrating that Pop architecture had existed before Pop Art, rather than vice versa. He proposed Albert Kahn's Ford Pavilion at the New York World's Fair of 1939 as the first example of Pop architecture because it was an advertisement, the precursor of all 'exclamatory hamburger bars and other roadside retail outlets'. An essential feature of popular culture was the disposability of everything including its aesthetic qualities. He quotes Leslie Fiedler: 'The articles of popular culture are made, not to be treasured, but to be thrown away.' Leaving aside his academic preference for crediting an architect with the invention of the genre, his thesis was that once architecture embraces commerce, it becomes Pop, subject to 'the same set of Madison Avenue rules' as popular culture – including, by implication, being thrown away.

He also noted that 'the collage-effect of violent juxtaposition of advertising matter with older art forms . . . was being widely discussed in architectural circles around the time of the Festival of Britain'. In a manner which today seems rather precious, this mixing of graphics and form can be seen in the temporary buildings of the Festival itself, which were far more exuberant than the permanent architecture of the period. The certainty of the buildings' swift demolition must have been a liberation for the architects involved.

Many of the early examples of what Banham called Pop architecture borrowed their forms from the Modern Movement. Stanley Meston, the architect of the original Golden Arches for McDonald's, introduced the parabolic arches to give the building a 'futuristic' look in 1953. He wasn't bothered that the arches had no structural function. Richard McDonald, one of the franchise's brothers, said later that 'it was fortunate the arches were not structural, since if a vehicle had run into one of them, it might have done serious damage to the building!' The life expectancy of Pop architecture has always been short. Commercial buildings like hotels and exhibition pavilions, or the interiors of shops and clubs, are really advertisements, built to last as long as the products they contain will sell. Harrison and Fouilhoux's Trylon and Perisphere, the centrepieces of the 1939 World's Fair, were copied in a whole range of consumer goods which today command good prices in antique shops. But the buildings themselves barely made it to the end of the fair. As *The New York Times* put it: 'If the builders of the Trylon were counting on a single season Fair, it might be argued that they timed themselves with 100 percent precision.'

The survival test for things in popular culture is whether or not people will buy them. In the purest form, these things are unnecessary, like fashion or entertainment. New styles are constantly invented to exploit the natural habit of consumers of becoming bored. Even when things are not improved by technical development, they are restyled to excite jaded palates. Permanent architecture cannot survive in this commercial environment; it is too durable.

One of the most transient forms of Pop architecture can be found in the world of popular music. The stage sets for outdoor rock concerts are conversion kits which change the use of space on an architectural scale. With equal ease they turn sports facilities and wastelands into transitory theatres for popular entertainment. They are large and expensive, incorporating technical equipment, decoration and weather protection, in structures which can take more than 20 trucks to transport from show to show. For the bands which perform on them they are distress purchases, brought about by the lack of facilities at the venues where they play, and the competitive need to add value to the tickets they sell. Greed and ambition drive bands to sell as many tickets as possible. These vices are endorsed by the huge public demand for tickets to the most successful shows; the Rolling Stones sold six million $35.00 tickets to their concerts during 1989-90. Left to themselves, the bands would present the cheapest shows they could get away with in the largest venues they could sell out. The fact that they present extravagant spectacles instead is a response to public demand.

The economic pressure on stage set design means that the materials and technology employed are just sufficient for the job. The sets are ephemeral; they have no use after the final concert. This is why, underneath the decorated surface, they are built from commonplace sub-structures of scaffolding and timber, assembled by hand from rented components. They are an entirely commercial architecture, sustained by voluntary public subscription and discarded as soon as they have passed their sell-by date.

See opposite ('The Wall' Tour), pages 106-107 ('Steel Wheels' Tour)

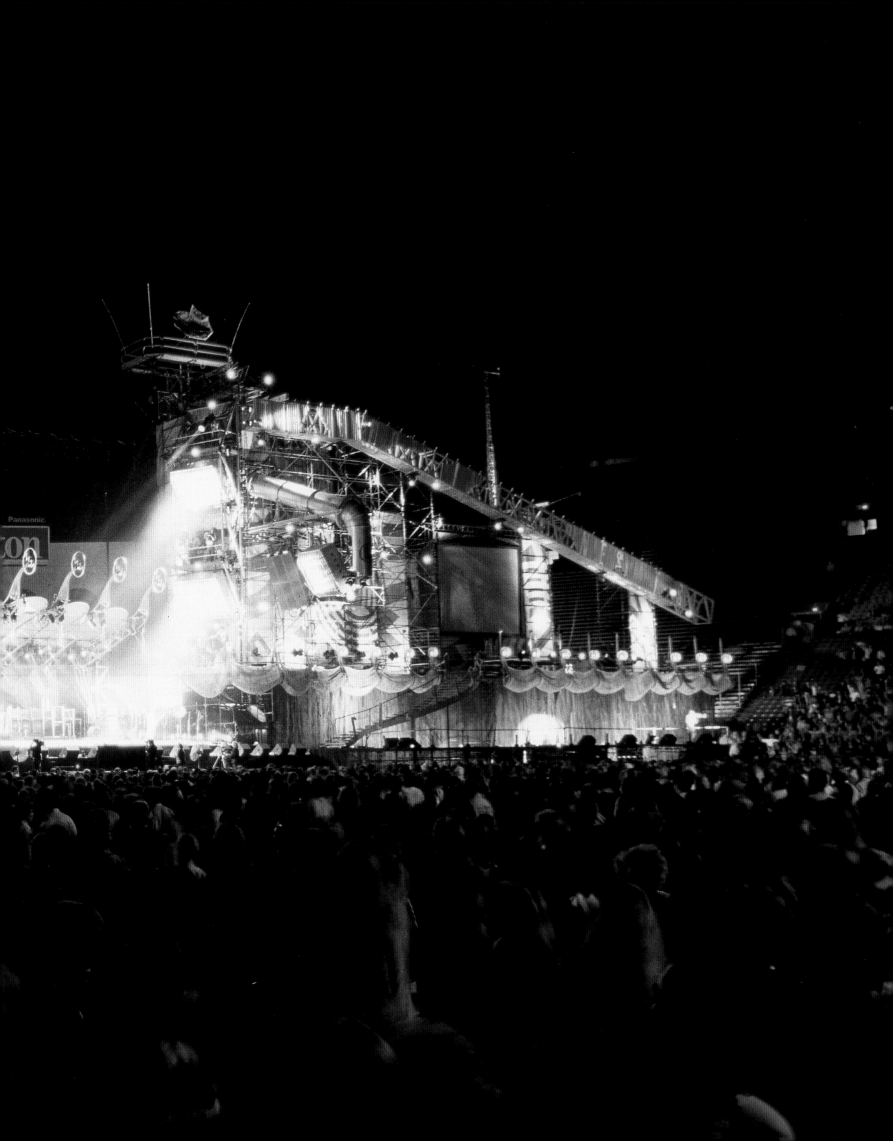

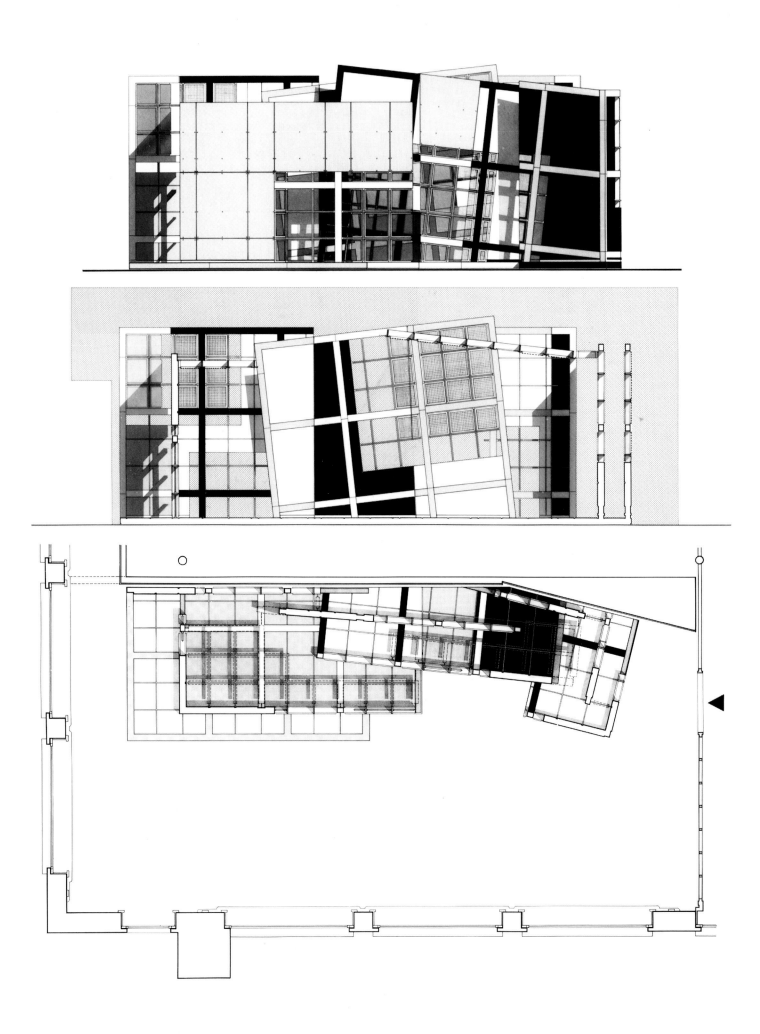

HIROMI FUJII

THE NAVE OF SIGNS

This project, as entered in the Europalia Exhibition which opened in Belgium in October 1989, provides a model of the concept behind my recent works. The theme of the exhibition is how matter is transfigured and becomes architecture – the emphasis is on transfiguration. My intention was to express in a concise way the transfiguration of not only material or form but the compositional system of architecture; ie, its structure. I selected metal as the material to be transfigured; similarly I chose the cube as the structure which was to undergo transfiguration.

This metal cube is gradually and repeatedly segmented, divided, and compressed, producing a dispersed space of layered fragments. In order to inscribe the segmenting, dividing, cutting, detachment, and layering of space, I began by using grids and colours as signs of traces, and then generating in them differences. The grids and colours, which are traces, induce mental operations such as suppression, displacement, and reversal; they make perceptible the presence or absence of things and the basic states of things such as reality and fiction (positive and negative), and inscribe spatial events such as segmenting, dividing, cutting, detachment, layering, and dispersion. This space is thus composed of elements that are related by means of mental operations in the depths of consciousness.

Compared to spaces that are integrated in a centralised manner through surface mental operations, this project at first glance may seem diffuse and dispersed. However, by introducing as the basic compositional language of this space those marginal elements that hitherto have been deliberately discarded because they were not thought capable of being coordinated or integrated, such as the unconscious or the mental operations of consciousness – ambiguity, diversity, and polysemy – it was intended to create a new spatial structure (ie compositional system) able to deal with diverse and complex conditions.

See opposite and below

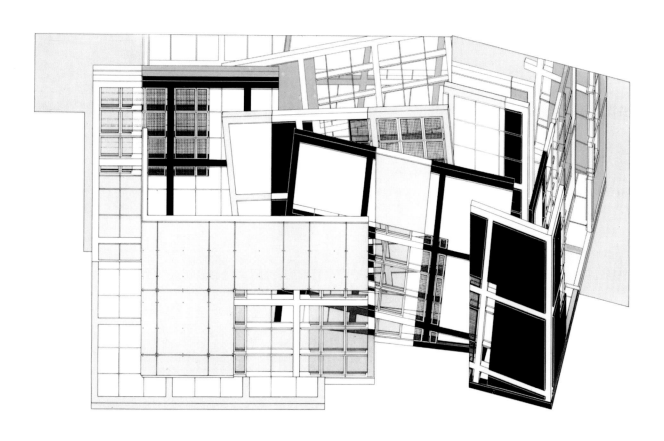

FRANK GEHRY – THE FIRST DECONSTRUCTIONIST
CHARLES JENCKS

'Just call me Daniel Boone', Frank Gehry said to me after I had called him that and everything else I thought appropriate: the Industrial Ad-hocist, the Father of the Botched Joint, the Son of Bruce Goff, the Noble Savage of Santa Monica, the Leonardo of Galvanised Sheet-Metal, the Malevich of Lighting and Rodchenko of the Non Sequitur (most influences are Constructivist), the Charlie Chaplin of Chain Link (he can look rather wistful disappearing into one of his industrial buildings, like Chaplin sauntering off into the horizon), the Over-Psychoanalysed Jewish Master-Builder, the Zen Priest of the Unfinished Finish, the Martin Escher of Reverse Perspective and Impossible Space, the First Deconstructionist Architect (still ahead of Peter Eisenman) and so on and on. The problem with Frank (soon to star in a film with Claes Oldenburg as 'Frankie Toronto') is that many labels work. He is, like many architects I have tried to pin down in *Bizarre Architecture,* almost unclassifiable. This is part of his strategy, like that of the clever Yankee backwoodsman; to escape detection by moving fast and shooting from behind trees. As Harold Rosenberg has written, the all-American art fighter like Jackson Pollock can outflank the European avant-garde by adopting more informal and pragmatic tactics. Instead of conducting his campaign according to orthodox military procedure – like the Impressionists or Surrealists moving through the salons in rational formations – Daniel Boone blends into his environment, uses whatever is at hand and picks off the ordered Redcoats one by one.

Frankie Toronto is telling me how he beat the over-psychoanalysed Peter Eisenman at his own game. 'About 1979 I gave a dinner for Michael Graves to introduce him to Max Palevsky, who wanted a multi-million dollar house. At the time Peter was trying to hold the party line of Modernism against the counter-attack of Post-Modernism and was losing on all fronts. One after the other the troops were deserting and going to the other side which increased his paranoia. So Peter tried to kill off Post-Modernism and wrote *The Graves of Modernism* to show what a turncoat Michael was. Because of my dinner party he gave me an angry call: "Frankie", he said in his New York Mafia voice, "I'm afraid you gotta lose a finger for that." And he lopped one off, or at least sabotaged a special issue of *A+U* on my work by telling Gandelsonas not to write the article. So when Peter came to LA for a visit I took him to an Italian restaurant where I know real Mafioso – who owe me some favours. After dinner I arranged for Clarkie to sit down next to Peter and put in the knife: "I hear you been messing around wit my friend Frangouch. The boys don't like suckers who fink on their buddies, understand? I'm afraid you gotta lose more than a finger Mr Egg-head." The blood drained from the East-Coaster's face.' Daniel Boone broke into a big grin and a hearty laugh; once again he had used his ready-made piece of industrial realism, his acquaintance with the netherworld, to beat the Big City Conspirator at his own game.

As a young boy in the Canadian suburb of Timmons, Ontario, Gehry had learned to play tough with the majority. Raised as the only Jewish boy in a Catholic neighbourhood he learned the role of the professional outcast at a young age. His grandmother used to bring home carp, which she would keep in the bathtub for several days, to prepare as *gefilte* fish for the Jewish Sabbath.

The rumour of these bathtub fish spread, and the boys would chase Frank home from school calling him a fish eater. This lesson was not entirely lost on Gehry; 50 years later he was asked, along with several other leading architects, to design furniture or objects for the Formica product called Colorcore. Unable to come up with something interesting – the material has a pristine finish opposite to a Gehry unfinish – he threw the plastic laminate to the ground in desperation. Luckily it broke and shattered into shards with very jagged edges. The rip joint, the imperfect fractures, inspired Gehry to create a fish-scale surface and from there a series of translucent fish lamps. With the same destroyed plastic he created coiled rattlesnake lights about two feet in diameter. The line of fish and snakes now sell quite well for over $20,000 each. Once again the creative outcast had succeeded in turning a mistake to his own advantage. The moral? If you're going to be chased home by a mob of prejudiced fish-haters, why not make them pay for it?

Architectural critics and others have speculated on Gehry's fascination with fish; his fish columns, lights and buildings. Naturally both Christian and Freudian interpretations are offered and Gehry, who has been in analysis for some years, does not discourage them. Like many other Californians, he regards psychoanalysis as a normal mental exercise; he also uses it as an aid to his thinking, and as a tactic to sharpen his perception of symbolic ambiguity, and assist him in outmanoeuvring the avant-garde. Thus it may actually be a mistake to think that Gehry's fish means, or reveals, anything profound. It may simply be a convenient symbol, an enigmatic sign that he knows to be potent and whose volume is, luckily, very practical. Like the elephant and dinosaur, which have also played roles in architectural history, the fish is most significant because it encloses a lot of space.

Gehry often proceeds by creative negation. He takes an existing prototype and reverses it, allowing the new rule of architecture to emerge after his negation. This process, related to critical analysis and the recent French philosophers' practice of deconstruction, has even been practised by architectural critics such as Demetri Porphyrios in his *Classicism is not a Style*. The negative definition may not tell us anything positive, but nevertheless, it acts as an allusion to the positive. Thus 'classicism is not a style' really means that 'classicism is a set of values' (as well, of course, as a style to which it alludes by negation). Several years ago Leon Krier met Gehry in a debate in Miami and proceeded to treat him with the same (dis)respect that his former schoolmates had shown. Krier, the archetypal European, was then breaking up cities into small village units, redistributing the income symbolically and decentralising the city figuratively. Gehry was also beginning to do the same thing although in an entirely different style (or non style). Krier was soon to re-create the European city as a reconstruction of Pliny's Villa – a set of small classical pavilions enclosing positive urban space. Gehry used plywood, sheet-metal, the dumb stucco box and raw concrete to create his answer; the 'Not Pliny's Villa' style.

This model is used in what is undoubtedly his most successful urban ensemble, the Loyola Law School. Laid out as a (non) palazzo and three (non) temples, it is a very effective collage of volumetric urban forms, recalling, in fact, the theory that had influenced Krier, *Collage City*. The anti-palace sets up a steady rhythm of windows, like a building by Adolf Loos, with the dark voids becoming their own new form of ornament. A (too) small glass temple breaks the centre while the side wings of the palace have eruptive staircases where there would have been corner towers. The street side of the (non) piazza is partly closed by a dark red chapel, easily the most beautiful Gehry creation here. It is made of Fin-Ply, a plywood which has been chemically treated to withstand weathering and resembles, appropriately, that *ad hoc* invention by Bruce Goff, plywood plus mahogany shoe polish. It is very well detailed both externally and internally, and were it not for the *démodé* materials, one might think it positively harmonious and classical. It is, rather, a stone Romanesque chapel built of the wrong material.

In any case, the (non) Classicism is quite an obvious response to the client's desire for a cool, rational style that recalls Roman law. It can be seen in the many (non) columns and the concrete pillars, minus their capitals and feet, which decorate each temple. It can be seen in the Acropolis planning, the tilted axes, the porticoes, and the rhythmical window wall. And the law students respond to it in an appropriate way. They walk around and pose in the piazza, mixing informal and formal clothes; one student I saw was wearing a white formal jacket over a bathing suit. They converse on the stairways which swing out over open space, they eat on the temple steps and lean against the colonnade as if at a cocktail party. Perhaps only in the Californian climate, or in the Mediterranean, can such an urban ensemble be used so effectively to create the public realm. Here the *res publica* really does exist again, and it is the very (non) image of Pliny's Villa. Its tough materials are the vernacular of the surrounding neighbourhood, one of the poorest and roughest in LA. It borrows this skin, in the same way a chameleon borrows its colour, for protection, but also to pull in the surrounding landscape and make a new (negating, but not negative) comment on this old urbane ideal of the public realm.

Thus Gehry's work has to be seen as a series of current strategies turned on their heads. This is the dialectical method of Duchamp, Dada and some Pop artists such as Oldenburg, whom Gehry knows and admires. It is also the method of the *bricoleur*, or French handyman, who makes old tools do new tricks. Unlike the scientist or classicist who tries to re-create the whole situation and its parts, the *bricoleur* tinkers and manipulates ready-made materials. The results are not high art, or science, in the accepted sense; the handyman does not try to create a jet engine. In part his is a conservative and reactive strategy in that it entails a response to a pre-existing situation. But Gehry does not aspire to be a Michael Graves. In the recent TV film *Beyond Utopia,* Gehry questioned the conservative tendencies displayed in the Portland Building, referring to it as the architecture of Ronald Reagan. Not long after, the unamused Graves, still the friend of Gehry, went off to the White House for dinner, perhaps determined to prove Frank wrong in some as yet unfathomable way. While Gehry one day may be invited into the Establishment, he will not, like Graves, be asked to build its temples. Or if he is, they will explode in unlikely ways.

His most eruptive temple is the California Aerospace Museum, a construction reminiscent of Duchamp's 'explosion in a shingle factory'. Like a Chinese garden it borrows the adjacent landscape by mimicking and enframing its parts. Odd disjointed shapes, leaning polygons and interrupted rectangles, recall the demi-forms of the nearby Exposition Park. An equation is thus made between the designed object and the *objet trouvé so* that they both become part of a larger whole. The environment near downtown Los Angeles is, like many American urban areas, a crazy patchwork of collaged forms all competing for attention. There is no European 'wholeness', no urban identity beyond a cacophonous rhythm of forms, no harmony of differences as in Amsterdam. There is no urban 'heart', or finished centre: the American city is, for the most part, a permanent building yard, and about as noisy.

The Aerospace Museum is an analogue of this city as well as of flight. Made from galvanised sheet-metal and other factory materials, it resembles the surface of an aeroplane hangar. A Lockheed F-104 Starfighter takes off on the side, like some aggressive rocket about to unleash its payload. And this plane announces the function of these distorted boxes like a giant Constructivist billboard. The welter of conflicting shapes conveys the mad, glorious dash of flying. It also suggests the contradictory aims of the aerospace defence policy, where billion dollar weaponry is built and destroyed for no other purpose than that of symbolism (which of course is quite enough).

Gehry has used the Constructivist method of compilation rather than composition. The individual rooms that were pulled apart in Loyola's freestanding temples have been conjoined at dissonant angles: a septagon looms out at a skew to the main 70-foot space which is symbolised by the black box and window below. But oddly, the internal space is not divided in quite the way it appears from the outside, and this 'lie' prepares us for the last Gehry paradox.

In a Greek temple stone represents the facts of construction, and ever since the Egyptians invented stone architecture it has had this representational function. Fundamentally, architecture seeks to make the transitory aspects of life both monumental and permanent. In a sense, with his (non) architecture, Gehry reverses this role and, as with the Romanesque temple at Loyola, transforms permanent material into ephemeral plywood. Most of Gehry's work, since designing his own house in Santa Monica, has been involved in this reversal process. It deconstructs, peels back and reveals, like archaeology, the botched and bungled inner layers which are hidden in any normal work. Like psychoanalysis, a favoured métier of the deconstructionists, the result may be a patchwork of disconnected elements in search of a story. Analysis, whether critical or psychoanalytic, is not necessarily synthetic or meaningful. It does not unite by idea, theme or aesthetic, nor does it try to change the world for the better. It simply shows the working parts in their semi-autonomous state.

As a process of design, however, this method results in an aggregation that is experienced as meaningful. Gehry is currently deconstructing three or four multimillion-dollar houses, ripping away their classical pediments, driving odd-shaped rectangles at a skew to their grids; generally destroying their equilibrium. The fact that some of these houses are ersatz classical partly explains this critical destruction, but another motive is positive: to provide contrast, smaller scale and the delight of incongruity. Whereas appropriateness and wholeness were the classical virtues, oddness and disharmony are the expressionist virtues 'employed' by Gehry. However, the opposite qualities of this dialectic have to be seen as necessarily linked, for no Gehry deconstruction is complete without its antithesis: a pre-existing, finished 'perfection'.

This can be seen in the Wosk House addition, which has been placed on the top of a decapitated apartment building in Beverly Hills. The pre-existing type, a five-storey stuccoed rectangle that is common in this area, still exists as a pristine, pink cube, its International Style surfaces and ribbon windows much as before. But set in juxtaposition to these simple harmonies is the arched window of the owner, Miriam Wosk, and her own little 'Not Pliny's Villa' on the roof. What planning authorities will make of this is an interesting point. It clearly violates every aesthetic norm in the book, and enjoys doing so. Like Antonio Gaudí and Bruce Goff, who also got away with unlikely additions, Gehry openly subverts conventional building codes. But is the Wosk House subversive architecture? As a generalised proposition no doubt it is. What if our cities returned to the medieval jumble implied by this *ad hoc* roofscape? The result might even be like Venice, Siena, or the back streets of Dubrovnik. It is well known, however, that planning legislators are determined not to let these mistakes of history recur. But Gehry proposes that they should, and it is for this reason that 'mistakes' are written into his deconstructions.

The north and south facades of the Wosk Roof Villa are broken up into seven and five discernible sections respectively. These parts do not correspond exactly to interior articulations – in fact the space flows, surprisingly, from the artist's studio on one side to her living room on the other. But, as if to break even this rule of non-correspondence, some shapes do hold discrete functions. For instance the spherical *Domus Aurea* of Nero (sic), now a blue not golden dome, contains the kitchen. This collides with the greenhouse/dining room and the pink volume of the elevator shaft. Collision City, that paradigm of seventies' ad-hocism, continues to jumble its way around the penthouse/duplex, with green tile smashed into Cadillac-golden ziggurat (the industrial car paint was used) and overlaid by a hairy pattern of blue tile shingles. According to Gehry these were meant to bring out the front corner. Above the stairway, skylights separate a black marble aedicule from the bowed roof studio. Thus, from the north side one can see ten volumes and eleven colours collide in humorous cacophony. They were originally intended, as it turns out, to recall temples on the Acropolis!

The disorganisation of this is more apparent than real, for actually the penthouse functions quite sensibly. A perimeter walkway and balcony provide light, space and access to the rooftop, one of the most unlikely spaces in Los Angeles. From here, one can not only step outside at any point, but also clamber over the flat tops of these collaged temples and survey the mountains, or a dramatic sunset through the towers of Century City. In nearly every way the seemingly arbitrary forms find an attractive function, and Daniel Boone disarms his critics once again.

When one analyses this deconstruction it turns out to be yet another example of reverse representation. If it's an acropolis, Gehry's first conception, then its brilliant industrial tile and glass have to be seen as anti-stone. The flat roofs are anti-pitch, the polychromy anti-white, the collisions anti-space, the cacophony anti-unity, and the balcony walk an anti-*temenos*. The point about these 'antis' is that they recall their antithetical 'pros' and in this involuted way the building can be considered strangely canonic. It is certainly pleasant and functional, and with Miriam Wosk's interior tiling and painting could even be considered as a 'finished' work of art. That Gehry should achieve such resolution of his deconstruction process is due in part to the existing building, used as a podium and πfoil, and in part to the tenacity of the client. De-architecture, such as his own house, is most successful when there is pre-existing material to operate on and a person, such as his wife Berta, to spur him on to the completion of his unfinished work.

FRANK GEHRY

THE VITRA DESIGN MUSEUM, WEIL AM RHEIN

This project in Germany, the first European commission to be won by the architect, encompasses three major parts: a seating assembly plant, its adjacent office, mezzanine and distribution areas, and a small furniture museum to house a collection of furniture (19th century through today) as well as a library and preparation of a master plan for the project – which also includes a new entrance road and gatehouse, a future expansion of the factory, parking for the museum and ancillary facilities.

The factory is a concrete frame construction with a stucco finish, skylights and large windows. The offices located on the north mezzanine have spectacular views of the adjacent hills as well as the museum and a Claes Oldenburg sculpture. This north facade faces the main factory as well as a backdrop for the museum. Ramps and entrance canopies flank this factory facade and make sculptural 'book-ends' to the museum. These different forms relate to each other and extend the visual impact of the project as a whole. These sculptural elements give scale to the big simple factory volume, and add to the campus-like environment. A consistent, albeit differentiated, formal vocabulary ties the various pieces together as one moves through and around the buildings. Skylights and clerestories are positioned to create various natural lighting conditions within these forms.

The museum building is composed of a catalogue library, office, storage and support spaces in addition to exhibition space. The galleries are treated as connected volumes spatially interpenetrating each other so that the exhibitions can communicate from one space to another. Each has a different character vis-à-vis natural light, volume, surface and scale, and although visually connected, they may all be secured separately. Natural light is introduced from skylights which are shaped to bounce and diffuse the light. This softens the light so that at times the space simply glows. The construction is plaster over masonry on vertical and inverted surfaces and metal roofing panels on sloped water-shedding surfaces. White plaster with titan zinc seemed appropriate for this area.

The master plan calls for several independent galleries to be added to the initial museum building and additional factories added to the west side of the new entrance road. Parking is to be eventually expanded at the west and south ends of the site.

see opposite and page 115

CHIAT/DAY BUILDING, LOS ANGELES

Following the Disney Concert Hall, the Chiat/Day Building is the second of Gehry's major projects to be built in the Los Angeles area. Sited in the Venice district, the offices consist in three principal sections, known to Gehry's office and company employees as 'Boat', 'Binoculars' and 'Trees'.

Each of the three linked sections has its own, wholly distinctive character, linked to that of the surrounding area – the Boat referring to the Pacific Ocean boatyards nearby, Trees to the dense forest which once dominated great swathes of the Californian landscape, and differently, Binoculars to LA's auto culture, forming a grand entrance for cars rather than for pedestrians.

Driving down Main Street from Los Angeles and Santa Monica towards the Pacific, the curvaceous, almost aqueous white lines of the Boat first catch the eye; this section flows easily into the centrepiece, Binoculars, of which more below, and then follows Trees, which houses the chief executive offices in an open-landscaped, democratic style; the elegantly stylised trunks, branches and canopy of this copper-clad section of the project complete the contrasts of the previous sections.

In Gehry's own words, the concept informing the Chiat/Day offices is that they are 'designed to work urbanistically in a community that is practically formless. I wanted the building to have differentiation on the street line to break down the scale of the long frontage, and to punctuate the entrance with something special.' The building's special focus remains the three-storey high pair of upright binoculars, which are both functional and visually appealing. The eye pieces serve as skylights illuminating the interior of the binoculars, which open up into a large conference room. And, as if to inspire bright ideas in the room, huge lightbulb sculptures, designed by artists Claes Oldenburg and Coosje Van Bruggen, hang from the ceiling.

Oldenburg, who was closely involved with the building as a whole, has said that the project was 'a departure from the usual antagonism between architect and artist. The beauty of it is that the sculpture is of equal weight with the other parts, acting as a pivot around which they revolve.' The interior office design of this advertising company eliminates the usual hierarchies, with all offices and furnishings essentially the same. 'My hope in the interiors was to make the place comfortable' says Gehry, 'and to create a place with a sense of humour.'

see pages 118-121

ZAHA HADID

FOLLY 3, OSAKA

Folly 3 for the Osaka Expo 1990 is located on an open plaza at the junction of several paths. A series of elements, compressed and fused, expand in the landscape and refract pedestrian movement through the site.

From afar, two vertically extruded planes signal the folly to approaching visitors who move along the ground or through the air by means of monorail. Horizontal planes serve the dual purpose of defining perimeters as well as inscribing a series of 'canyons' within cantilevered walls. These canyons extend through the site and are distinguished by spaces which vary in compression.

Five ramps, varying in length and thickness, stretch along the ground plane. These lower elements are juxtaposed against the set flow of planes above. The result gives rise to a series of coves, where visitors may seek refuge from the arduous and overwhelming exercise involved in a day's sightseeing.

See pages 122 and 124

MOONSOON RESTAURANT, SAPPORO

The project as an interior contradicts its exterior enclosure. The constraints of the conventional building created the desire to break away. The result is a hybrid of compressed, dynamic inside and static outside. The twofold programme of a restaurant with formal eating and relaxed lounging is stretched between two synthetic and strange worlds of opposite character: fire and ice.

The ground floor in cool greys (materialised in glass and metal) was inspired by the seasonal ice buildings of Sapporo. The tables emerge as sharp fragments of the raised level from the rear, drifting like ice across the space. Above the ice chamber whirls a furnace of fire in brilliant reds, yellows and oranges. A bar which tears through the ceiling of the ground floor spirals up to the underside of the dome like a fiery tornado bursting a pressure vessel. Elsewhere a plasma of biomorphic sofas hybridises eating with lounging, allowing for an infinite configuration of seating types with moveable trays and sofa backs that plug in at any point.

See pages 125-127

VITRA FIRE STATION, WEIL AM RHEIN

We concentrated on one zone of the vast Vitra factory complex, from the main gate with the chair museum to the other end where the fire station was to be located, designed as the edge of this 500-metre-long zone. The zone itself becomes an artificial landscape, potentially containing such facilities as a workers' club and sports field. The proposal for the overall scheme is not the definitive delineation of the final project but proposes a dynamic pattern to allow the spaces to develop gradually.

The fire station's point of departure is a series of layered screening walls, and its programme inhabits the spaces in between the walls which in turn are punctured and broken according to the functional requirements. The main puncture comes from the movement of the fire engines, perpendicular to the linear flow of the walls and the landscape. Sliding open the doors in a wall will reveal the fire trucks behind, parked under a large roof.

At ground level, one beam contains the shower and changing area, interlocking with a second beam containing the fitness area, which again is linked to the outdoor fitness and barbecue garden. A stair in the intersection of the beams at ground level leads to a third which stretches between two raised terraces. As one passes across the spaces one catches glimpses of the large red fire engines, the main focus of this landscape.

See pages 128-129

MEDIA PARK, ZOLLHOF

The programme for the site and for the area as a whole focuses on accommodating new creative and media businesses, together with shops and culture and leisure facilities, to transform old Düsseldorf Harbour into a new enterprise zone. The water's edge, not the street, is seen as the active part of the site, animated with sports and other leisure activities; we propose for it an artificial modulated landscape, protected from the street traffic by a building which functions as a wall, and which contains the studios and offices. On its ground level are the more public-related businesses (galleries and showrooms) and above, those requiring more quietness. The wall's street side is plain and solid, while on the waterside the surface is open, partly articulated in relief, to allow for different floor depths according to needs. Where there is a wish to create a larger unit and create a particular corporate identity, then a section of the wall breaks free, as with the advertising agency, which breaks into a whole series of slabs.

The ground behind the wall accommodates most of the public facilities (shops, restaurants, cinema) and underneath the advertising agency are deep spaces for technical studios. A big triangular plane cuts the site, sloping against the wall and piercing through it underneath to form another entrance to the street. From here most of the shops are accessible. For these a system of interlocking free forms is devised underneath the slightly raised ground.

See pages 130-133

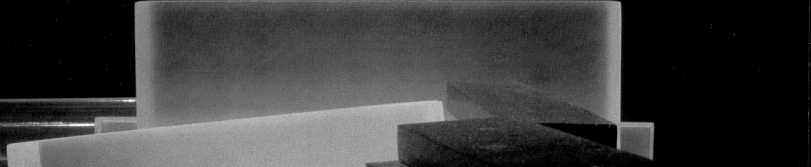

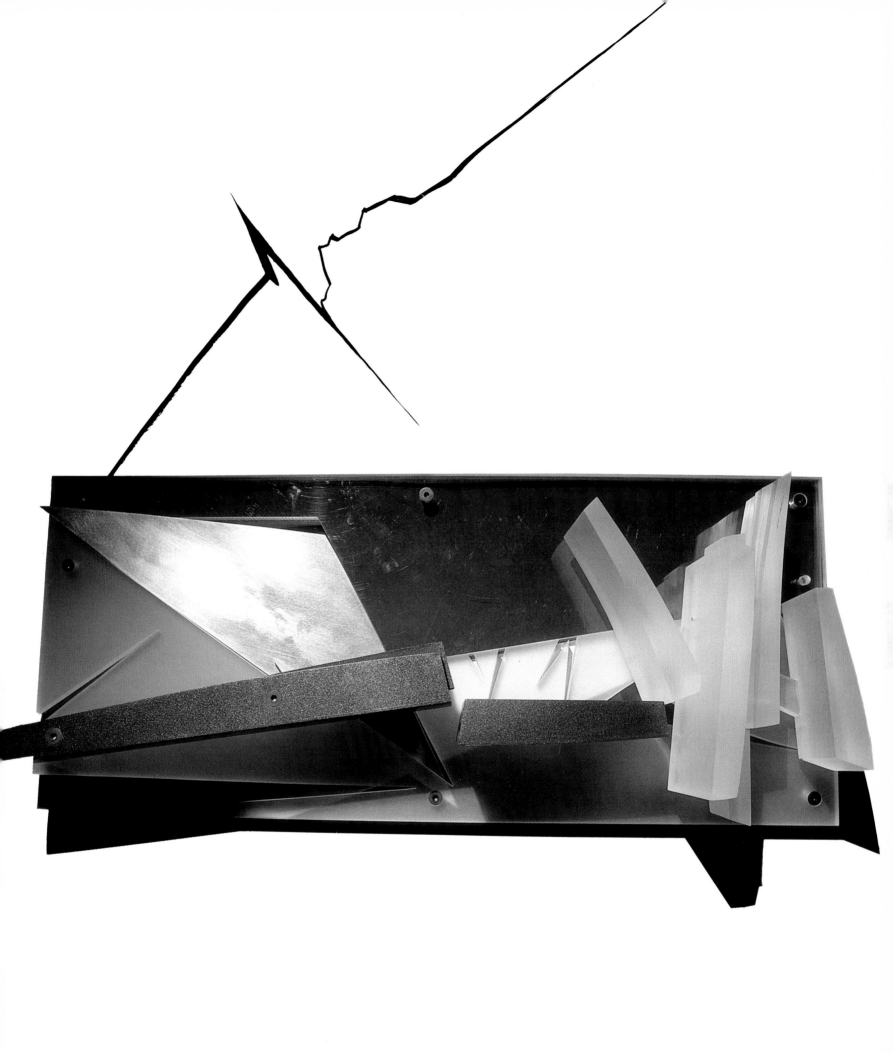

ITSUKO HASEGAWA
ARCHITECTURE AS ANOTHER NATURE

The history of humankind is one of continual development and domestication of the earth and destruction of nature. Nature in the wild is not a comfortable place for human beings, and so human beings have created comfortable environments by standing up or adapting to, and transforming nature. The world human beings create, physically speaking, is a mass of artifice, yet deep down it is underpinned by nature. Nature ultimately encompasses all of human existence, and the spaces created by human beings represent an environment, albeit on a new and different level. The character of that environment is closely tied to the way society and technology have developed historically.

It is not only developments in technology and society that are causing great upheavals but the tempo of those developments. In the past change was gradual and human beings could be sympathetic to, and maintain harmony with nature, but the speed of technological changes today is rapidly bringing about not just changes to the earth but its destruction. We sense that advanced technology is changing our lives, but we can no longer perceive with any clarity the nature of the technological society in which we live, much less its details.

Today, it is clear that society can no longer simply accept and depend on the modern Western mode of thought. Although those of us living in Asia, with its Buddhist background, ought to be searching for social ideas of our own, we tend to spend our days consuming, distracted by the notion that we can somehow change our lives through material objects. We lack any theory with which to respond to new conditions. As we become materially richer, we begin to sense the superficiality of our lives.

Faced with this situation, people are increasingly focusing on what might be called the primary landscape within themselves, the non-modern as opposed to the modern, the non-urban as opposed to the urban, the non-artistic as opposed to the artistic, the local as opposed to the universal, the indigenous and the ethnic, and the idea of ecology and a relationship of interdependence with nature. Many people are now concerned with the environment, and their concern extends from their immediate surroundings to the globe as a whole. One of my aims is to reconsider architecture of the past, which was adapted to the climate and the land and permitted human coexistence with nature, and to see human beings and architecture as part of the earth's ecosystem. This includes a challenge to propose new design connected with new science and technology.

We also ought to think seriously about restoring architecture to the people in society who use the architecture. It has long been my wish to explore ways of allowing users to participate in a true dialogue with the architect. In designing private houses,

I have tried to enter into dialogues with clients and to work jointly with them. Just as I, as an individual, am a part of society, even as I stand outside it, architecture too is a part of the city into which it is introduced. It is important that I do not discard my subjective self, but I must also be willing to look objectively at myself.

These thoughts led me to the conclusion that a building that is used by many people, whatever its scale, ought to be designed not as an isolated work, but as a part of something larger. In other words it must have a quality of urbanity. The city is a changing, multifaceted entity that encompasses even things that are in opposition to it. My second major aim has been to try to eliminate the gap between the community and architecture by taking such an approach to public architecture and to give architecture a new social character.

I believe any new building must make up for the topography and space that is altered because of its introduction, and should help to create a new nature in the place of the one that used to be there. I feel any new building ought to commemorate the nature which had to be destroyed in order for it to built, and ought to serve as a means of communicating with nature. The theme of my work is 'architecture as another nature'. We must stop thinking of architecture as something constructed according to reason and distinct from all other forms of matter. In creating spaces we must recognise that human beings are a part of nature. Architecture must be responsive to the ecosystem as all of human existence is ultimately encompassed by nature.

To put it another way, architecture ought to be such that it allows us to hear the mysterious music of the universe and the rich, yet by no means transparent, world of emotions that have been disregarded by modern rationalism. We need to harness both the spirit of rationalism and the spirit of irrationalism, pay heed to both what is international and what is local, and recognise the nature of contemporary science and technology in trying to create an architecture for the society of the coming era.

The idea of 'architecture as another nature' is one that has met with sympathetic response from citizens, and I believe it can endow architecture with a social character. In the Shonan-Dai Cultural Centre I created an open, garden-like space at ground level by burying 70 percent of the total floor area below ground, with much of this underground portion facing sunken gardens; because of this the building is in a certain aspect 'Landscape Architecture'. In effect, a second surface level was created. However, there was opposition among local people who were not accustomed to such underground spaces, and discussions with them about such matters began a whole series of meetings. People have quite different perceptions and tastes. In the process of design, the spaces sometimes reflected the subjective views of the architect and at other times they reflected opposite views. This give and take during the design of the Shonan-Dai Cultural Centre enabled me to think about the relationship between architecture and society.

I have consistently taken an *ad hoc* approach to architecture rather than an exclusionary stance. Having completed the Shonan-Dai Cultural Centre I now realise quite clearly that I want to create an inclusive architecture that accepts a multiplicity of things rather than an architecture arrived at through reflection and elimination. The idea is to make architecture more realistic through what might be called a 'pop' reasoning that allows for diversity as opposed to a logical system of reasoning that demands extreme concentration. Such an approach represents a shift to a feminist paradigm, in the sense that an attempt is made to raise the consciousness of as many people as possible.

Human beings were born to live in a relationship of interdependence with nature. We are adaptable to change and are physically and spiritually rugged enough to live practically anywhere. I believe this 'feminine' tolerance and consciousness can help to dissolve the system in which we are presently locked and bring about a regeneration.

To sum up, buildings as well as human beings are born of nature, receive their images from nature, and return to a more profound form of life through death and destruction. Another nature will come into being when ideas of the global environment, traditional modes of thought and the 'feminine' concept are married to today's technology. The idea of architecture as another nature is one I will continue to espouse until the arrival of the meta-industrial society and the creation of spaces that are both natural and comfortable to human beings.

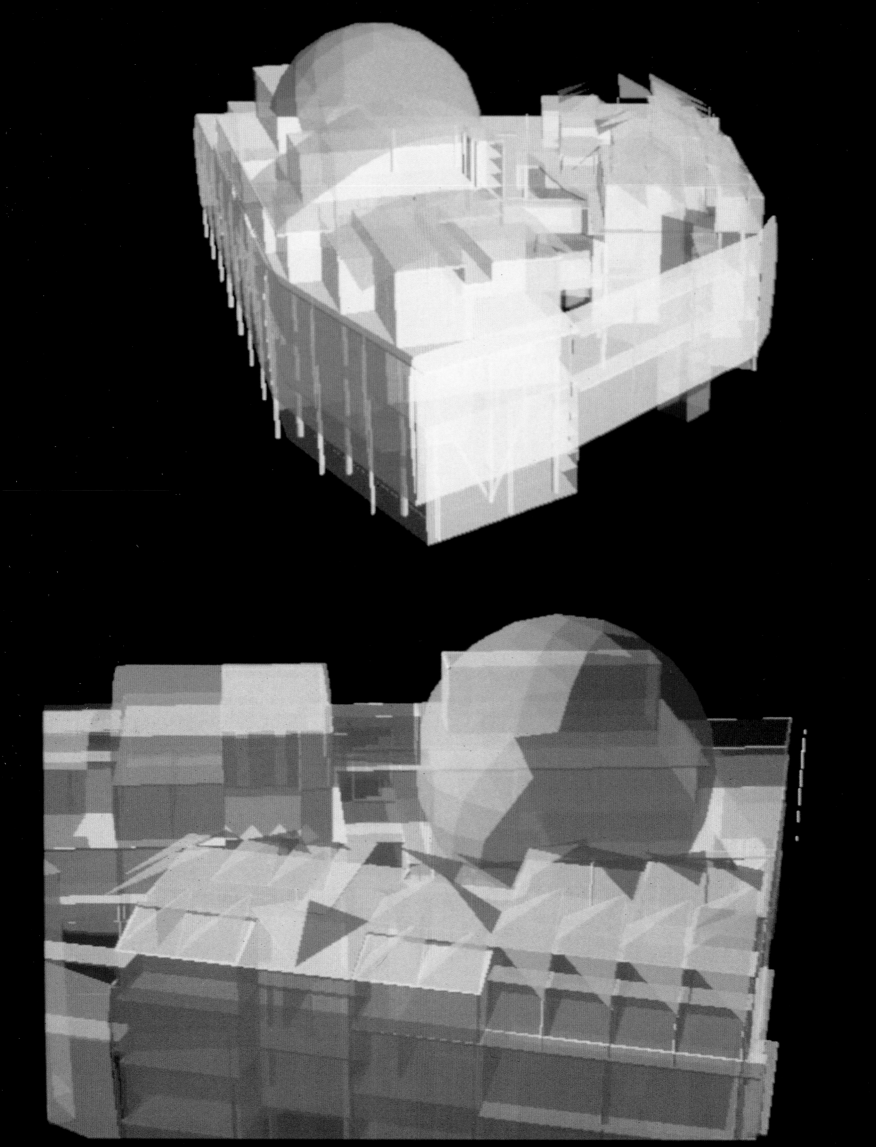

ITSUKO HASEGAWA

HOUSE IN NERIMA, TOKYO

The client wished to rebuild according to the plan of the house he was used to, so there were fixed criteria including the house's overall dimensions and even the exact size of the client's desk and the L-shaped bookshelves around it. The building consists of a main house for the client, a novelist, and his wife, and a separate house for their daughter, also a novelist. An entrance stairway and inner courtyard separates the two houses. On entering one climbs upstairs to find a roofed area with walls of punched metal that allow winds to pass through; an outer room accessible from both sides. Climbing further upstairs one comes to an observatory for viewing the moon, a platform from which one can see the high-rise buildings of Ikebukuro and Shinjuku. Further in the distance, Mount Fuji and other mountains can also be seen. Inside, of particular note are the living rooms in both houses which are lined with white acrylic boarding and punched aluminium fittings resembling Japanese *shoji* or lattice framework, creating an inner space delicately separated from the outside. The space created is thus wrapped in a semi-transparent veil which admits a beautifully fine light. A concrete box serves as both foundation and cellar, at ground level the main structure is wood and above is a curved roof of linked steel deck plates. The roof looks like a single giant wave enveloping the various spaces and structures beneath it.

See page 134

BIZAN HALL, SHIZUOKA CITY

To create space for garden areas, and to secure sunlight and air circulation for the building, I slightly rotated its position, so that it stood at an angle 15 degrees skewed to the sides of the site: this created triangular spaces at three corners of the site. The lobby block, consisting of an entrance lobby and display lobby, thus became a keystone-shaped space with a perspective effect. The same shape was used for the gable roof of glass and punched aluminium that covers the stone-paved approach running from the gate to the lobby block. To minimise noise disturbance the main auditorium is surrounded by two walls with a gallery in between. Sunlight and air enter through the ceiling, from the inner courtyard above. The small studios and rooms also get fresh air and sunlight from above. There are five fixtures in the ceiling of the auditorium to let in sunlight and fresh air which act both as five-colour light prisms and conduits to introduce air from all directions. Together with the coloured grid made up of pillars and beams they create a serene space that offers a variety of experience to the visitor.

See page 137

CULTURE AND LEARNING CENTRE, SUMIDA

Sumida Ward is a traditional working-class neighbourhood in Tokyo, where the old popular culture lives on and traditional handicrafts are still practised. The Centre had to be rooted in this area, had to be in harmony with it. On a site that was not quite quadrangular, I arranged three separate volumes to form a plaza. This plaza connects with two neighbourhood streets, facilitating movement in the area. The southwest volume accommodates assembly and communication spaces, a hall and a planetarium. The southeast volume contains an information centre and a library above the entrance hall. The third volume has study rooms and a branch office of the ward government, and on the top floor are counselling rooms for children. The parts are linked by bridges that help expand the services provided by the centre. Each volume is defined by translucent screens, giving order but without closing off spaces entirely in what is a crowded area. The layered translucent screens articulate space in ways that suggest traditional features such as the *shoji*, *sudare* and *koshido*.

See page 138

SHONAN-DAI CULTURAL CENTRE

Following discussions in the community about two-thirds of the volume is accommodated in a modernistic box-like structure, buried underground. In order to promote roots in the local community and a better understanding of the world and the universe, various representative spheres that suggest a futuristic, cosmic environment, and clusters of pitched-roof structures that suggest the woods or a village of folk houses, have been built above the ground. The plaza is a man-made garden with a stream, pond, greenery, and various shelters. Devices activated by light, wind and sound, a tower of wind and light, and a 'tree' with a built-in clock have also been installed.

See page 140 - 143

NAGOYA PAVILION

The pavilion holds an interior theatre for 200 people. A variety of materials are woven together to create an expansive aerial garden of delicate light and breezes. A rest area, covered with milky white cloth, presents an image to the eye like the craggy peaks of China's Kweilin. A high mountain, ten metres in diameter, has been constructed from a variation on a cross section of a Fuller dome. Fibre-reinforced plastic and punched faces form the bulk of the mountain, while the whole is enveloped in the green of the surrounding nature. Colour has been added by pebbles and marble, laid down and mixed with a glittering array of seashells.

See page 144

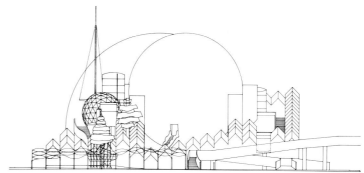

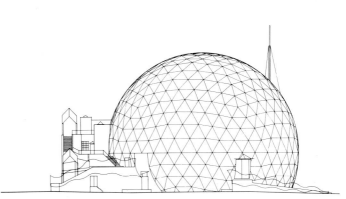

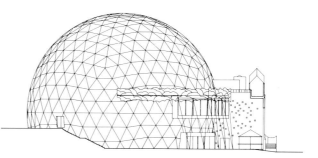

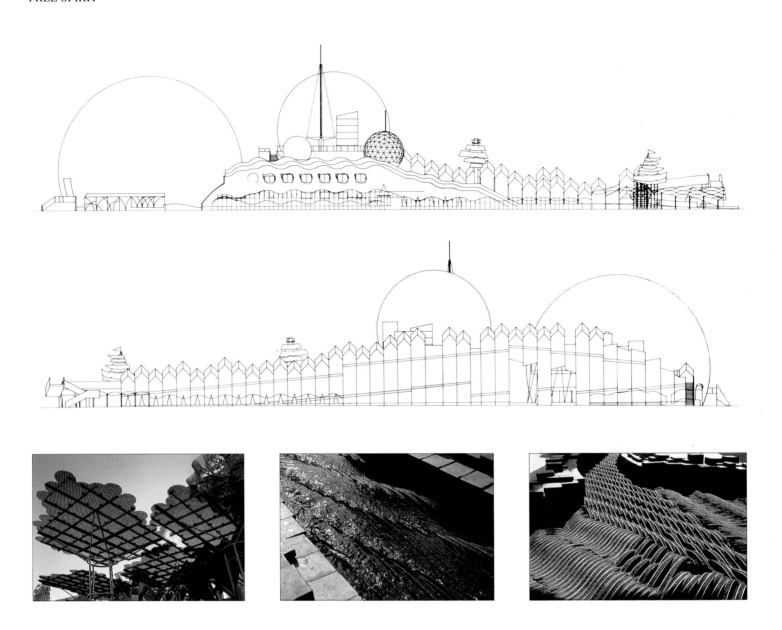

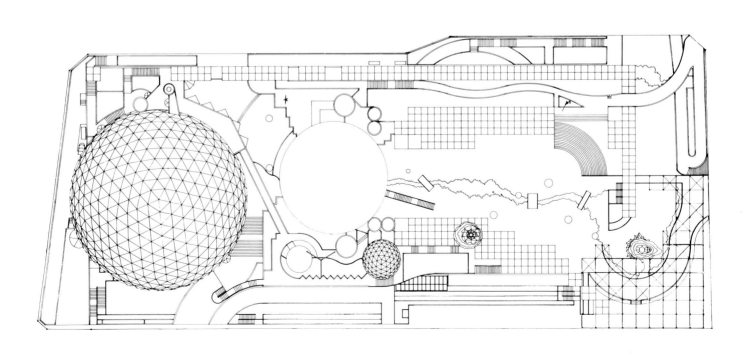

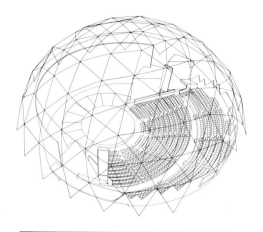

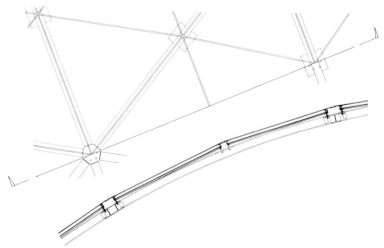

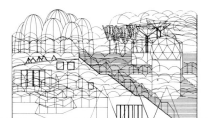

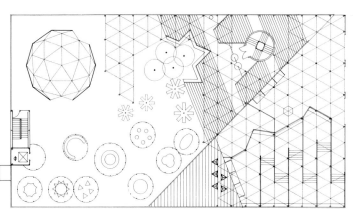

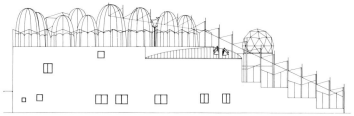

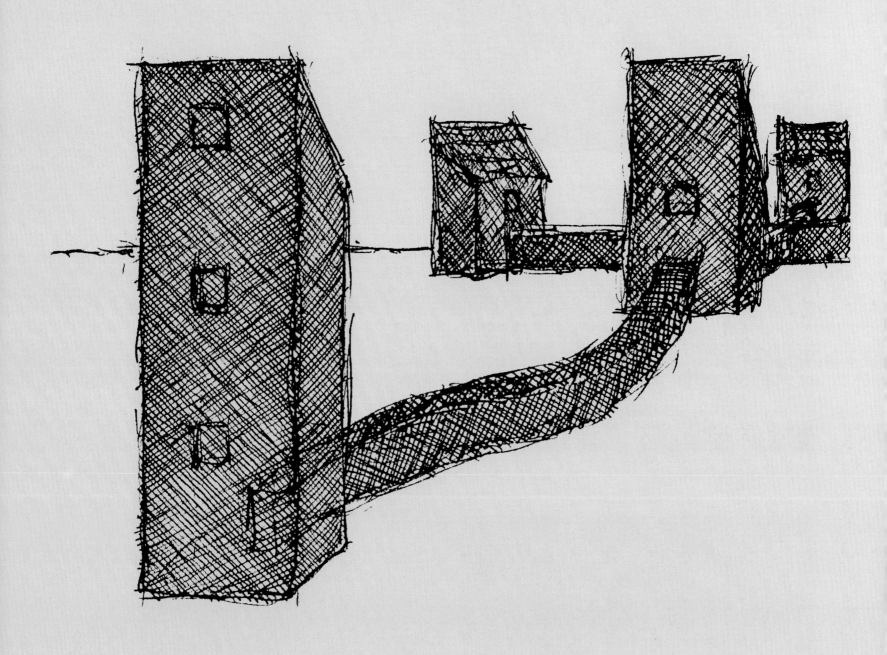

JOHN HEJDUK

THE POTSDAM PRINTER'S HOUSE/STUDIO

For the last four years I have been working on a major project called Berlin Night, and from this I submitted a single element, entitled The Potsdam Printer's House/Studio, to the Berlin Tomorrow competition.

I have donated this work as a plea in opposition to super/master/grand planning, which has destroyed so many significant places. I believe in the modest, incremental growth of cities. I am suspicious of grand schemes (they usually destroy the soul of place). I have therefore entered The Potsdam Printer's House/Studio in the hope that its scale and size might give a relative clue as to the particular atmospheres possible.

See opposite and pages 148-149

GRONINGEN CITY MARKER
Book G

During the past 15 years, I have developed a singular method of practising my beloved discipline architecture. I have worked out of a room in my house. The room measures seven feet by nine feet. From this room have come the thoughts on a new way of looking at architecture and at the construction of structures. The way is osmotic, by a form of osmosis. I am also a teacher and I fabricate books. When I work on my drawings, I listen to music and I read. When I take a break from my work/room I go into the garden which my wife Gloria has so . . . tenderly and lovingly created.

Like her the garden is a source of tranquillity and inspiration. Together we live a simple life, an almost 19th-century life. She speaks for herself and has graciously taught me about music and literature . . . and about the growth of life. We cherish our privacies and we love literature . . . the silent word. Within this atmosphere work proceeds, structures are built through the social participation (almost medieval) of students, of architects, of engineers, of artists, of faculties, of a community of souls (throughout the world).

In this way the following structures have been built: The House of the Musician/The House of the Painter (Berlin, Martin-Gropius-Bau); The Collapse of Time (London); Object/Subject (Oslo); Security (Oslo); House of the Suicide/House of the Mother of the Suicide (Atlanta).

I proposed that The Tower of Cards, The Tower Named Groningen and The Joker's Perch be realised by the City of Groningen, the Netherlands, for their city project 'Marking the City Boundaries', by the same method which put into place the above projects – by community participation.

The Tower of Cards

Thin metal plates mounted upon a metal frame.
Tower dimension: four-sided structure,
one side from ace to king of hearts
one side from ace to king of clubs
one side from ace to king of diamonds
one side from ace to king of spades.
An observation: 13 cards high; 4 suits of 13 cards = 52 (weeks). All the numbers of the Tower of Cards add up to 364; 364 + 1 (the Joker) = 365 (days).

The Tower is a fixed timepiece.

When we play cards we pass time in a fixed position.

Within the vehicle we will pass time (tower) in a fixed position. The colours of the Tower are the colours of the deck: white, black, red, yellow.

A Dutch analogy.

A Tower of Letters, Spelling: Groningen

Ten cards high, from ace to ten.
Only one side of the Tower will have letters.
White letters on a black ground.

The Wheel of Fortune (Joker's Perch)

A pole of 48 feet high, a wheel mounted on top with 12 spokes. The wheel is horizontal but slanted at 15 degrees. On it sits the three-dimensional Joker, legs dangling, one arm holding on for support, the other outstretched with a rattle. The Joker faces the Tower of Cards – fixed time.

– A trilogy is put in place.

See pages 150-153

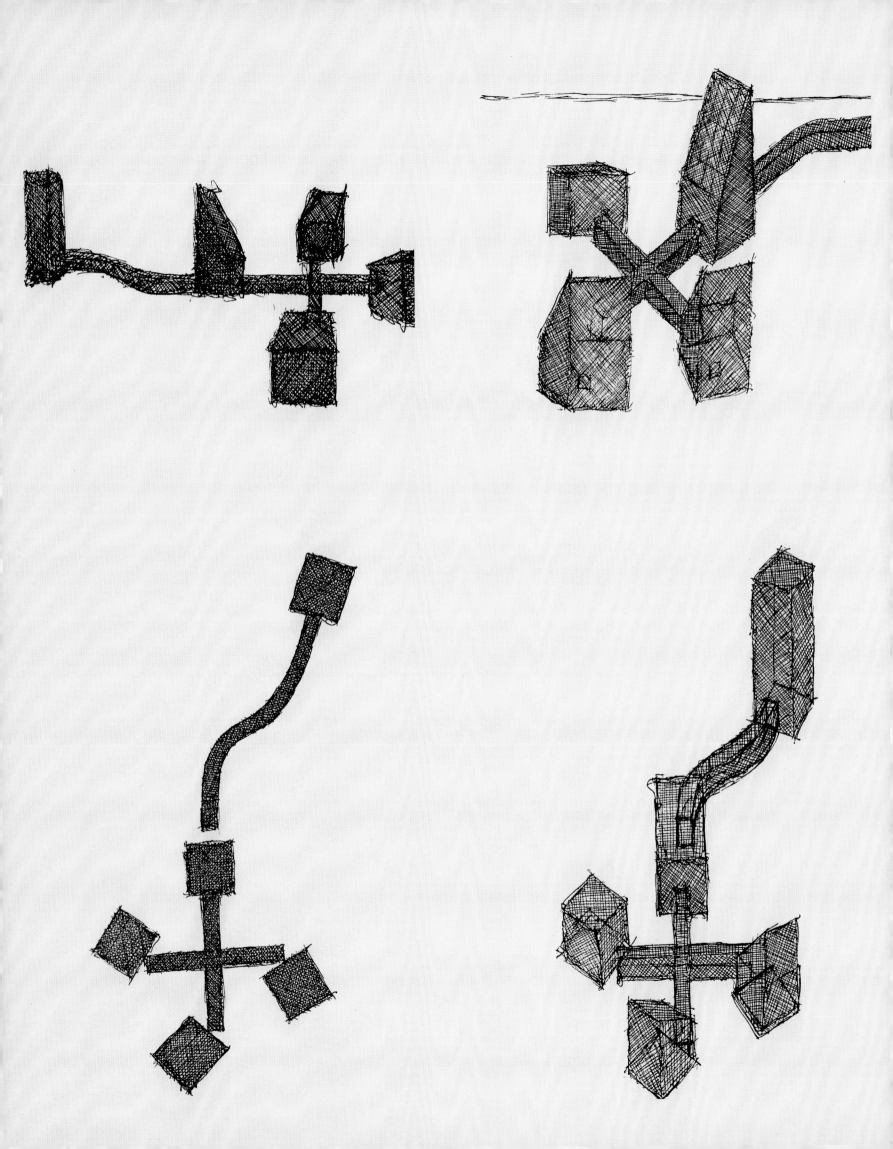

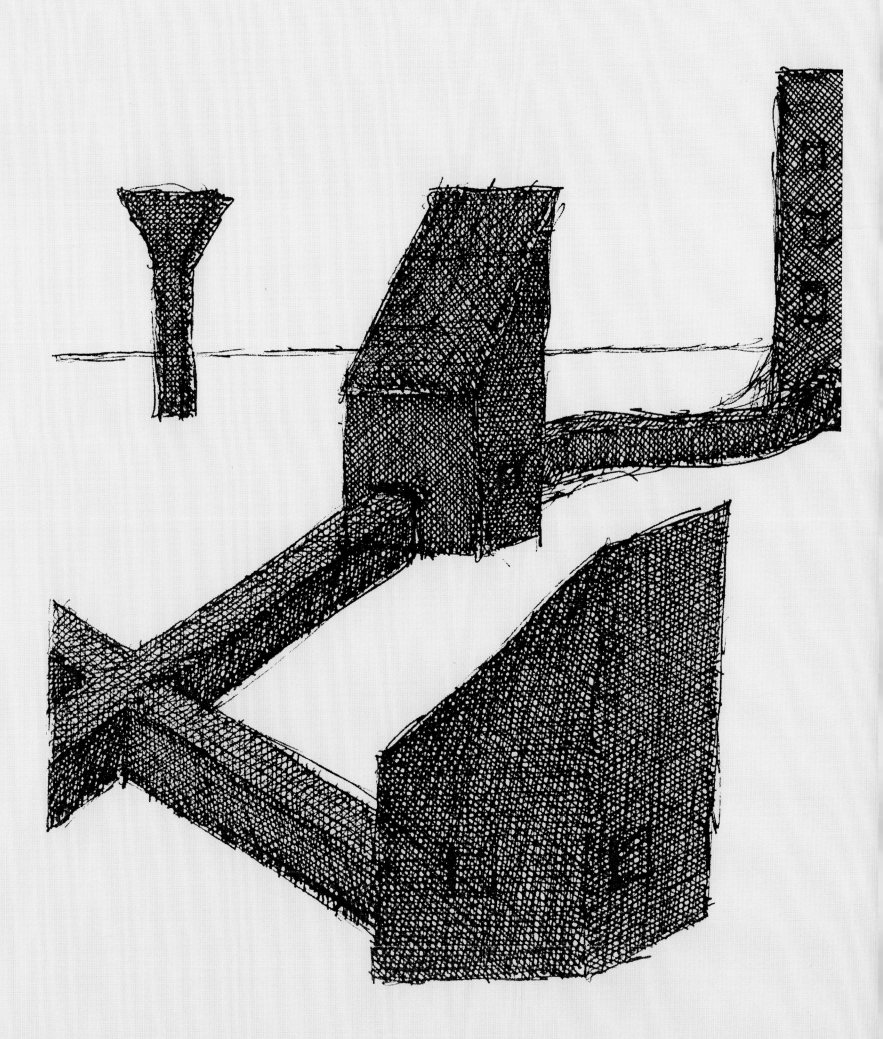

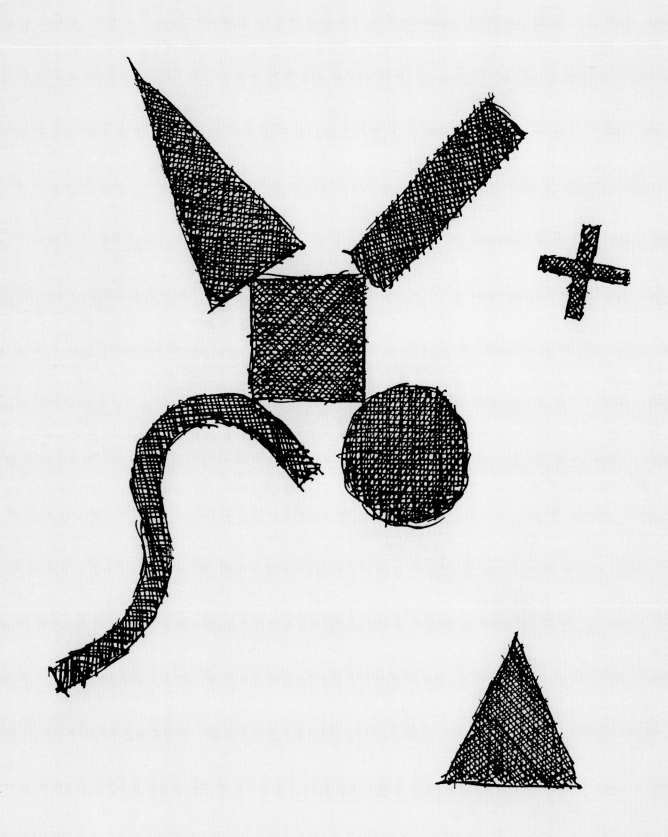

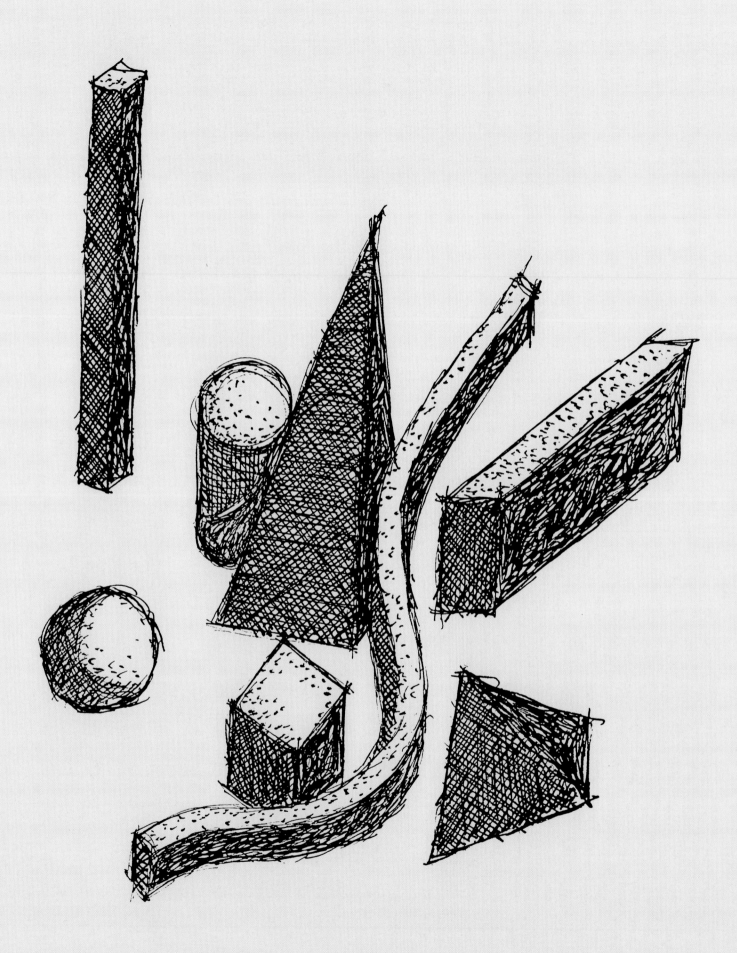

PHILIP JOHNSON

THE BROADCAST CENTRE, TORONTO

Construction on the 1.7 million-square-foot Broadcast Centre, the headquarters of the Canadian Broadcasting Corporation, began in October 1988, with the building due to be completed in 1992. Housing state-of-the-art production facilities, and at the same time accommodating an unprecedented degree of public access, the building will be one of the most modern of its kind in the world, combining specific technical attributes with the kind of monumentality required of a leading national cultural institution: sited on the periphery of an area of downtown redevelopment, the building was designed to function partly as a new civic centre.

Design consultant Philip Johnson, working with John Burgee Architects, developed a space-liberating and cost-effective plan consisting in the use of a basic ten-storey building as 'bedrock', set in a supergrid of columns and beams 30x30 feet square; positioned within this context are a variety of important additions and interruptions. There are three major television studios on the roof, standing out as perceptibly discrete elements, the largest and tallest of which is clad in red-plated aluminium. Two of

the studios, clad in blue reflective glass, are placed at an angle to the building and project out from the roof and facades, extending down the sides.

The main entrance is defined by a silver glass cylinder, forming an entrance canopy and extending to the roof where it becomes fully circular. Each of the building's facades forms a wholly distinct impression, and on the north, east and west sides angled and expansive green glass curtain walls break through the grid, extending up to the roof. Inside, large atrium corridors restate the building's exterior facades and converge from all the public entrances. The 300-seat radio studio on the ground floor, designed to accommodate orchestra concerts, combines a classical music hall with modern broadcast facilities.

Materials throughout are man-made, hard-edged, metal and glass, fitting the building's purposes; as Johnson says, 'It's a functional building. It's simple, it expresses its purpose. We didn't try to be decorative. Colour is expressive of what happens in the building and its role is very important when you want monumentality and the materials are simple.'

See opposite, below and pages 156-159

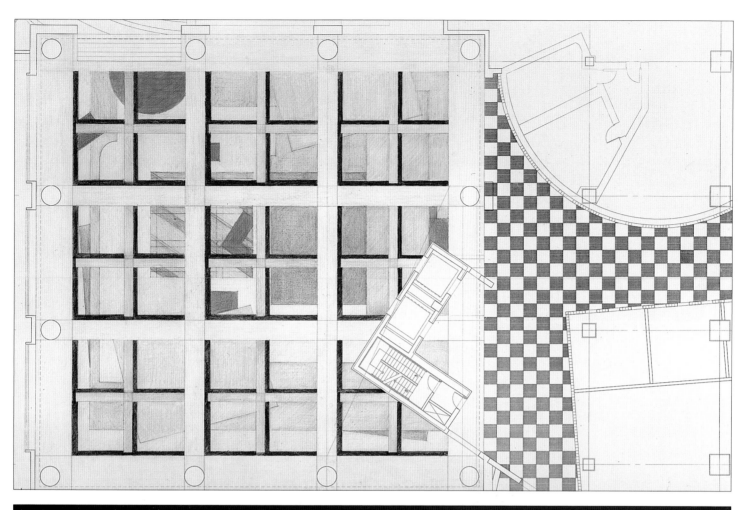

KRUEGER & KAPLAN

'ANALOG', COLUMBIA UNIVERSITY, NEW YORK

This first Analog was built for the School of Architecture at Columbia University. It is a dogma-ray oscilloscope. In order to provide easy access, it is mounted in the central skylight within the school, suspended between the real world above and the jury space below. From this position, the Analog peers through a window into the library monitoring the morgue of history where the latest architectural idea is a Xerox away. At 20-minute intervals, determined by timing motors and the rising oratorical foam of the reviewers below, the 'scope' dances, tracing out the pulse of café dialectics, as the jury kicks back to light up another Gauloises. After each 'review', the Analog shifts into its inactive mode, resuscitating its badly abused lungs. The Analog is not only caught in tension between these institutional spaces, but, as well, between ideological positions of a fundamentally political nature. We would like to dedicate this piece to that one daredevil student willing to risk their degree to cap another gushing bibliographic well of dogmatic gas.

The project was commissioned by the Graduate School of Architecture, Planning and Preservation at Columbia University as part of the 'Installed Mechanisms' exhibition. Located in a skylight of the underground Avery Extension at the level of the architectural library, the construction is also visible from the lower level exhibition area and the exterior plaza above. From this central position, the work confronts the school, the library and the general public. Timers activate lighting and electric motors at irregular intervals. The movement of the two motors through linear actuators upsets the balance, causing this suspended work to pitch side to side to the alarm of the students and librarian. After each periodic outburst, the unit comes to a rest, rhythmically inflating and deflating a latex bladder attached to the body by means of the syncopated reversing of two industrial blowers.

A bent steel truss of welded quarter-inch rod is sheathed in 18-gauge cold-rolled sheet Crosby-clamped to the frame. The head assembly is welded low-carbon plate supporting the mechanical and electrical hardware featuring two Bodine 1700 RPM AC motors, the shafts of which are attached to two Rohlix actuators that translate rotary motion into linear thrust as well as a control panel on which is mounted the motion control components including relays, motor-start capacitors, switches and timers. Due to its capacity to repeatedly disturb student concentration in the Avery architectural library, the librarian requested that the plug be pulled on this terminal patient prior to the closing of the exhibition. Calm and pest control has now been restored to the stacks.

See opposite

ART PARK, LEWISTON, NEW YORK

At Art Park we produced a work of rudimentary intelligence, one capable of taking a number of courses of action based on the status of environmental sensors. The infra-red motion detectors that sensed the presence and location of viewers in the vicinity of the object triggered one of the programmed sequences of activity stored in the memory. This project is no grandmaster chess challenger, and represents the field of artificial intelligence only at the most primitive level, but it does attempt to slip out of the Pavlovian leash by proposing a new field of investigation in machine psychiatry – artificial personality.

Just as artificial intelligence can be considered machine-simulated intelligent behaviour, so artificial personality is machine-simulated modes of behaviour. It is the relationship between the stimulus and the nature or manner of response that leads to the attribution of intentionality – this is a machine with an attitude. In order to facilitate this perception, we manipulated the timing and sequences of activity undertaken by the work in response to the presence of visitors, to convey a number of psychological states – arousal, defensiveness, aggression, paranoia, boredom and confusion (confusion was the easiest).

The work was suspended between two cliffs created by the demolition of a tunnel serving a now defunct railway line that ran along the gorge of the Niagara River at Lewiston. A trail now occupies the old right of way, effectively confining the approach to the piece to one of two directions. Motion detectors were oriented to intercept these approaches and to sense movement directly below as well. When approached, the on-board computer activated any or all of 15 automatic automotive power antennae, three fog lamps and a number of truck running lights positioned within the piece.

Programmed responses were provided for the firing of any sensor and for all combinations. As the work is directional, it responds differently to an approach from the front than to one from behind, or from two directions simultaneously, or from below. Additionally, loops in the programmes read the sensors intermittently to detect changes in position. If watched passively, the work would acclimatise to one's presence and go dormant, reviving with the movement to leave. A group of people milling around below the work could keep all sensors activated, resulting in the most agitated response.

This choreography is central to building the perception that one is being watched. The nature of the change in response to one's pattern of movement leads not only to an understanding of the personality of this 'thing', but its attitude, by its very nature, becomes a commentary.

See pages 162-163

DANIEL LIBESKIND
FISHING FROM THE PAVEMENT
(Architecture Perfected)

Sedition is rooted in education which only appears to equal the whistle – sound dissolving the face's angry citadel.

A fully equipped talent is attuned to the sea. Rum for sketchy farewells, static abattoir. I am praising the city by spilling six

phantoms on snows of evident docility.

– Taste excess with your cranium or advise the togaed attacker stranded on an oriental amphora that tall Saxons float in shame,

ring shaped columns do not bend, Ghenghis Khan ridicules restrictions –

Are you entranced by fourteen hundred theorems, a dappled rabbit, cows bleating in the attic, ineffable apples? After all the

Universal Savant is airborne on the back of a billion Sibyls who shape cameos for few cents while flying.

As for repair in the loving eruption, open scissors. I think of drinking diorite: testing a pedestrian conundrum

with theatrical homicide.

Edified disgorge identity by vomiting the declaration of an alias.

Weeds. Migration of promiscuous and Dutch thorns. End.

Is Kaddish comprehensible to a misanthrope? Chess logical to undertakers? Incomparable Sibelius composing in a

video arcade, – tourist of enduring rest – tendon pulling Nordic veal to Venice. Damnation, militant flies, Virgil, young

ladies made of ice-cream.

No tantrum with respect to you – a Jew with plenty of time pouring sentiment into the Kabbala. Violet-blue dripping

without terror: a liability.

Dumb achiever – filtering the bride's airy song is typical of the involuntary turn. In the Tiber ridiculous Edwardian furniture –

possibility for exegesis.

To heck with Ecce Homo! – asset in eggs, dust storm. The inventory of conflict confirms the ghost, casts each

soul in a minor key – sixth on the diatonic. Last atom oddly stranded at the terminal while you – tautological

darling – knock on my formaldehyde prism without angles, without lines, using a zero metaphysically corrected by a six

finger guru. A cherubic picador, peaceful survivor of Armageddon's circle, calculates the position of star while the horoscope is brimming with spontaneous tenderness.

Love violates the Old Litigant inside the guts of Buddha who trusts the heretic's arid little hovel – opens the eternal rune to a theorizing which smacks of analphabetic's antic. Mistletoe chaise longue which is pleasing? – a libertine's lie!

Never flee the linear figure, Pax, ancient Latin goddess, a gymnosophist from Pakistan.

The heart spills its lilacs, echoing what Titus Flavius Sabinus Vespasianus revealed about the Atlantis: steer effluvium receding, perforating the white quad with apocalyptic salt. Alliance of numbers with affliction and ectoplasmic emission.

Sweet oppression: clear photo of the international beast. Cutting with a terribly serrated knife mirrors eternity, refined harm.

Poor lightrope, selfish nectarines.

Sobbing, a condemned woman resolves to put lipstick at the scaffold. Pod instinct throwing ogive vaults across debility; awesome dots, orthogonals of salty fluid.

Erstwhile theophany: discharge from a roving beast's eye, beauty criticizing the colossus. Audacious faeries made of nuclear chromosomes form into threads, split lengthwise, associate with Don Juan's ovoid.

Enamoured with the medically depilated reflection races – are occidentals tired of animal mortar? Is a pneumatic NT built for sliding down Reason's annulated cadaver?

Distraught as medals thawed in Eve's tresses are the professors fussing in Erebus, humming.

– Kiss egglike, crushing the sea.

– What extinct gizzard can hush these innuendoes, guests?

– Flame, the puritan's guile!

One ought to kiss the Wailing Wall without swallowing an intrusive stone or hear the Song of Solomon played on a knife.

Chained to a steep rock the gallant idolater deigns to bear his pain calmly – asks for lozenges – proud ant! If he could only hear pachalik music, Istanbul's crone, the omniscient whispering traditional curses . . .

The rightists consecrate each menhir with a writhing movement of their wrists, reminiscent of figures in demotic writing of ancient Egypt. Curious delight: screaming with wrath rivals of the Sun Chasers make offerings of their nails to authorities, shaking a radish at the camera.

Rambunctious pinnacle, – dreadful monument on which a furious youth glows like a chromospheric flare, incinerated, god in his swollen hand. Magnificent illustration of cowards whose rings enter through the mouth in order to fire the official with aversion to dust. The bishop's phallic culm, pleasing enough though half-red, flying in particles, lashing the bearded occupant to the marrow.

Rougher activity than usual in the systole but everything on this little knee seems satisfactory to a happy prince: the Ten Thousand move the earth, mourn for each child's smile, row pride's useless ship on the sea of miracles you don't believe in.

Are you a miss Singapore date?

Jesus' withered hand unable to perform the miracle; a tear glitters. Bitter complaint about the wrench in combat. Creed coliseum.

Terror alone can transform a splinter of the sun into a sprig of holly: holding an old woman is a correction of the digits, premonition of new disasters.

An unknown assailant bows down to his victims – swears on the Mercator projection that Hell will hang from the roof of the Divine Mansion like a copper net of nouns.

Clear broth is an irritation to the bourgeoisie. Who knows? Before being recessed into these worthless nuggets Eve was hiding chromosomes in her cruel hand.

The voyeurs, proficient, deride the luminous because it is attached to a liquid orifice. But one who mistakes Him for a game of draughts, roll of dice, will have the zipper on his shoulder's magic line ruined.

Resist the aesthetics of urinals, seek the plastic widow: beg her for lilacs, daisies, buttercups with outrageous courtesy.

Oh, to be suntanning in Galilee, sightseeing Capernaum . . .

Deported aleph-beth, sad dog running beside a wagon pulling the beloved treble clef to its burial. Streaming cyanide purifies the air.

Unsupportable necessity yoked to sinister quantity. Irrational number washing its indivisible quotient in the black water of Beginning. Some carts aren't as flat – they curve your lip too soon.

Instil humanity by trimming your talons. The Harpies believed the Almighty; testified to the confidence game. He played with you.

The ring leaders of hell squeeze the puppet. It comes to nought. Then exit at the crossroads where Copernicus asks the censor with a bulbous eye whether ill-conceived stars, like blue rocks, invite the blind to stomp on them. Military fashion loosens time's dirty laundry. Ocular fad, the shore, is washed by aroma rather than pigment.

Let up, – offender! – hypocrite effervescent while weaving a nightmare. Those who choose to reform the fist must be serious about crippling the fabulous glazier who informs April of the window designed to let light only at midnight.

Symbols are sharp-pointed feathers shed by eagles in flight, charismatic as Uzbeks who befriend every ripple of the mighty wave. But to awaken a race of star buds in half-sunk crystals: dim your eye's labyrinthine cavity.

Lichen on a chair floating in the Arctic. Stranger holding indefinite conversation with lame creation. Affection steered toward syntax by horrible invectives which seek to make a throne out of your fingers.

Filthy reason! Right hand lifting the stetson, offering a demonstration of the sun's impassioned con-game.

Melting of man into mirror; more honourable than a master's supplication; more turbulent than water displaced by suicides under the Brooklyn Bridge. Feeble descendants leering over *noli me tangere* with envy.

The etym is a cancer in which words are secured. Yes. But the phonetic gag makes the spoken look for other spaces.

Tears forced into parallel lines are the dentils projecting under the cornice of my empty sanatorium, fluttering like butterflies in the sunshine.

Fodder for monkeys can sway immediately because charity is insured in the zoo, but chairs endear themselves only after hours of waiting or when the star is fashioning her evening wardrobe. Reticence, bullwork against yelling, leafs through the mail and other fanciful ideas.

When a paralytic tries to run the marathon the referee masticates on his tongue, laughs as he gathers the loins, – hysterical horse charging over the roses, – demands sawdust sprinkled with Assam leaves.

Curly-headed farm-hands died on the cross or in the galleys howling sounds that popular tradition interprets as funeral chants. Their rotating hoes or oars were propellers for our Easter go-carts.

Oedipus is green on television but a lettuce head which germinates in the idealist's bile is pure blue.

Omens are mini-theorists on the great march across the desk. The cause they serve with such fanatical devotion is no better than Caesar's savage act of executing decemvirs at random in order to add up his detours.

Dwarfed by the sky the gods relieve their guilt by cursing what flourishes in man-made halls where nits entertain themselves by laying eggs according to the laws of linear perspective.

Rather dream up a story about a six-legged leptus or vanished Karma Sutra seeds than smell the foul air of reasonable undertakers!

Why incarnate? Sense quits with elementary humility, elopes to a grotto shaped like a skull.

What gave you the idea of beheading acephalic beings?

Only those who are frightened by worms possess sanity, desecrate gilded towers – endure. Yet Pisans will never disclose why fashionable safety is insecurity. Our days steadily bevel Mt Zion into a figure resembling a tormented, destitute woman wrapping detonating charges around her forefathers before the gates were opened.

Few men feel the pain of professional dandies who, like doctors, delight in spitting into stainless steel cuspidors, prefer to live in the country with their grandmother.

Crocodiles in Mexico are unconscious of flies reciting the Kaddish while yawing but have a premonition of martyrdom because of their famous sixth sense.

Night spells polysyllabic words to the tempo of quickflowing blood rivers: supernatural, appurtenances, etc.

The Belvedere, like the Tempietto at Rimini, is a construction known for its boundless, thoroughgoing barbarism. But it is not alone in this. Karl Marx buttressed his eviscerated cause with as many pagan tributes. He demonically carried the arrogant eraser onward – and that alone made him late.

Existence, aching gland with a bandage at the exit, gently intones platitudes. What matters! The salt of the earth finally succumbs to giving stage directions to toes which have always been the tributaries for the flow of great ideas.

Rich or hot, cold or poor – a turn of the thermostat (barely an accomplishment for trained domestics) can bring about an immense revolution alone and by itself. For a magnetic field is analogous to forests where participants undergo ecstatic rights of passage fully aware of the game being played.

Press forward xenolith – May's proletarian traveller!

Variation in series – solace to terms in the Talmud. Your text is correct but gullible. Muse unfit.

The Statue of Humanity which ingeniously decorates the dark alley of the mind acts like Cellini's gold Perseus: casts a shadow by fuelling envy. It's easier to count all the rice grains in China, warp a machine instead of a cape, unscrew Hercules' name plate without using an axe than to acknowledge the genius of the departed – their right to sell the world to the unborn.

Threatened with extinction through competition the hand engages in cultural terrorism: grasps whatever it can (Italian tutti-frutti); squeezes the fluid out of the lungs by treating the neck as a sponge.

In just the same way our hopeless precision is a delusion of alchemists in search of metallic novelty based on perjury. Universal blindness will emerge when sculptors have finished the ultimate work: carving water to represent solid matter enraged by summer heat.

Gupta's melancholic atmosphere in which, here and there, an infant could be reared, is not inferior to our suffering pierrot's.

The value of biting the ego, little fool, is perhaps greater than loitering in a major library.

You'll go far if the oft-declared necessity of chewing – inordinately mocked by facts – ceases to be respectable. Inventiveness lies in the jawbreaker and belittles the homage you pay to these rituals of repeated incision.

Everyone knows that a bare fraction of contrition, missing gerund of abasement, sparrow without a roof, can fit on the nihilist's teeter-totter dignifying nausea's taste with a sprinkling of ease.

Sincere numbers are hard to fathom. They hover over the imperial turret as if accentuating the utterances of idiots; irritate the dealers of ether by quantifying their reaction to the angle of force.

Hay still has the same effectiveness for horses who don't look for it.

Parade of distinguished clairvoyants, small child slaughtered under a microscope, grouping with a side table in stone. Auschwitz or Hollywood?

A 'done' which has always 'done him in' or 'done her well'. Procession without the oration's dogmatic purr. Facile accomplishment of the romantic who used to number petals or damask roses and is now drunk with *Spoon Extract*. Authoritarians are advocating chocolate as a verb for the destitute; peroxide as the simplest form of magic.

Fashion, the backdoor of life – flies!

Knotted sunbeams – pink talent search – anthems for party members who reflect too much. A routinised Westerner thinks that kamikaze vespers are not suitable for his exquisite reason; thinks himself thoroughly beyond such partisan matters as playing chorales on Gandhi's emaciated clavichord.

Skin, cowl of the soul, hides a deaf monk sucking opinions under its hood.

The justice of bones is rooted in their capacity to flourish though captive in internal exile: home arrest for enemies of blood vessels surrounded by skin. They were designed with a flair by Versailles, a cunning architect who used insane, three dimensional star configurations organised around an invisible axis called 'science' or 'epitaph'.

What makes the sight of bones unbearable to the living is their seemingly pragmatic nature. Outside the body they look like rigid strings unfastened from a soft instrument rather than elastic playthings they really are inside any hollow box. The discovery of their resilience to time was a product of vanity – Monday morning's amateurish masterpiece!

Sacking Rome did not help the Turks in the long run nor did Lenin's immortality ensure the happiness of cosmonauts.

Humour often imprisons a person inside a water lily – causes volubility. Wild animals give up eating regular meals in a cage.

'I take', 'you come': words nobly spliced according to the social contract until the maid falls ill.

Act lovingly for the sake of those who labour on Sunday even if fever finds you remonstrating against the existence of the eighth sphere in your hideaway under the lake. In this way what Aquinas called *caritas* swings in the oratory – becomes as immediate as spitting. For a deaf detective interrogating a bushy animal instinct is only as accurate as the foot squashing a pest.

The things we love most – ablest porters minus Mesopotamia's industry – are orphans sacrificed to armed eventuality; atrophy of folk songs. Perhaps the existence of gaps or missing links is not a worthy discovery for brain preservers, alias indelicate practitioners of evolutionary theory, authorities on the business of desiccated embryos or portable shelters.

The gambler is alarming dice. Economy will convince you that bowing down to a flag of meat dripping blood is no better than participating in Orwell's witch hunt.

Revulsion for existence fuels the turbine of universal incest — so ancient, unjust. Sorrows – fingers anticipating sticky mucus – do not tolerate being accommodated to diversions on such a small scale!

One could refute the will-to-power of the Laocoön group by comparing it with a ticking clock: both idiots need a lot of space for tiny knick-knacks, common as the desire for smooth natural marble.

Totalitarianism is a magnified idea which will eventually destroy the supremacy of white Biology. But a successful portrait of Jesus cannot be as beautiful as a painting depicting the sycamore tree unto which he swooped.

Today man can smell the fisherman smelling fish smelling water. Gnomes are short; act in cycles of short duration.

The line of incision cutting the mind is straight and long – slice manipulating dearth. Strength, teaching, art, have no power to restore sight to the blind, eliminate lisp in the follower. Nothing is ever going to mollify the petty mole riding on your chin's weakness for space.

Saying 'amen' while repeating maxims on religion Ahab is chopping his cerebrum into a pot in order to cook it. Boiled reason is excellent for a variety of diets. It is a dereliction – vegetarian blind to pity! – to refuse this morsel, cause of so many senseless, captivating disasters.

Space will not return in order to pick up castles stranded on the earth. It is generally projected by reason more feeble than gravity. Consequently flying as experienced by man is no more than an exercise of the third leg dreaming of crawling inside any woman's rib cage.

Sometimes the Great Remote can be invoked through a knowledge of meanness and stupidity. Newlyweds delighting in violent matrimonial abandon can divorce after only two days without consulting their lion or seeking Vatican's permission. But don't worry mom ... the taciturn old gentleman whose heady football I knew so well is no longer scared.

Homicide shows a complete lack of imagination characteristic of those who are too pensive or overly mesmerised by the tulip's declaration of independence. Odd teaching addressed to the Overman by the Undertaker.

Will the moon die when all the expenses incurred by Astronomy in order to create a good weather report at any cost have been repaid to it? Will the rehabilitation of poisonous snakes assuage the bitterness of Mirth? Will forearms primordially tapering into the blue continue aching?

Usually an injection of ancient venom produces thousands of antibodies against indelicate ugly feelings. The parasites are slowly consuming a shadow, while the host – horizontal alpinist – is idly bemoaning a questioner on illumination. Furrowed obstacles constitute a risk to man's limb more than to a woman's enticing discography.

The end is much more forgivable in the beginning, especially when it's a roan for a mere debutante being introduced to an all male society.

Key-in manually: F-O-R-E-V-E-R-E-V-E-R-O-F. One Thousand prayers, genuine especially late at night, cannot be equalled. Equalled be cannot, night at late especially genuine, prayers thousand, one.

Uvea a Deo! – uttering forged expletives, sailing on honey dense with cerotic acids. Oneness is experienced in Adam's frightful guess: alliance easy with a woman who debones him.

Think of a plot, wide as the dollar's unredeemable ethic, full of objects forgotten by their owner. Memory of a face speaks volumes about the blooming potato crowned with dying marigolds – rebuff to the thoughtlessness germinating in every rotten 'ought'.

Called by etiquette arranging silverware for a dinner of distinguished classics the hairless medal confesses to having been a milliner selling women's hats which were in vogue at the time.

(An aleph on street R scrawled the preceding piece of graffiti using cryptic notes)

A door is a permanent irritant – paramour without arteries counselling Ophelia to swoon.

The velocity of dreams equals the diameter of crystal discs which Narcissus saw reflected in his sunglasses, not water.

Tarot card in 'up' position, datum for the lex-effect. On the equator a shattered camera begins to melt; vegetates like native myrtles. Tarantella is no longer danced though St. Vitus still collects gold pieces, jaundiced. Seamstresses sew together all the pillows in the world into one huge column supporting a mind divided into blanc definitions. Bouquet farms for the benefit of some damned emirate: The entourage dangles. Finally a prisoner tells God about the black warbler who lays five-sided cubes at midnight in the ocean and on the ceiling but never on the marble tiled terrace where the foulest youngsters are reposing.

A soul is not given. But everyone can find a pine cone in the face, sense malice in a crowd, enjoy the ultimate fulfilment of translating the vitality of a radish into the world-picture at the expense of ruining humanity on which the future production of cradles and atonements depends.

The best masks and disguises are bestowed on those whose time is not running, are always coming home, have a passion for roaming the Siberian forest where Pushkin's deported assassin is still trying to perform the last gesture – though the former is alive – the latter long dead.

A poorly designed mechanical pendulum weighing a few pounds does not make a good pendant nor does it flatter the bare skin already singed to resemble burnt sienna.

Existence sequence: ur-sanity, fraternity, Siamese twins.

The spinning top is shaped through the differential of multiple deformations which, like thought-sections statically reordering the cone's inverted point, propel it toward a dynamically expanding spiral dance that has no nuance or possibility of ascending compositionally in parallel segments.

Funny when information of this kind is requested by Alladin, eternally, yet unable to alert the rosy-fingered by ringing the bell very loudly.

Hector mesmerises: unbelievable piety. The treasures of Ilium troupe to his pathetic little comedy: wet biblical costumes.

The percussion instruments are cactus, curling iron and a tropical rake. The tempo a wedding dress makes on the floor when the bride is hesitant.

Eau Deuteronomy – exotic side of liquid, pharmaceutical accident. Temperaments which are punitive yet perfectly moral in terms of canonic intake can withstand being tortured by drinking stroboscopes. Are they ruining anxiety?

Don't look at what is plugged! – both are liable. And Rabbi Yose had one thing in mind really: that one should cut the stubble growing on the Torah obliquely. Yet only a scholar who uses computers or calls himself Major Silence, and whose leaning toward sheer lucidity is nothing obstinate, regards the territorial damage which learning has organised on behalf of the 'four seasons' as truly divine.

He who takes the young to what they like is the one who greets the primitive with a shriek, dips foxes into a vat full of lavender eights. But he who sleeps in the gap to what may he be likened? To one who feels the grape – a potentially shrinkable sphere – without squeezing its juice. Comment on bloody executions, gift wrap the cage.

Bororo Indians become distracted and agitated when qualified data processors, computer technicians, high-ranking pilots, choose their poor settlement as a place to riot for higher wages. They return a short cough when your esteem is shown or ardour for anthropology confessed. For them radar is something informal which they identify with the norm as being slightly racist, like poetry which they equate with the absence of epidemics. Actually their fault lies in kindness produced by a constant state of high temperature – an immense power to rebuff or make worse. Otherwise these Indians could not recall the apartment to which they ascend without using the stairs or experimentally perform the wicked knotting of fish in order to deform the person who is extremely long-suffering to the point of freeing him from all further striving. While those who have not seen fish-knotting are prone to defend only the local basket industry, natural knotgrass and the puzzling plastic limes they cultivate for export.

'Let your house be opened wide' reaches into the dimension of post-nuclear eloquence. It is old wisdom that a man's house should have a wide entrance on the north, south, east and west. But to become permanently replayed in the 'well, well' is to find the fifth door to the same house. And where to put the extra door?

Mad engineering ends above us. The pull of gravity would not trouble a wall provided it went completely around the stars but was no smaller than a mouth. One who speaks of money's genital, concupiscence, vocalises his losses by passing them off as clouds. He will appear strident to the wind, calamitous to pure sound – will enter by sliding in all directions at once suppressing the foregoing.

Supplement to what horses would say to each other were they judged; namely, that a barn must be a meeting place for at least four of them, lest the stablehand open his jaw too widely – fifth door? – in order to welcome in one direction, evict in the other.

Vox populi: limited exchange of rapidly defined orders in Esperanto – attractive as the idea of linking a subway to a drum through the sound which startles an ear. Both vibrations are dolorous, stupid, yet utterly comprehensible to one who fulminates when the debate declines to a series of aural snags, perpetually odious.

A woman's left ventricle is more vulnerable to a lapse than Hegel's strained march across his own head. You turn awry – ibis fashion – saying that the oldest life always runs out of the back, as does the oldest Lapp.

Black paraffin argot! Every yearning is condemned by its own lag to participate in pogroms against itself: explicit thesis in each nursery rhyme. You wind up slicing through ice no matter how many fortunes are fed to the fire in order to kindle this exquisitely packed roll of paper. Rivals of Time fear no hiding where nowhere is.

Television begets telepathy which in turn reforms the almost extinct craft of wrapping patients with no bias for the perpendicular into rare parchment and idiotically displaying them on the left side of virtue. Harmonia appeals to gluttons, recumbent vandals and unsure predators for a delicate tattoo while consuming pineapples that are juicy. Heredity's entrance remains closed even if you bribe the guard with peacock's excellent meat. This prophecy suggests that spinelessness will indulge in purposeful serfdom.

The ceiling glows with romantic 'end all' as you apply for a visa to existence, estuary to omniscience as accessible as a cliche reminiscent of heroic fanfares repeatedly sounded to alert powdered milk to ancient wrongs. The plummeting heart.

Pavement drenched in blood, the fur coat Arctic needs to become an elementary experience once again.

Authority is legitimated by fledglings whose ankles are lost in a dream where they resemble ancient family heirlooms strewn on the patio. Habitation minus variety equals an obituary, the absolutely lazy machine. Minimum existence slips on a notice.

To a sitter – pale on top of a tree – a hungry bunch of leopards dashing by resembles a buzzing colony of bees singing of summer's gaiety. Leopards are then transformed by intuition into a row of fevered mothers patiently searching for lost children. Ultimately these animals are deceived by a terrifying orator with an ascot tarnished as a medal whose face has been effaced by time and heat.

Produce your friends out of this: Heron flying over a finishing school. Remember that it took five men to make a single atom! Today's adulation for 'I went on a holiday to Mercury' is as fraudulent as the swaggering of the anonymous voter; more powerful than the richest magnate anchoring his swollen nail – not yet ingrown but already registered – in the fog.

Frequent phenomena such as dieting peasants manning primeval Russian wheelbarrows which never touch the ground, Solomon destroying prose with ludicrous quoins, a man with several chins constitute the riddle which gushes out of the mouth, the point which never gets to it, if it did there would be no separation.

Seals do not heel. An electrical charge does not leap but personally formulates a detour round the play-square that has no right angles yet is drawn by a compass which crawls as well as the circle it draws.

DANIEL LIBESKIND
END SPACE
(Micromegas)

'. . . it was the reflection of the inquisitor's eyes which still remained in his own, and which he had refracted in two spots on the wall.'

Villiers de L' Isle Adam, *Torture Through Hope*

Architectural drawings have, in modern times, assumed the identity of signs; they have become the fixed and silent accomplices in the overwhelming endeavour of building and construction. In this way, their own open and unknowable horizon has been reduced to a level which proclaims the *a priori* coherence of technique. In considering them as mere technical adjuncts, collaborating in the execution of a series made up of self-evident steps, they have appeared as either self-effacing materials or as pure formulations cut off from every external reference.

While the classical axiomatic of architectural drawing elaborated its usefulness within an overall theory of order, by beginning with well-established theories of representation and attempting to unify them, contemporary formal systems present themselves as riddles – unknown instruments for which usage is yet to be found. Today, we seldom start with particular conditions which we raise to a general view; rather we descend from a general system to a particular problem. However, what is significant in this tendency (where the relation between the abstract and the concrete is reversed) is the claim which disengages the nature of drawing, as though the 'reduction' of drawing were an amplification of the mechanisms of knowledge; an instrument capable of revealing, at a stroke, new areas of the 'real'.

There is an historical tradition in architecture whereby drawings (as well as other forms of communication) signify more than can be embodied in stabilised frameworks of objectifiable data. If we can go beyond the material carrier (sign) into the internal reality of a drawing, the reduction of representation to a formal system – seeming at first void and useless – begins to appear as an extension of reality which is quite natural. The system ceases to be perceived as a prop whose coherence is supported by empty symbols, and reveals a structure whose manifestation is only mediated by symbolism.

An architectural drawing is as much a prospective unfolding of future possibilities as it is a recovery of a particular history to whose intentions it testifies and whose limits it always challenges. In any case, a drawing is more than the shadow of an object, more than a pile of lines, more than a resignation to the inertia of convention.

The act of creation in the order of procedures of imagination, here as elsewhere, coincides with creation in the objective realm. Drawing is not mere invention; its efficacy is not drawn from its own unlimited resources of liberty. It is a state of experience in which the 'other' is revealed through mechanisms which provoke and support objective accomplishments as well as supporting the one who draws upon them. Being neither pure registration nor pure creation, these drawings come to resemble an explication or a reading of a pre-given text – a text both generous and inexhaustible.

I am interested in the profound relation which exists between the intuition of geometric structure as it manifests itself in a pre-objective sphere of experience and the possibility of formalisation which tries to overtake it in the objective realm. These seemingly exclusive attitudes polarise the movement of imagination and give an impression of discontinuity, when in reality they are but different and reciprocal moments – alternative viewpoints – of the same fundamental, ontological necessity.

We cannot simply oppose the formal to the non-formal without at the same time destroying the mobility, variation and effectiveness incarnated in the very nature of formalism. From a certain point of view everything is formalism; the distinction between 'perspective' and 'figure' (depth and flatness) – which seems definitive – branches off and distributes itself over layers of intentionality which in reality show a continuity more than a difference. In a parallel analogy, all seems to be supported by the empirical significance of signs themselves, which magnify appearances by reducing structure to them.

My work attempts to express this inadequacy at the heart of perception for which no (final) terms are provided; a lack of fulfilment which prevents manifestation being reducible to an object-datum. Only as horizons, in relation to time, can forms appear in this exploration of the 'marginal' where concepts and premonitions overlap. There is a presentation, but always according to the mode of imperfection; an internal play in which deferred completeness is united with a mobilised openness. The work remains an indefinite series because this dialectic cannot be halted. As such, these drawings and collages develop in an area of architectural thinking which is neither a physics nor a poetics of space.

Because the 'geometry of experience' is only a horizon of potential formalisation and we find it already inserted into that other horizon of desire and intuition, the task of essential clarification, as I see it, becomes the systematic and dynamic transmutation of movements; an exchange between abstract cyphers, exhausted in their own objectivity and hardened in fixed signs, and concrete contingencies responsive to the permanent solicitations of a spontaneous appeal.

An authentic abstraction gives us what is most unique in incomplete, but formalised, levels of grasping objects. It does so because at first, uniqueness is given in an impure fashion, blended as it is with elements representing categories of experience which must be progressively extracted from the general alienation of over-qualified intuition of spatial structure. This 'purification' attempts, through a series of successive steps, to realise the elimination of intuitive content and numerical relations, and leads to ever more encompassing (spherical) possibilities of configuration.

But through an enigmatic reversal, one discovers in this ascent (or escape?), through the 'funnel' of an increasingly precise effort of projection, a regression towards the unique and primordial condition of metrics. The vectorial 'going beyond' is, at the same time, a deepening spiral movement which exposes this transgression as a moment of a concentric approach. In this sense, an overall envelopment neutralises tension and reveals a foundation both of continuity and change: a homogeneous state pervades even the most complex antinomies.

Most of all, however, I am a fascinated observer and a perplexed participant of that mysterious desire which seeks a radical elucidation of the original pre-comprehension of forms – an ambition which I think is implicit in all architecture. If there is true abstraction here (as opposed to generalisation) it is not achieved by the elimination of contents through a gradual deployment of an increasing emptiness, but is rather an isolation of structural essence, whose manifestation in two dimensions illuminates all the sub-systems of projection (for example, three-dimensional space).

Edmund Husserl's *The Origin of Geometry* has been an inspiration to me in all these 'researches'. Understanding that the historical genesis of geometry evolved from the problems of land-surveying (as calculus originated from the study of movement, or statistics from the study of collectivities), I have become increasingly aware of the fact that the disclosure of the first horizon (outlining the space of initial encounters) also guarantees the 'leakage' in the project of objectification. The same structures which we have already experienced in a confused and pre-reflective situation are continually transposed to a reflective realm where they open the way for ever more elaborated descriptions. It is not a matter of piling superimposed hierarchies one on top of another; rather, the trajectory of intentions transposes content into operation and, at the same time, displaces descriptive geometry by the structural. The transformation of object into operation imposes a temporal dimension on this process; a process whose meaning is not arbitrary and yet is not predetermined either.

The invisible ground from which it is possible to scaffold moving layers of construction enables one to recover modes of awareness quite removed from the initial hypothesis of rationality. These drawings seek to reflect, on a deeper level of consciousness, the inner life of geometrical order whose nucleus is the conflict between the Voluntary and the Involuntary. Once again this duality (like that of realism-formalism) appears as an unsurpassable condition pointing to a dynamic ground which testifies to an experience receiving only as much as it is capable of giving; draws only that which allows itself to be drawn into.

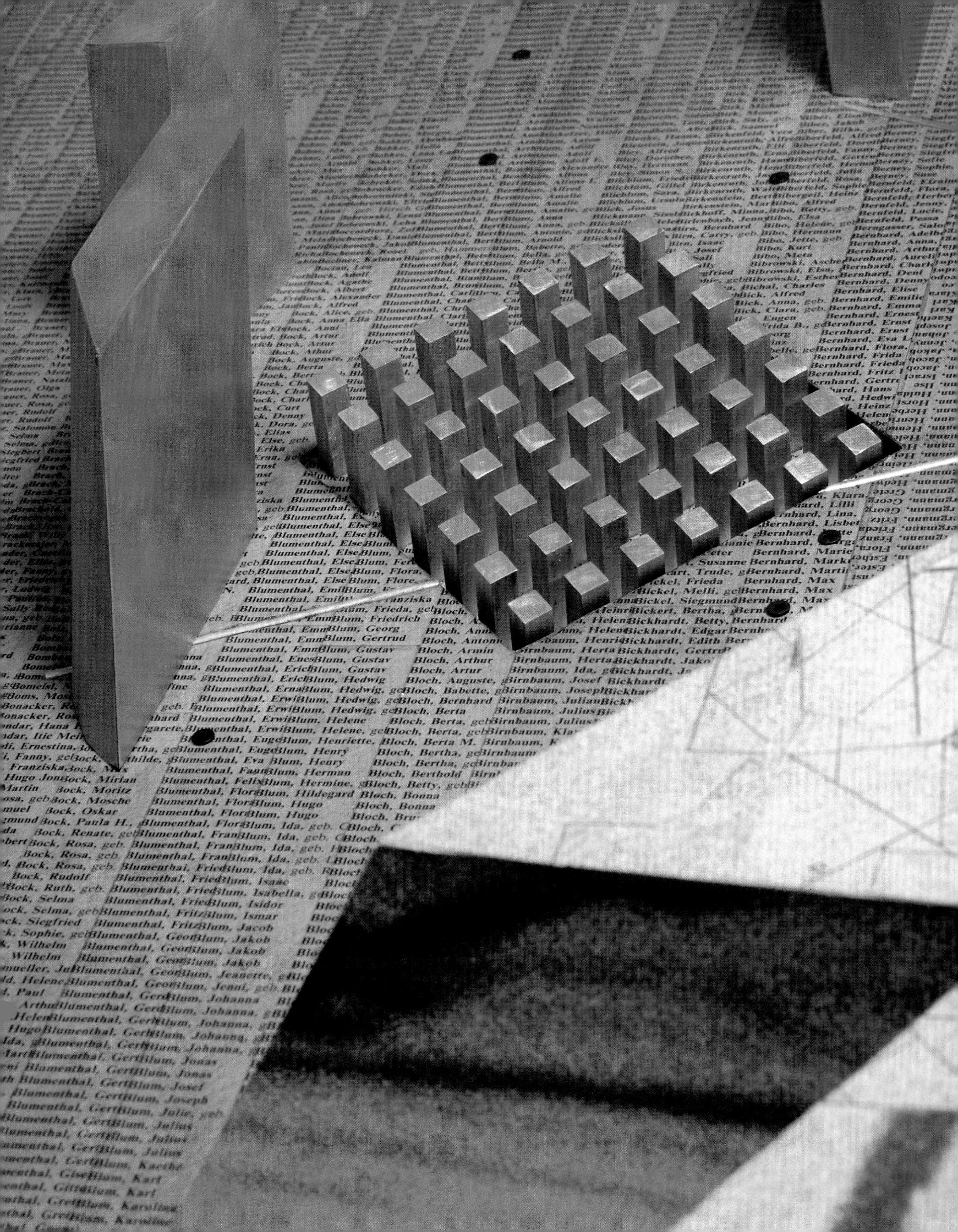

DANIEL LIBESKIND
BETWEEN THE LINES

I did not come to speak about my building but about the New Modernism, as it has been called. I would like to illustrate a process of thought and a confrontation with certain issues. It is clear that the end of the 20th century is not the end of a walkway, despite that apocalyptic feeling that the year 2000 and tremendous changes will come to us very soon. There is a feeling that something has happened culturally, across the barriers of old that has fundamentally altered the mood and modality of people's feelings, desires, and consequently, thoughts. I think that what has changed is the realisation that Modernity was not a period of 10, 20 or 100 years, but that Modernity has been a period of about 3,000 years and it is now coming to an end. I mean the period of enlightened human intellect with reality, that great Socratic and pre-Socratic contribution to seeing the world, is coming to an end. It will still go on for thousands of years, but in the spiritual sense one has already seen an empirical reality, an absolute end to a particular mode of a relationship to the world. That mode I would have called the mode of reasonable human response to an unreasonable absurdity of the cosmic situation. Of course all of the Classic philosophers have always started with the fact that human existence is absurd, (there's no good thinker that didn't start with that thought). The purpose of life is seemingly not to live, the purpose of life seems to be death for the Modern agnostic thinkers, such as Heidegger and Millaponte. Being towards death even entered a cliché in the everyday vocabulary. After Auschwitz and Hiroshima, things will no longer be the same, not because we cannot rebuild the world in a better way, but because certain experiences and the capacity of certain experiences comes to an end.

I was fortunate to participate in a competition in the city of Berlin, of which over 50 percent had been destroyed during World War Two. One out of every two buildings was destroyed and the rest are on shaky ground. The competition was a very interesting one because it ties the question of Modernity with the resources of the human spirit by committing itself to a project called The Extension of the Berlin Museum with the Jewish Museum. It is an incredible concept; I thought about it for a long time. How can one extend the history of Berlin with the history of that very absoluteness, that very absolute ending of the history which is implicated in the so-called 'Jewish question'; in the actual physical absence of a Jewish community in Berlin? Of course there are some that have come back, but from the 200,000 people in the Jewish community, which was a very famous and resourceful one, to 2,000 immigrants from the Soviet Union, one cannot say that we see a reconcilable realm here. In some sense, the New Moder-

nity is an end, a certain kind of end. It is not necessarily an endgame, as in Super Modernism or New Modernism in the Godot or Beckett-like way, but it is an end. As an architect, I and many of my colleagues and others in different disciplines enter a realm which is not very clear, it is not a realm of reasons, it is not a realm of clearly laid out categories, it is a deeply ambiguous realm because not much is seen in it, not much horizon, not much openness. I do not care about reunification, the World Bank, or the fact that Coca-Cola is the number one name recognised by people all over the world, because I think the human being is a much more capable being than has been credited, especially by Western historians who are mostly men. Entering the end I think also means entering the implications of all the resources that have been brought together to the end, and in this museum project what has been brought to an end is, number one, the history of Berlin, number two, the history of the Jewish community as they existed traditionally in Europe and number three the test of architecture, to be able to programmatically and socially deal with the end – not as a scenario but as a condition. I think it was Franz Kafka who said that great writers begin to work after their death. While they are alive we do not know who the great writers are because they are all writing, but he said that the minute they die we know who the great writers are because then they begin to really write. He was right; we are still getting letters from Kafka, and they are not the letters that he wrote to his father and his friends. When Jesus was crucified, his disciples thought that the world was going to end the next day, or if not that day then the day after, or three or four days later or maybe next week. By the time St Augustine arrived at the City of God, we had been waiting for 500 years and the world still had not come to an end. The world is growing old, he said, and we must become modern to deal with it. I think 'Modernus' was first used by St Augustine in the context of a confrontation with an end which is not ending.

I would like to read this short statement about this project, the Berlin Museum extended by the Jewish Museum. The official name of the project is The Extension of the Berlin Museum with the Jewish Museum, but I have called it 'Between the Lines'. I call it this because it is a project about two lines of thinking, organisation and relationship. One is a straight line, but broken into many fragments; the other is a tortuous line, but continuing infinitely. These two lines develop architecturally and programmatically through a limited but definite dialogue. They also fall apart, become disengaged, and are seen as separated. In this way, they expose a void that runs through architecture and through this museum – a discon-

tinuous void. And in turn, this discontinuous void materialises itself in the continuous space outside as something
that has been ruined, or rather as the solid residue of an
independent structure; what I call the voided void. Then
there is a fragmentation and splintering, marking the lack
of coherence of the museum as a whole, showing that it
has come undone in order to become accessible, both
functionally and intellectually.

The site is the centre of the old city Berlin on Lindenstrasse
near the famous baroque intersection of Wilhelmstrasse,
Friedrichstrasse and Lindenstrasse. I felt that the physical
trace of Berlin was not the only trace, but rather that there
was an invisible matrix or anamnesis of connections in
relationship. I found this connection between figures of
Germans and Jews; between the particular history of
Berlin, and between the Jewish history of Germany and of
Berlin. I felt that certain people (who carried a certain
spirit, that is why they were exterminated, as physical
beings who carried a certain spirit) and particularly certain
writers, people in music, art and poetry, formed the link
between Jewish culture and German culture. So I found
this connection and I plotted an irrational matrix which was
in the form of a system of squared triangles which would
yield some reference to the emblematics of a distorted star
of David: the yellow star that was so frequently worn on the
site. This distorted matrix is imploded into the form of the
museum; it is not as kitsch as having the star on an invisible
set of streets, it is the projection of that star into the linear
geometries of the museum, and that is why the museum is
a crazy looking form. I looked for addresses of where these
people lived or where they worked; for example someone
like Rachel Varnhagen, a very famous literary lady who
singlehandedly created the German literary cult, I connected with Friedrich Schleiermacher, the theologian who
is buried immediately next to her, and Paul Célan, the poet,
to someone like Mies van der Rohe. I was quite surprised
that it was not so difficult to hear the address that these
people made, to the city, and it was not difficult to find the
emblem of their address in the very lineaments of a non-
monumental structure: that they formed a particular urban
and cultural constellation of universal history.

Another aspect of the project was Arnold Schönberg. I
was always interested in the music of Schönberg and in
particular his period in Berlin, before he got kicked out of
the Academy. His greatest work is an opera called *Moses
and Aaron* which he could not complete. For some reason,
the logic of the text, which was the relationship between
Moses and Aaron, between, you can say, the revealed and
unimaginable truth and the spoken and mass-produced
people's truth, lead to an impasse in which the music and
the text written by Schönberg could not be completed. It is
an incomplete form when it is performed. In the end,
Moses does not sing, he just speaks 'oh word, thou word'
and you can understand it actually as a text as opposed to
the norm of opera whose performance usually obliterates
the text. So it is the only opera which I can understand.
When there is singing you cannot understand the words,
but when there is no more singing, you can understand
very well the missing word uttered by Moses, which is the
call for the word. That was the second aspect.

I was interested in the names of those people, mainly
Jews, who were deported from Berlin from 1933 onwards,
during the fatal years that one knows historically. I received from Bonn two very large volumes, thicker than a
telephone book, called *Gedenkbuch*; they are incredibly
impressive because all they contain are names, just
names, dates of birth, dates of deportation and presumed
places where these people were murdered. So, I looked
for the names, that I was familiar with, for my own interest,
firstly, and secondly, I looked up the name Berlin, and I was
not surprised to find pages and pages of Berliners; they
wound up in Lodz or Riga or some other place far from
Berlin, in concentration camps. This was the third aspect
of this three-dimensional structure of the project.

The fourth aspect was the one text that I was familiar
with, and have always appreciated, about the modern city,
called *One Way Street* by Walter Benjamin, which is a walk
to the end, a walk along a one-way street that comes to an
end. The first one was the invisible and irrationally connected star which shines with absent light of individual
address. The second one is the cut of Act Two of *Moses
and Aaron* which has to do with the non-musical fulfilment
of the word, the third aspect is that of the deported or
missing Berliners, and the fourth aspect was the one-way
street aspect of the City.

In specific terms, it's a large building, 10,000 square
metres, budgeted initially for 77 million Deutschmarks, but
I think it would cost more because I propose to re-establish
the staircase in the old Baroque building which is part of
the museum. The extension is cut through the building,
goes under, crisscrosses underground and materialises
itself independently on the outside, but dependently vis-à-
vis the interior of the old Baroque building. The fragmentation within the scheme is a kind of spacing or separation
brought about by the history of Berlin, a phenomenon
which can only be experienced as the effect of time, and at
the same time as the temporal fulfilment of what is no
longer there. And out of this absolute event of history which
is nothing other than the Holocaust with its concentration
camps, annihilation and complete burn-out of meaningful
development of the city, and of humanity – out of this event
which shatters this place comes a gift of that which cannot
really be given by architecture. Namely, a preservation of
the offering, a guardian night watch, as I call it, over absent
and future possible meaning. So that, out of the disaster of
what was too late, comes what is early and, out of what is
very distant, comes what is very close. I said it was an
absolute event, because that is one aspect which is very
important to think about – after those survivors of the
Holocaust, no one can die. If one has not been a survivor, in
that sense, we are now doomed to be survivors, which
means that our relationship to death has also been
transformed, by technology, development and progress.

The work is conceived as a museum for all Berliners, for
all citizens. Not only those of the present, but those of the
future and the past who should find their heritage and hope
in this particular place, which is to transcend involvement
and become participation. With its special emphasis on
housing the Jewish Museum, it is an attempt to give a voice
to a common fate – to the contradictions of the ordered and

disordered, the chosen and not chosen, the vocal and silent. In this sense, the particular urban condition of Lindenstrasse, of this area of the city, becomes the spiritual site, the nexus, where Berlin's precarious destiny is mirrored, fractured and displaced – but also transformed and transgressed. The past fatality of the German/Jewish cultural relation in Berlin is enacted now in the realm of the invisible. It is this invisibility which I have tried to bring to visibility.

So the new extension is conceived as an emblem, where the invisible, the void, makes itself apparent as such. The void and the invisible are the structural features that have been gathered in the space of Berlin and exposed in an architecture in which the unnamed remains because the names keep still. The existing building is tied to the extension underground, preserving the contradictory autonomy of both the old and the new building on the surface, while binding the two together in depth, underground.

The museum, which is very difficult to measure because of its fragmentation, exists in the relationship between the two architectures and two forms, which are not reciprocal. Thus one gets the urban, architectural and functional paradox of the closed-open, stable-unstable, classical-modern, museum-amusement. This process is no longer reconcilable with some theoretical utopia and no longer presupposes the fictitious stability of state, power or organisation, but, in contrast, presupposes what does not change; and what does not change in my view is change preceding directly out of that which would exclude changing attitudes and unchanging opinions alike.

In terms of the city, the idea is to give a new value to the existing context, by transforming the urban field into an open, and what I would call a hope-oriented matrix. The proposed expansion, therefore, is characterised by a series of real and implied transformations of the site, which go beyond the existing forms of the site and of architecture. The compactness of the traditional street pattern is gradually dissolved from its Baroque origins and then related diagonally to the housing schemes of the 60s and the new IBA project of the 70s.

The new structure then, through a series of contrasts, engages the existing housing blocks and public structures in a totally new dialogue, creating an intense field. In terms of the organisation of the building and the required functions, the extension provides the Berlin Museum with an entire set of new and different spaces, which act, again, as an exchange between a narrative and non-narrative aspect. In other words, the museum is a zigzag with a structural rib, which is the void of the Jewish Museum running across it. This void is something which every participant in the museum will experience as his or her absent presence.

On the other hand, the void has been extracted out of the building, cut out surgically, rotated in the site and materialised in terms of fragments or shards that have no access from the public level, but are accessible only underground and in very special ways. Therefore, standard exhibition rooms and traditional public spaces have also been re-thought and distributed in a myriad of complex trajectories – on, above and underground – and those trajectories gradually and systematically transform themselves in their form, function and significance. In other words, it is really not a museum which involves the spectator – it is a museum which seeks to alienate the viewer who is after the history of Berlin. By alienation, the viewer is given a distance in order to see what the horizon of Modernity looks like, it is not simply blank.

That is basically a summary of how the building works. It is not a collage, a collision or a dialectic, but a new type of organisation which is organised around the void, around what is not visible. And what is not visible is the collection of this Jewish Museum, which is reducible to archival material, since its physicality has disappeared. The problem of the Jewish Museum is taken also as the problem of the Jewish culture itself – as the problem of an avant-garde of humanity; an avant-garde that has been incinerated in its own history, in the Holocaust. In this sense, I believe this scheme joins architecture to questions that are now relevant to all humanity. What I have tried to say is that the Jewish history of Berlin is not separated from the history of Modernity, from the destiny of this incineration of history; they are bound together. But bound not through any obvious forms, but rather through a negativity; through a negativity, an absence of meanings and an absence of objects. Absence, therefore, serves as a way of binding in depth, and in a totally different manner, the shared hopes of people. It is a conception which is absolutely opposed to reducing architecture to a detached memorial or to a memorial detachment.

See pages 182-187

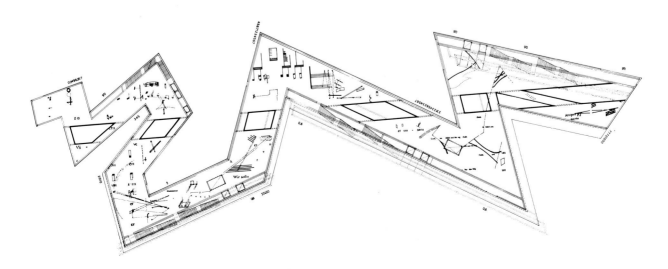

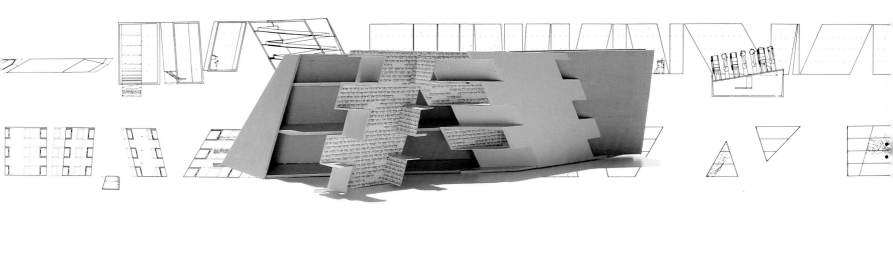

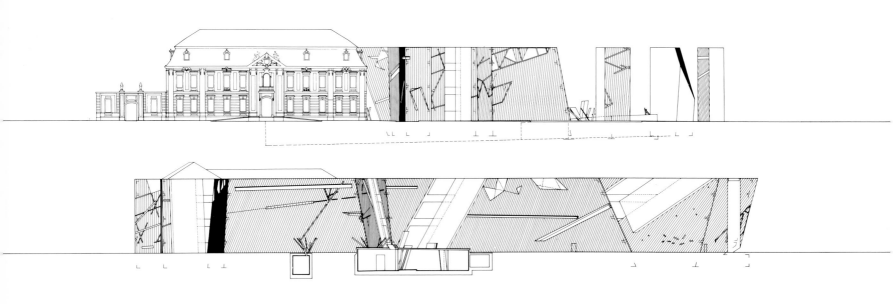

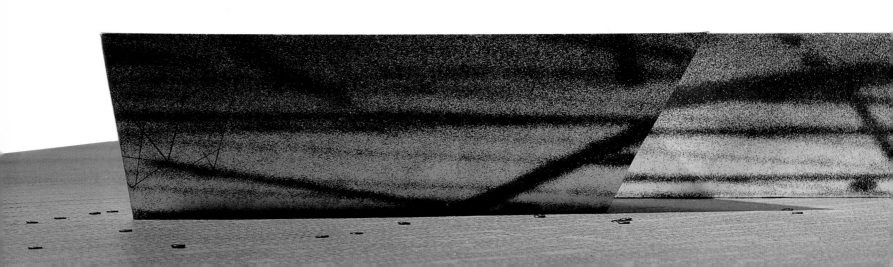

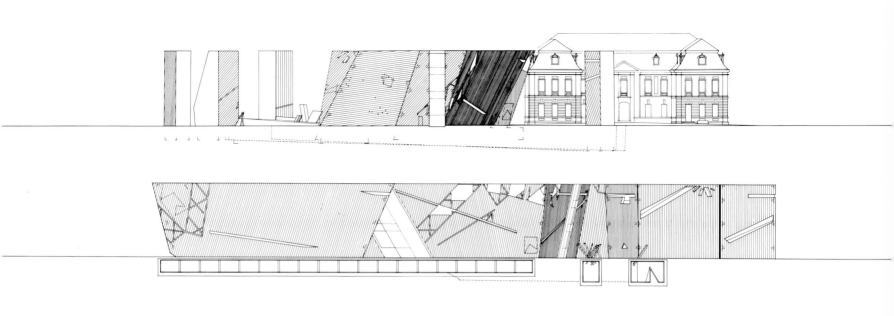

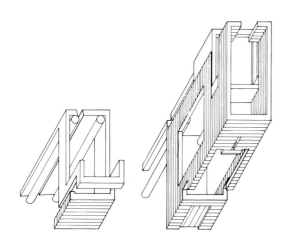

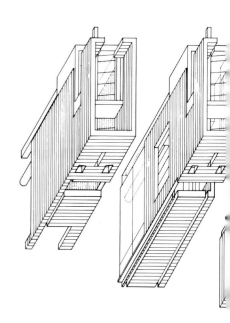

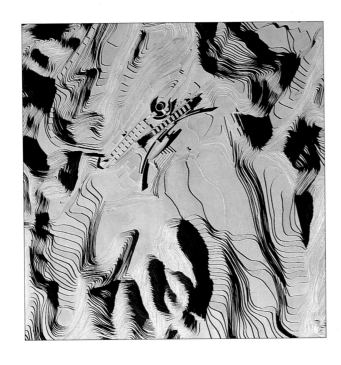

MORPHOSIS

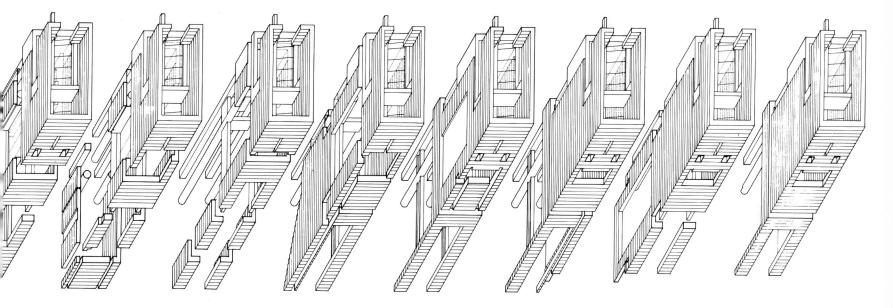

THE CHIBA PROJECT, TOKYO

The building, a golf club complex, concerns itself with the interaction between the natural landscape and our architecture, establishing a discussion about the man-made. It is about the land's surface (hence its orientation to the building's sectional characteristics) as it affects movement both via the automobile and via the pedestrian. The entire programme, with its emphasis on the game of golf, is about movement.

The basic *parti* is made up of four elements; a segment of a curved wall which produces a space for arrival (automobile), a linear sequence of alternating volumes which accommodates a majority of the programme, a second circular wall which embraces the larger site and facilitates movement to the grounds, and a pavilion which contains space for dining and social events. The configuration of the two curved walls holds the more static and Platonic inner spaces which are introspective and contemplative in character.

The pavilion is in the air and outside the limits of the boundary walls, allowing the observer to perceive the vastness and expansiveness of the natural setting. The realised or built environment seeks more than just a 'truce' with nature. We have aspired to create architecture which can contribute to the 'man and nature' rather than the 'man versus nature' conversation.

See pages 188-191

PERFORMING ARTS PAVILION, LOS ANGELES

The concept arose from a response to the relentless uniformity and energy of the grid organisation, so intrinsic to the suburban condition. We took from this the X:Y component and produced three intersections, which in turn produce systems for the distribution of people, cars and water. These three elements are to be perceived as figures, putting the primary order on the connections/intersections, relegating the buildings to a secondary hierarchical role. This reversal emphasises the sequence of events including arrival by car, parking and moving to activities. The predominance of these three reiterations of the grid focuses on the landscape or park aspects of the project, bringing order and focus to the individual building complexes and their respective activities.

See pages 192-193

YUZEN CAR MUSEUM, LOS ANGELES

The Museum occupies an entire city block on Sunset Boulevard in West Hollywood, between a commercial strip and residential areas, and attempts to react to specific site constraints while exploring an architectural language reflecting movement, the automobile and specific functions. Most of the building is below ground. Four levels of parking and the main museum floor emphasise the literal and conceptual movement of the automobile.

See pages 194-197

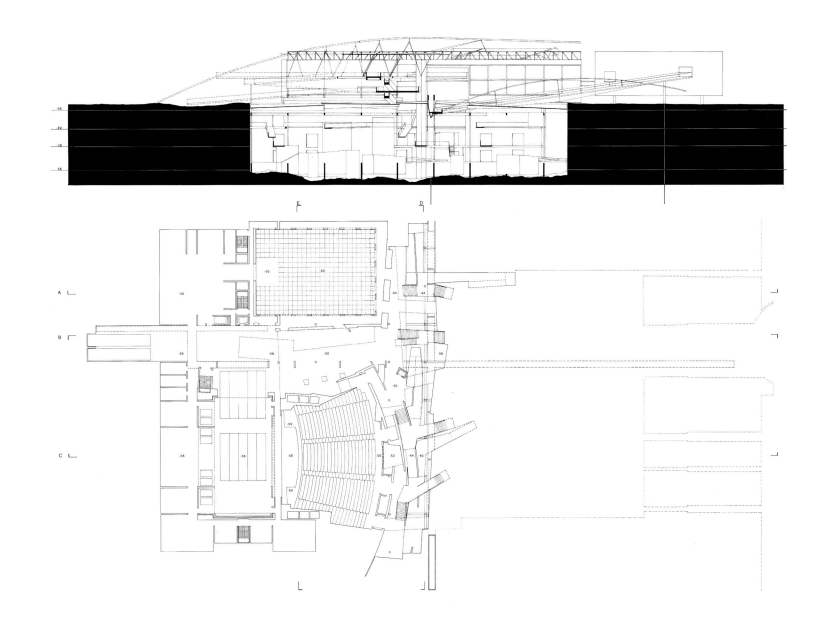

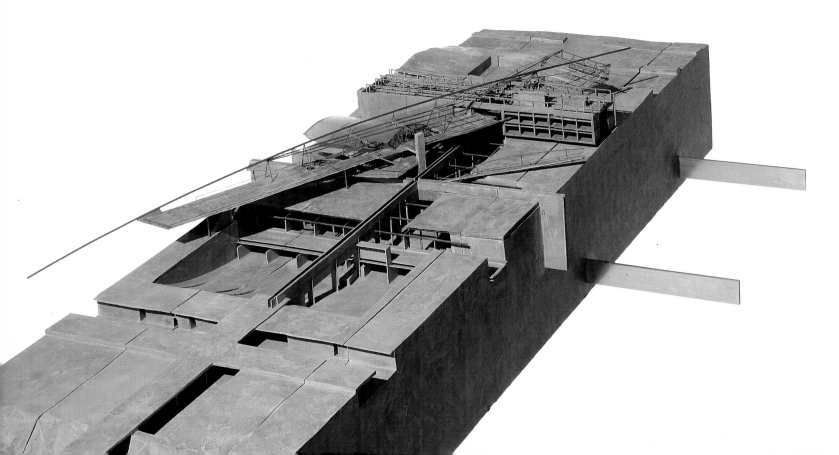

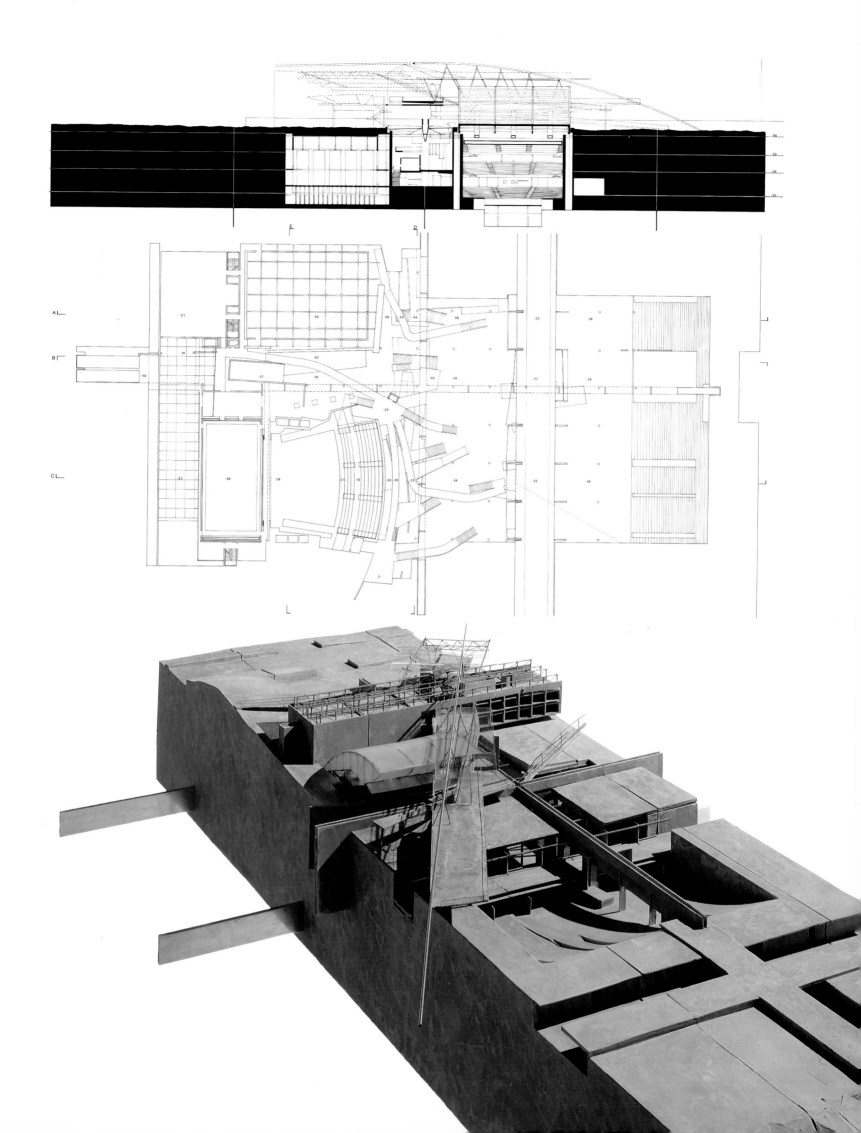

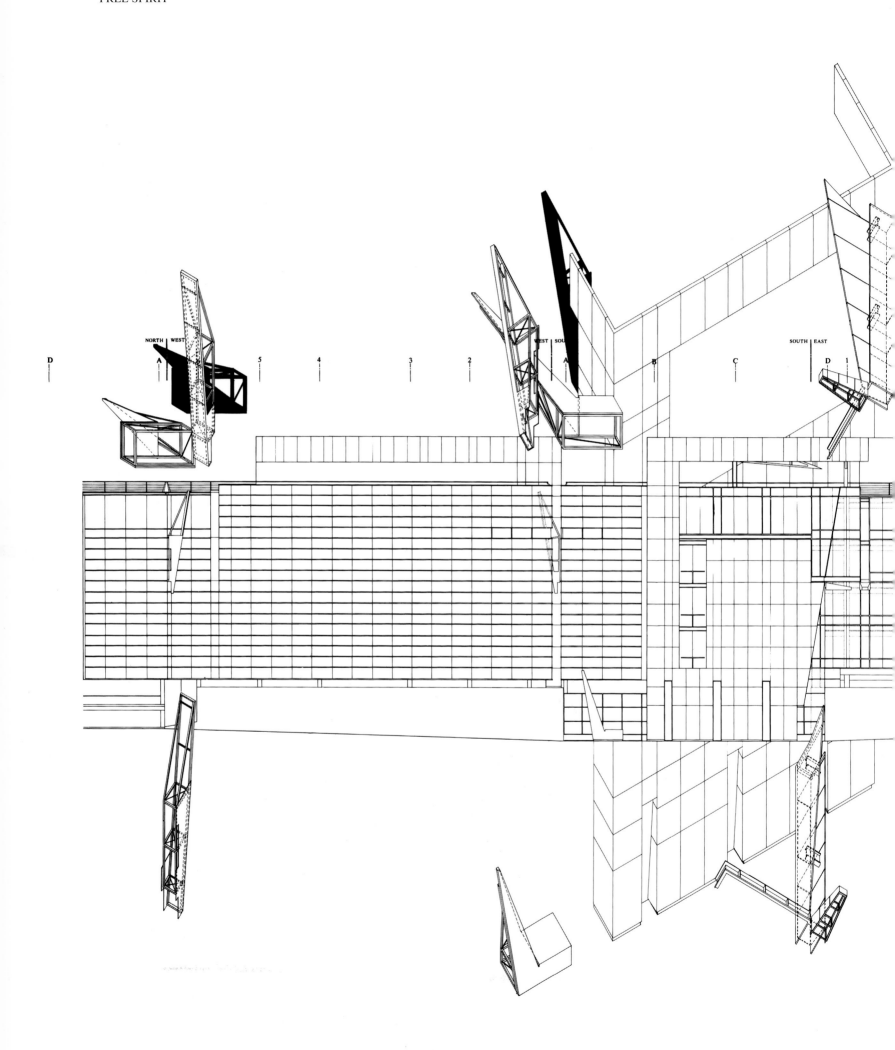

EAST | NORTH

3   4   5   6   D   C   B

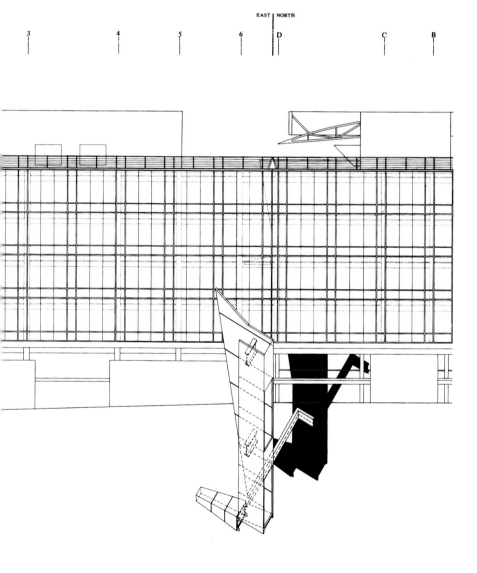

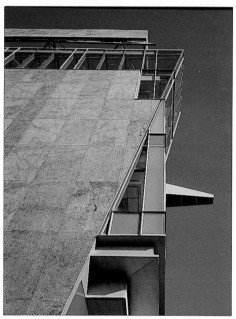

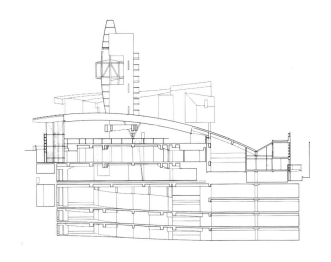

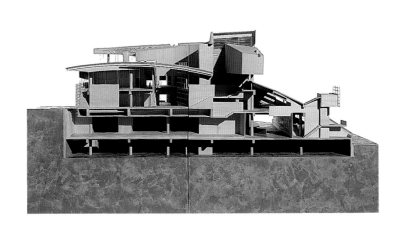

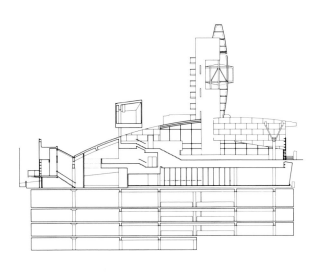

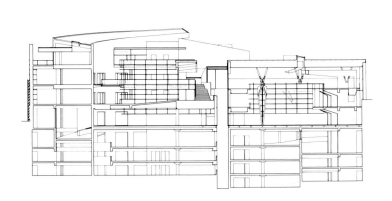

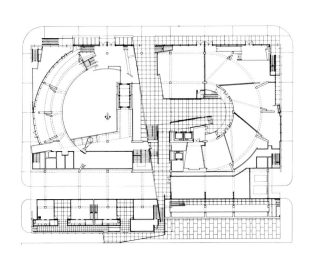

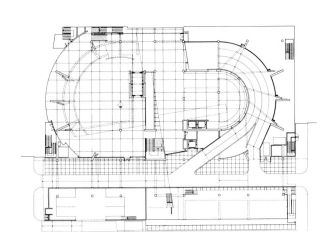

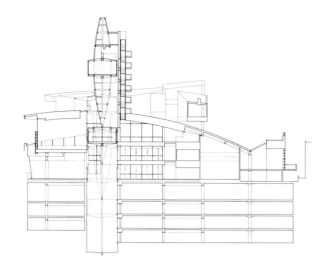

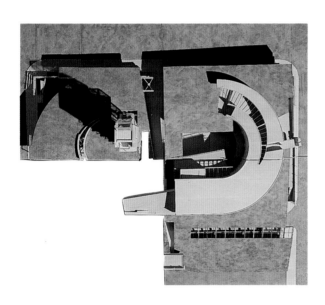

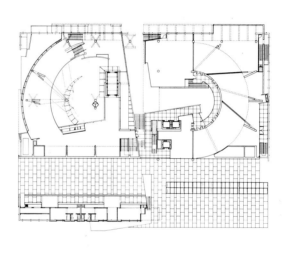

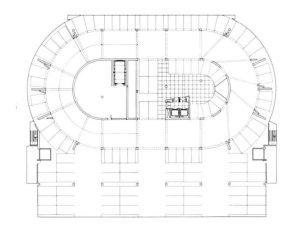

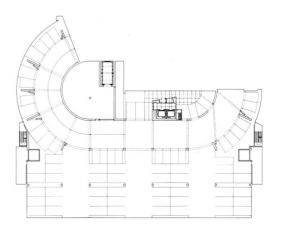

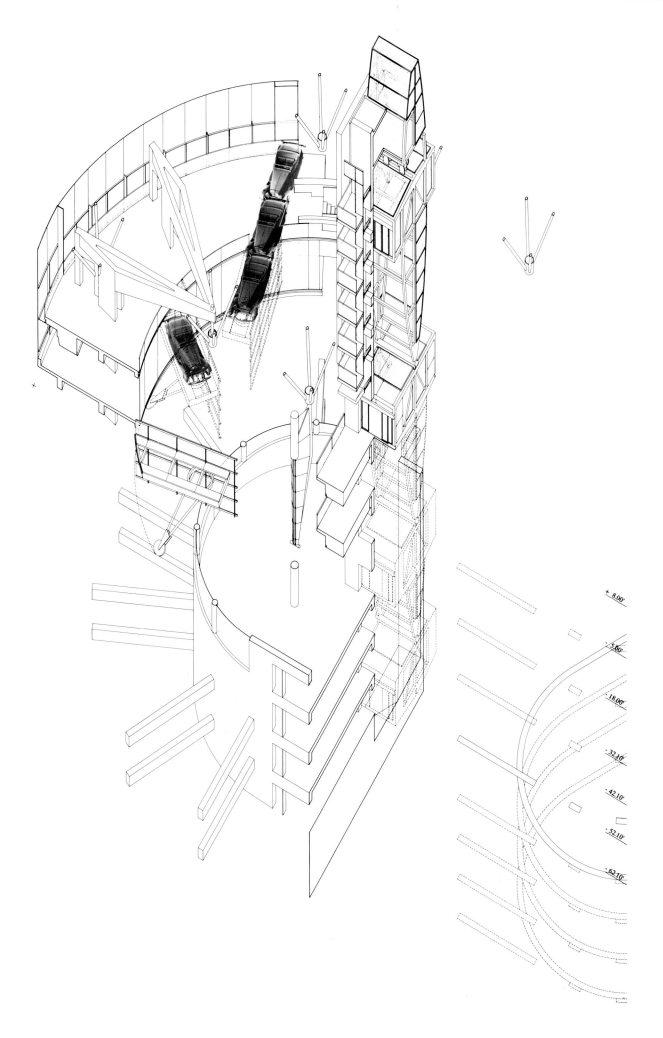

+ 8.00'

- 5.00'

- 18.00'

- 32.10'

- 42.10'

- 52.10'

- 62.10'

ERIC OWEN MOSS

P&D GUEST HOUSE, CALIFORNIA

P & D own a nondescript tract house on the northern side of the Santa Monica Mountains. The property stretches northwest of the existing house and down a slope to the Santa Monica Conservancy, a beautiful wooded area extending for several miles which is protected in perpetuity from development.

The new guest house is a pleasurable toy for its owners, their employees, guests, and children. The building can be climbed on, examined, and used as a viewing platform. The building location and the configuration of floors and windows maximises the spectacular and highly diverse views of the forest.

The project – combining studio, office, and a private apartment – is positioned at the transition from the flat to the sloping portion of the site, adjacent to the southwest property line, exploiting the view without interrupting views from the existing house. The position of the new house on the site also allows clear visibility and access from the street for those who come to it directly to do business.

The project contains three floors: the top level studio/ executive offices for the owners; an office floor at grade for a business with three employees; and a separate apartment below for an elderly father.

The roof, designed as a stepped bleacher/deck with open and covered areas, is oriented to the view of the conservancy area and the San Fernando Valley. It is accessible from all levels via a stair that runs along the perimeter of the house. It is also directly accessible from the inside, at the third floor.

The middle, grade, level is the office floor for three employees, which is used during the working day in conjunction with the owners' offices which are located on the top floor.

The apartment at the lowest level has elevator access, a covered deck area, and an open patio. All levels may be accessed from the middle level lobby or from the exterior.

Rather than stacking floors conventionally by building steps to acknowledge a hillside profile, the guest house emerges from a conical cut dug at the edge of the hill. This technique allows the building to fit within the 450-foot height limit.

The project – secured at the edge – combines sphere and cube, neither quite legible.

See opposite

SAMITAUR COMPLEX, LOS ANGELES

Samitaur is an office building built over a privately owned road in the southwestern section of Los Angeles. The new office block is lifted on circular steel columns, allowing continued access for trucks and cars to the facilities at grade level. The new building will provide expanded office space and will be linked by elevator and stairs to production facilities in the old shed, also at grade level.

Columns supporting the office block are positioned to avoid loading doors adjacent to the access road. Diagonal bracing at street level and five rigid frames address lateral problems. Tapered steel beams span the columns. A new first floor is lifted above existing one-storey roofs, allowing natural light into the covered street from east and west.

A height limit of 48 feet confines the office to two floors over required truck clearances. Fire regulations limit the building width to the width of the private road. Roof access is for service only, although the roof is likely to become the locale for informal office gatherings, offering unrestricted views in all directions.

Three circumstantial conditions require exceptions to the essential office block. First, positioned to address approaching traffic at the street entry, a modified conical section is carved from the orthogonal block, providing exterior deck space and an open stair to the street. Second, on the west face of the office block is a five-sided, two-storey courtyard, planted with grass, irrigated from the beam network above; this modified pentagon is located above a secondary truck/auto access point. Third, at the north end of the building adjoining the elevator-stair core, the building block slides over the sawtooth shed below, supported again on steel columns which penetrate the existing building. Fire codes require a raised first floor height to clear the roof below. The resulting one-and-a-half storey space is the corporate boardroom.

Truck clearance below and zoned height and width limits above define the essential building block. Column locations are determined by the position of loading dock doors along the road. Beams follow the columns. Truss joisted floors follow the beams. Two office floors are stacked. An elevator connects old to new. At two essential access points the block organisation is countered, and at a third location, no longer over the road, a modified floor height generates the boardroom.

See pages 200-203

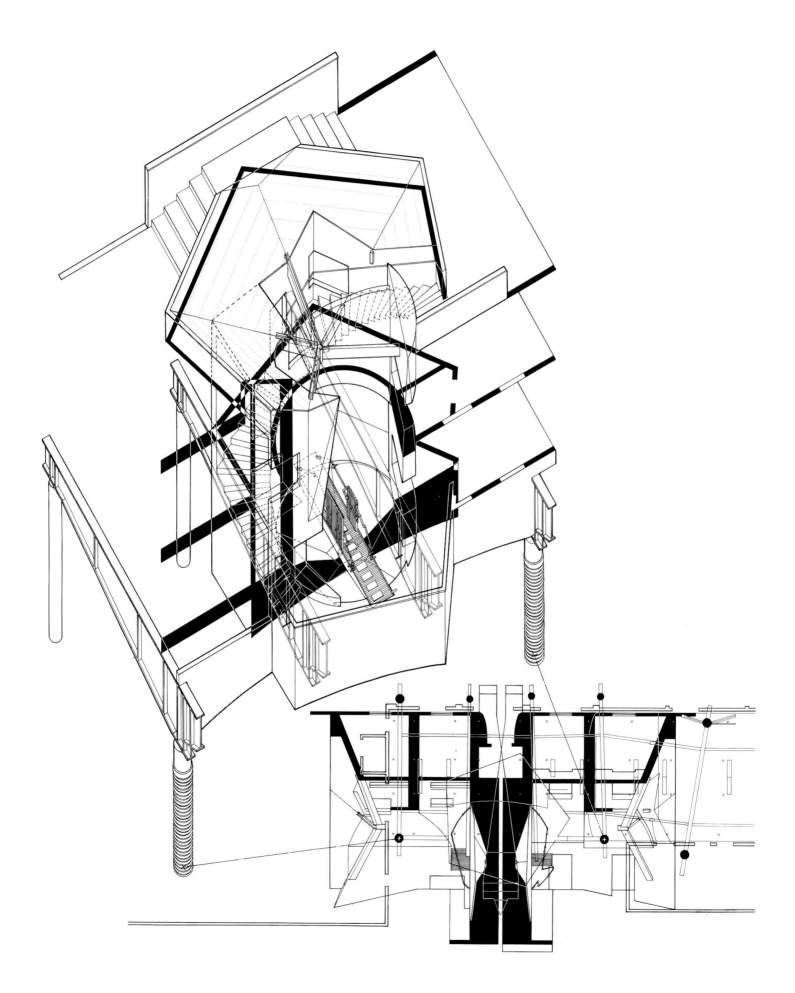

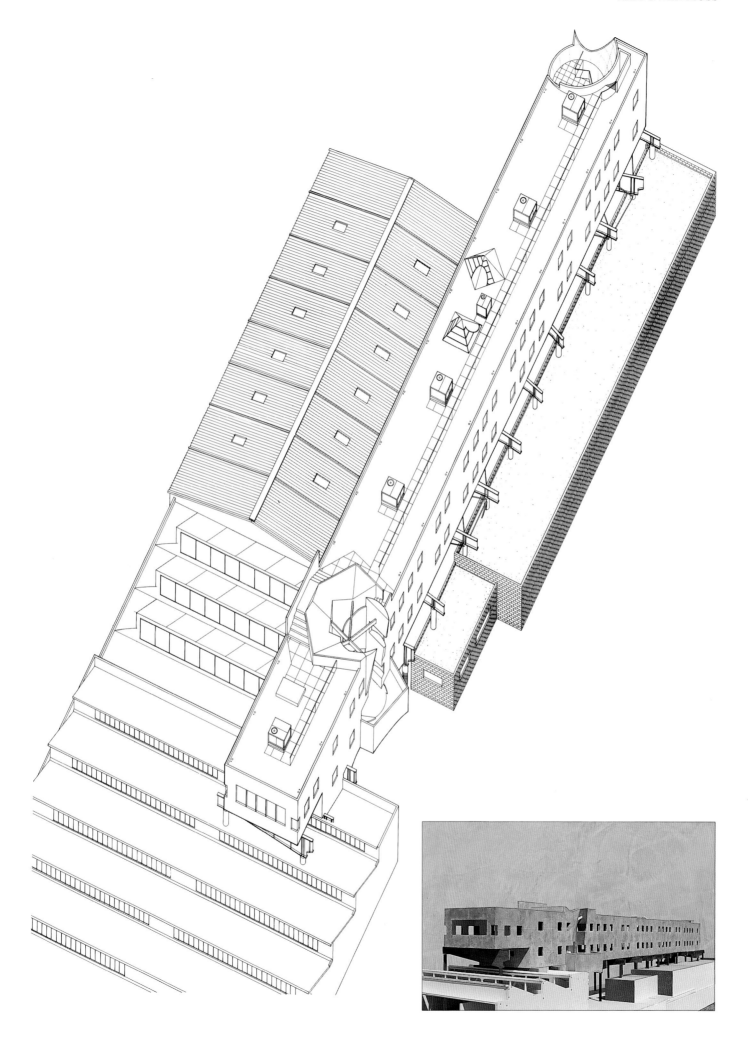

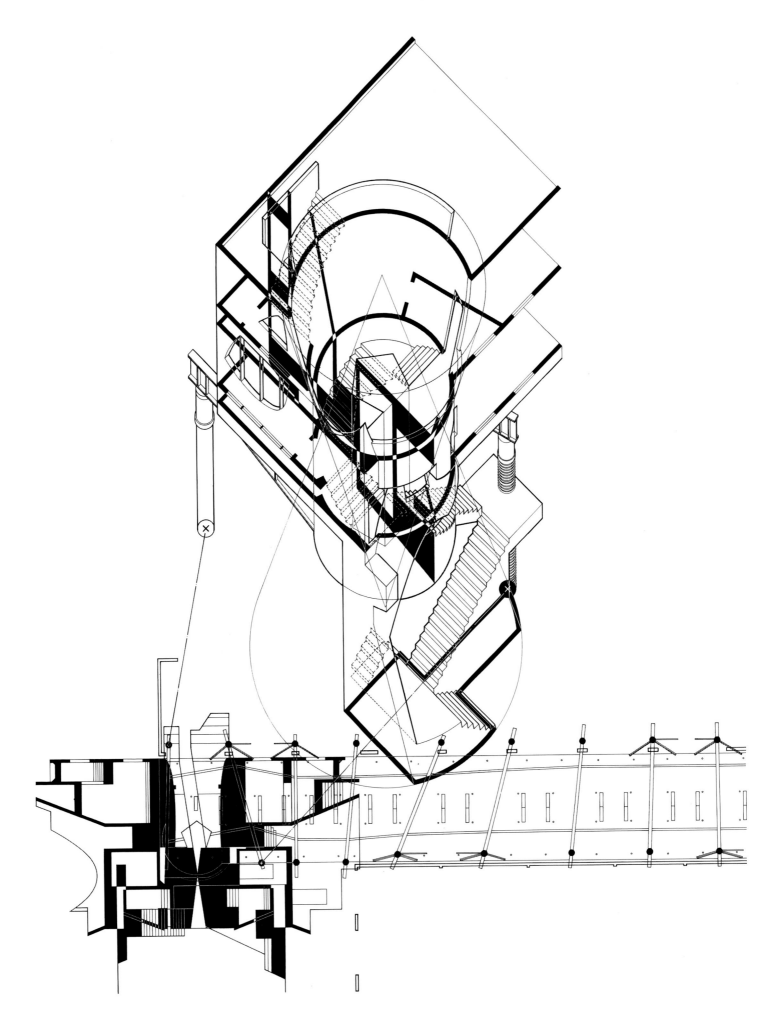

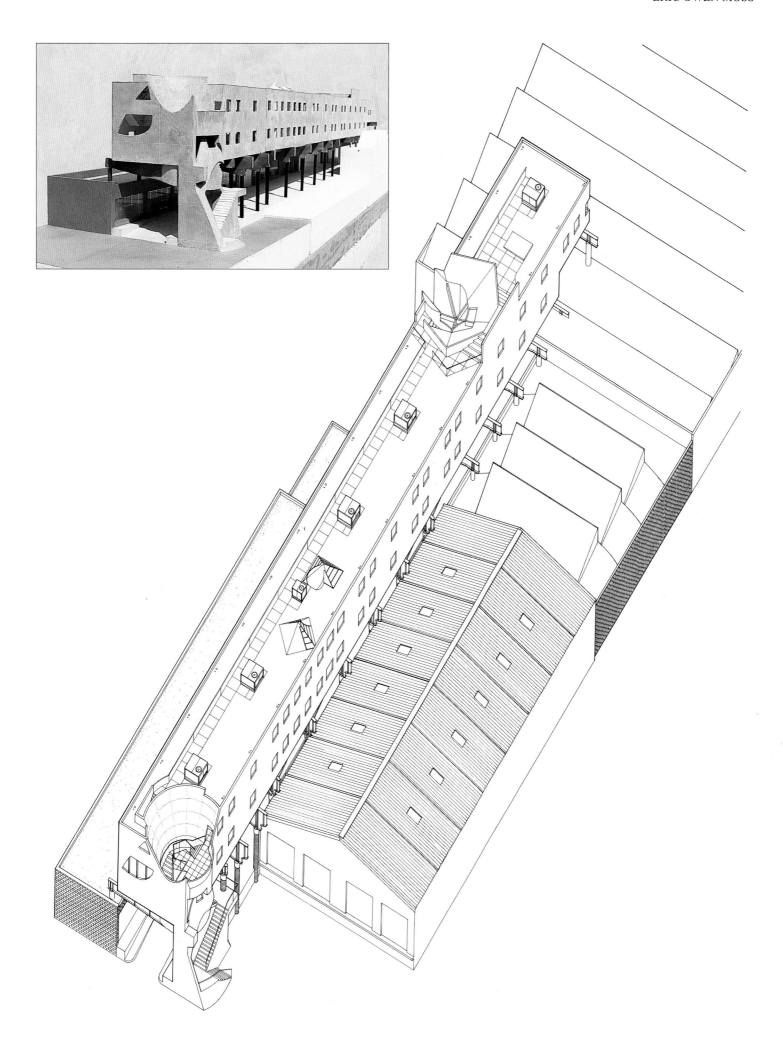

JEAN NOUVEL

THE MEETING LINE, BERLIN

In nearly three decades, the political schism of Germany has produced an entirely unique situation in Berlin. A completely different urban and architectural model has developed creating a dual city with two centres. Now that the Wall is down, hopefully this bipolarity will dissolve. However, it will require a thoughtful approach and a slow path so that radical mistakes are not committed in the name of rapid progress. Political decisions could cause major changes in traffic patterns. Despite these potential changes, we formulated a number of hypothetical situations to lay the framework for our proposition to the Berlin Tomorrow competition. It seems likely that the main political institutions will be located along a loose axis running from Brandenburger Tor to Alexanderplatz. A cultural promenade could be imagined running from the forum to the museum complex situated near the Dom. The Friedrichstrasse is likely to become a major business and commercial axis.

As for the canyon that was once the Wall, we see a major opportunity to create a new core for public animation, day and night. The lobotomy and mummification of space that played such a tragic role in the life of the city now seems irrelevant. Its transformation into a place of renewed life will come to symbolise the hope and optimism of Berliners.

Friedrichstrasse: light it up, colour it, enlarge it, deepen your visions. It would be irrelevant to laboriously fill the voids. It seems more sensible to use (and abuse) the characteristic anomalies and surprises.

The anomalies: empty lots on each side of the street, squares in progress, more remnant than deliberate; large walls, blind and sad; bridges for the S-Station and Checkpoint Charlie. The surprises: perspectives at the end of crossing streets; needles and domes emerging above and between the buildings.

Propositions: to make public the spaces on both sides of the street and to express the ground forcefully by way of dotting, painting, informing, lighting, bordering, lining; to light up every empty wall with narrow 'billboard-buildings' so that Friedrichstrasse will be bathed with light, colours and the logos of the firms which occupy it; to animate the bridges of the Station and Checkpoint Charlie with digitalised light-news and electronic billboards; to create in the perspectives between buildings additional emerging objects, totems, new symbols for public buildings and corporate firms. To suggest a deeper field of vision and consciousness of the metropolis.

The Meeting Line: to mark the end of a situation which was considered fatal, to reinforce the desire that these horrors should never repeat themselves and to eradicate the existence of a no-man's-land under constant surveillance from watch towers, I propose to create along this long scar a 'meeting line'. This will be crossed by a series of streets, long-closed and new. A sinuous space, a sort of golf green, shining with small optimistic lights and coloured like the crossing of a golf course with a computer grid. Along this ribbon, different sequences will take place linked by covered walkways for families, joggers, cyclists, young lovers.

There will be lively spaces devoted to shoppers, meditators, peeping toms – all the good and bad crazies of the metropolis; there will also be a series of spaces equipped with shops, bars, restaurants and night-clubs, flower shops, book shops, candy stores and bike stores – vigorous images of life. There will be housing and office buildings along the way, offering great views. In this way the city will dare to look at itself again and smile in its new mirror and at its new reality.

See opposite, below and pages 206-209

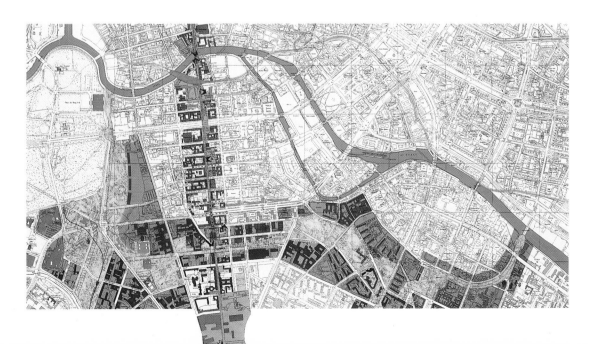

Die Meeting Line

OMA

CHECKPOINT CHARLIE, BERLIN

There has been a dramatic shift in the circumstances surrounding this building (situated opposite the site of the border crossing of the same name) which has now resulted in a change of use. Initially a collaboration between the military and the municipality of Kreuzberg, the ground floor was planned as a service faculty for Allied troops, while the upper levels were given over to apartments of various sizes in response to a shortage of social housing. A distinct podium base, which separated these two functions, was intended to make the division between them clear.

Checkpoint Charlie intentionally echoes the forms of the Wall and viewing towers which were once so close to it. Direct metaphors such as the roof, which is clad in polished metal, and seems to fly over the building like an aeroplane wing, continue this formal theme, making an unmistakable reference to specific events in the history of the city.

Despite all its physical and metaphorical connections with the past, Checkpoint Charlie also contains an equally timely set of signs that allow it to escape purely contextual categorisation. By doing so, it manages to exemplify the irrepressible optimism that now pervades Berlin itself.

See opposite, and pages 212-213

THE BYZANTIUM, AMSTERDAM

The duality of this site is unique. One side is bordered by the most urban area in the Netherlands, the other by a forgotten enclave of rural charm, the Zandpad. Only 80 metres from the metropolis is the continuation of arcadia.

This contrast is the theme of the building; the design attempts to do justice to the two very different environments by using a metropolitan scale to screen the idyll. Thus a very exciting transition between two opposing landscapes is created.

The main mass of the building is a long core of dwellings that runs east to west through the middle of the site, so that neither the park nor the Tesselschadestraat is overwhelmed. This 'vertebral column' is traversed by three cross beams, creating a block of building with one axis and six ramifications. The advantage of this construction is that its total volume is subdivided into a great many different parts, each of which is able to respond to the site's variants through scale, materials, colour and programme. The concentration of the main volume of these structures in the middle zone, and their subsequent elevation, makes the whole block surprisingly transparent from all sides. In this way only a minimal impact is exerted on the environment.

The complete construction rests on two subterranean parking layers. On the surface level, along Stadhouderskade and Tesselschadestraat, the urban facilities form an 'L' shape. Stage-like parking lots for the residences serve to isolate them from the urban area. Apart from the main axis, the three finger-like structures bordering on the park are reserved for dwelling purposes, with the offices to be situated on Tesselschadestraat.

Beneath the backbone of the main axis is a gallery which runs from the asphalt of Stadhouderskade (parallel with the Vondelpark) to the most pastoral area, an adjoining small, sloping park. Double sliding 'windows' make up this gallery, with small premises for the building's residents on the arcade's stage. All the dwellings are accessible from the gallery as are the glass fronts of the offices. The quantity of glazing has resulted in a transparency that is marked even for the Tesselschadestraat.

Following the example of Van Eeghenstraat, the blocks at Vondelpark are situated like villas in front of the residential section. On the corner of Vondelpark and Stadhouderskade a wedge-shaped structure has been erected, rising out of the stage. Most of the public urban facilities have been located here. The structure is divided into discs so that, viewed in perspective from the entertainment centre in Leidseplein, it can be read as a wall with signs.

As one of the most charming features of Vondelpark is its narrow entrance broadening into an elegant vista, it did not seem proper to interfere with the park's original design.

The corner of the site is occupied by a restaurant; when the weather is fine the south facade can be opened up, forming a terrace along the Zandpad and creating a mobile platform in front of the first floor. It will be a satellite going across the Zandpad, making a direct connection with the park possible, while the buildings at Stadhouderskade can be regarded as a tailpiece of the west wall functioning as a backcloth for Leidseplein. The corner of Tesselschadestraat provides a pivotal point for the urban facilities. It is marked by a low tower, making the building part of a typically Amsterdam tradition of low skyscrapers which compensate for their lack of real height with a wealth of turreted motifs as can be seen at Amerikan, the Hirsh building, Hotel Centraal and the Telegraaf.

The office strip in Tesselschadestraat consists of ground-floor showrooms with entresols which can be easily reached from the gallery. Over these are positioned a complete layer of offices, which are articulated through separate buildings with separate addresses which can also act as independent units.

Overall the intention is that this building should prevent the usual draining experience of city life.

See pages 214-215

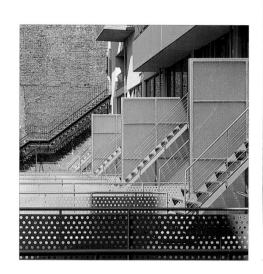

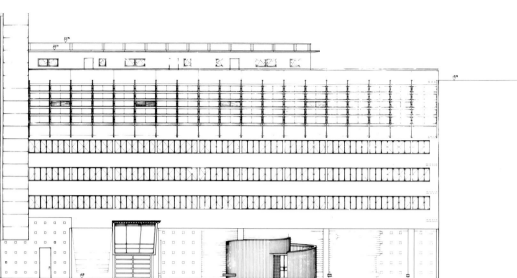

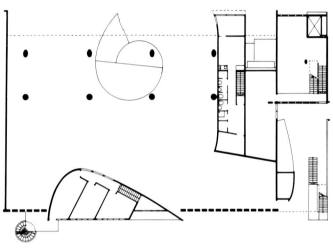

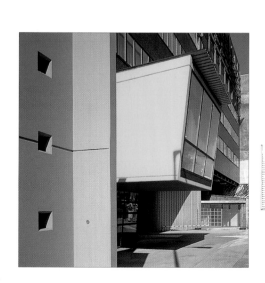

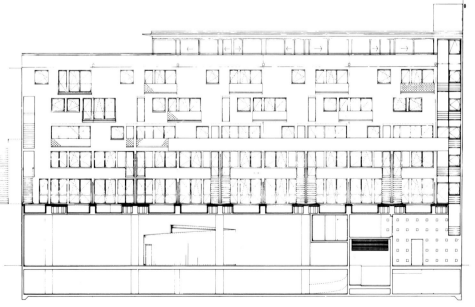

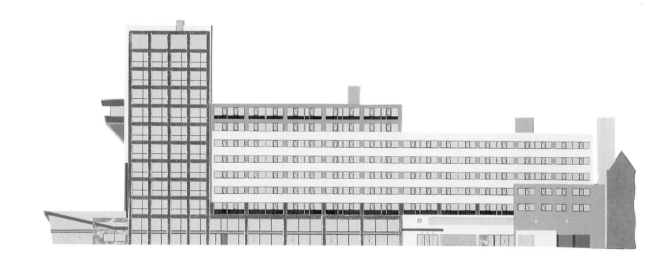

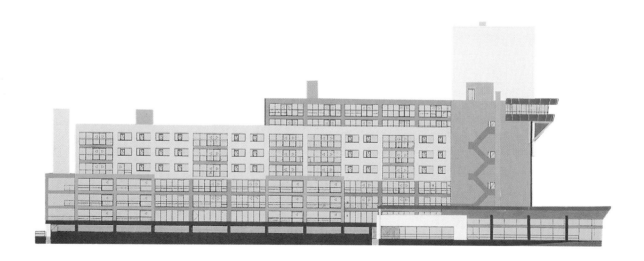

PHILIPPE STARCK

'LA FLAMME' ASAHI BUILDING, TOKYO

A black polished granite urn placed upon a luminous glass staircase is topped by a 'flame', covered in matt gold. The aim of this building when completed, not far from the Asakusa temple, will be to gather together young creative Japanese, giving them the means for research as well as practical skills. It is drawn in an essentially symbolic spirit. Here, the luminous base plays with energy and the urn with mystery, while the flame states this is a place of passion. This building is the first important pawn in the war staged between large Japanese firms through architecture.

See opposite

TEATRIZ RESTAURANT, MADRID

Situated right at the centre of Madrid, the Teatriz, which at the beginning of the century was a theatre, was blessed with a number of beautiful volumes. Therefore, the conversion called for delicate manipulation on the part of the architect. There were no, or next to no, references left to the auditorium. The stage, however, was respected: 'The theatre here retains some beautiful traces from the past.' As Starck comments: 'This is the first time that I have managed to balance the parameters of fantasy, rigour, and sympathy as well. The strong and novel idea for me was that one could give emotion whilst remaining friendly, make up a fantasy whilst remaining rigorous, and create ambiguous places whilst remaining elegant. It is a juxtaposition of semantic touches. Whether this is beautiful or not does not concern me.'

See pages 218-219

SALON COPPOLA, MILAN

The spirit behind Starck's projects has always been integral to his work; as he says himself: 'It is always more a question of spirit than anything else behind my built work. Three years ago L'Oréal asked me to design a collection of furniture for their hair salons with a view to distributing the work, for L'Oréal, Maletti in Italy and Takara Belmont in Japan, which together form the largest and best salons in the world. They would group together to manufacture and distribute my furniture: The Starck Collection.

'They also decided to set up a salon in every city in the world in order to show an example of the use of furniture and styling. L'Oréal wanted me to make types of decoration, murals and things – which I knew wouldn't work, as I thought it would be far better to show a few examples which people might then apply to their own interior decoration, taking an element from here, and another from there, gradually building up something themselves. It therefore became an exercise in re-evaluating hair salons.

'The way in which I entered the project was, as always, from a critical point of view. I studied hair salons a little and their furnishing, and noticed that they were deteriorating, in the sense that a hair salon is a place where people go to become more beautiful, to blossom out, and you find yourself in a harsh, constraining contraption. It is supposed to be a place of pleasure, of flourishing, but instead it is somewhere where women feel panicky about what is going to happen to them.

'At the beginning of the project I thought that the title was significant – notice that it is hair "salon", not "factory"; so from this came the idea of redesigning all the furniture as that which could exist in a salon or living room, as opposed to the average room of hair-washing sinks aligned as if they were in a factory. The object was a collection which would abandon the machine; rather, it would veer towards the human, making it a place where people go to make themselves look and feel beautiful. I don't believe you can do this if you are feeling scared. Coppola expresses the idea of feminine beautification with dignity, without any affectation; it is dignified femininity.'

See pages 220-221

PARAMOUNT HOTEL, NEW YORK

Paramount is on the same Broadway block as several major theatres, including the Imperial. Originally built in 1927 to a design by Thomas Lamb, who also worked on the Ziegfeld Theater and the original Madison Square Garden, redesigned and reopened under new management in August 1990, the hotel is now according to its proprietors 'the embodiment of hotel as theatre, with a constantly changing cast of characters in its guests and visitors'. To achieve a suitably grand and dramatic atmosphere for this undertaking, the interior design was entrusted to Philippe Starck.

His inimitable style is seen throughout the 610 guest rooms, whose furnishings, he says, are more than inanimate objects. At once restful and humorous, the rooms are intended to distract as well as comfort overnight visitors; in the single rooms, guests are greeted by an oversized version of Vermeer's masterpiece *The Lacemaker*, hanging over a pristine white bed. According to Starck, the maternal figure concentrating on her needlework creates an aura of soothing security throughout the night.

Elsewhere in the hotel are to be found a marble entrance foyer, an original, Joan Miró-inspired ceiling of lights, a gold-leafed, gravity-defying staircase and furnishings by (amongst others) Marco Zanuso, Franco Albini, Jean Michele Frank, Antonio Gaudí and Jasper Morrison.

See pages 222-223

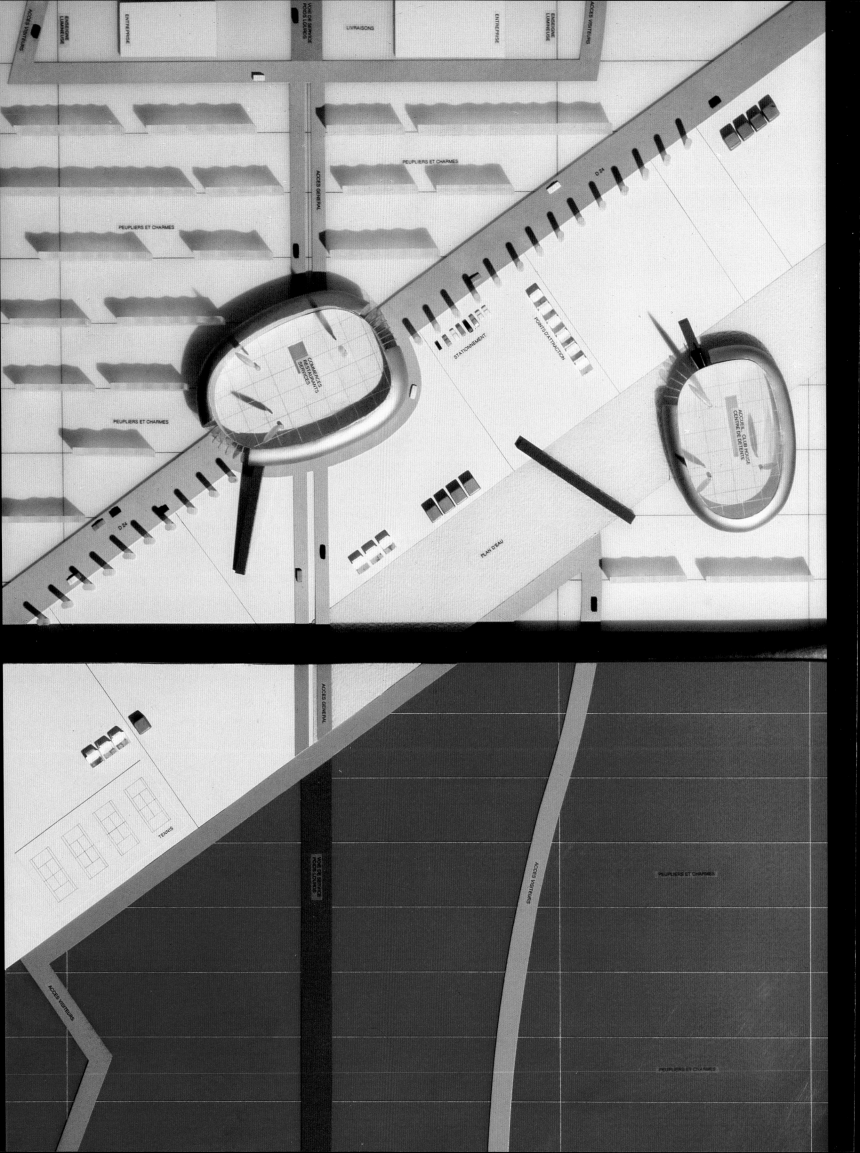

BERNARD TSCHUMI
THE ARCHITECTURE OF THE EVENT

Architecture has always been as much about the *event* that takes place in a space as about the space itself. The hall where I give a lecture might have been used for a banquet the night before; next year it could be a swimming pool. I am not being facetious: in today's world where railway stations become museums and churches become nightclubs, we must come to terms with the complete interchangeability of form and function, the loss of traditional or canonical cause-and-effect relationships sanctified by modernism. Function does not follow form, form does not follow function, or fiction for that matter. However, form and function certainly interact, if only to produce a shock effect.

If 'shock' cannot be produced by the succession and juxtaposition of facades and lobbies any more, maybe it can be produced by the juxtaposition of events that take place behind these facades in these spaces.

If 'the respective contamination of all categories, the constant substitutions, the confusion of genres' as described by critics of the right and left alike (from Andreas Huyssen to Jean Baudrillard) is the new direction of our times, it may well be used to one's advantage, to the advantage of a general rejuvenation of architecture. If architecture is both concept and experience, space and use, structure and superficial image (non-hierarchically), then architecture should cease to separate these categories and should merge them into unprecedented combinations of programmes and spaces. 'Crossprogramming', 'transprogramming', 'disprogramming': these concepts stand for the displacement and mutual contamination of terms.

My own work in the 70s constantly reiterated the thesis that there was no architecture without event, without action, without activities, without functions; architecture was to be seen as the combination of spaces, events and movements, without any hierarchy or precedence among these concepts. Needless to say, the hierarchical cause-and-effect relationship between function and form is one of the great certainties of architectural thinking – it lies behind that reassuring *idée reçue* of community life that tells us that we live in houses 'designed to answer our needs' or in cities planned as 'machines to live in'. And the cosy connotations of this *Geborgenheit* notion go against both the real 'pleasure' of architecture in its unexpected combinations of terms, and the reality of contemporary urban life in its most stimulative, as well as unsettling, facets. Hence, in works like *The Manhattan Transcripts*, the definition of architecture could not be form, or walls, but had to be the combination of heterogeneous and incompatible terms.

The incorporation of the terms 'event' and 'movement' was no doubt influenced by Situationist discourse and by the 68 era.

Les événements, as they were called, were 'events' not only in action, but also in thought. Erecting a barricade (function) in a Paris street (form) is not quite equivalent to being a *flâneur* (function) in that same street (form). Dining (function) in a university hall (form) is not quite equivalent to reading or swimming in it. Here, all hierarchical relationships between form and function cease to exist.

This unlikely combination of events and spaces was charged with subversive capabilities, for it challenged both the function and space: such confrontation parallels the Surrealists' meeting of the bicycle and umbrella on the dissecting table.

We find it today in Tokyo, with its multiple programmes scattered throughout the floors of high-rise buildings: department store, museum, health club, railway station, putting-greens on the roof. And we will find it in the programmes of the future, where airports are also simultaneously amusement arcades, athletic facilities, cinemas and so on. Regardless of whether they are the result of chance combinations or of the pressures of ever-rising land prices, such non-causal relationships between form and function, or space and action, go beyond poetic confrontations of unlikely bedfellows.

Foucault, as recalled in an excellent book by John Rajchman, expanded the use of the term 'event' in a manner that went beyond the single action or activity. He spoke of 'events of thought'. I would suggest that the future of architecture today lies in the construction of such events.

For Foucault, an event is not simply a logical sequence of words or actions, but rather 'the moment of erosion, collapse, questioning or problematisation of the very assumptions of the setting within which a drama may take place – occasioning the chase or possibility of another, different setting' (Rajchman). The event is seen here as a *turning-point*, not an origin or an end (as opposed to propositions such as 'form follows function').

Just as important is the spatialisation that goes with the event. To quote: 'There are events in the space we construct ourselves to inhabit: heterotopia.' Such a concept is entirely different from the ethos of the Modern Movement, which sought to affirm certainties in a unified utopia, as opposed to our current occupation with multiple, fragmented, dislocated terrains.

After Foucault, Derrida expanded on the definition of 'event', calling it 'the emergence of a disparate multiplicity' in a text about the *folies* of the Parc de la Villette. I had constantly insisted, in our discussions and elsewhere, that these points called *folies* were points of activities, of programmes, of events. Derrida elaborated this concept, proposing the possibility of an 'architecture of the event' that would 'eventualise', or open up, what in our history or tradition is understood to be fixed, essential, monumental. Derrida had also suggested earlier that the word 'event' shared roots with 'invention'. I would like to associate it with the notion of 'shock' – a shock that in order to be effective in our mediated culture, in our culture of *images*, must go beyond the definition of Walter Benjamin and *combine the idea of function or action with that of image*. Indeed, architecture finds itself in a unique situation: it is the only discipline that by definition combines concept and experience, image and use, image and structure. Philosophers can write, mathematicians can develop virtual spaces, but architects are the only ones who are the prisoners of that hybrid art where the image hardly ever exists without a combined activity.

It is my contention that far from being a field suffering from the incapability of questioning its structures and foundations, architecture is the field where the greatest discoveries will take place in the next century. The very heterogeneity of the definition of architecture – space, action and movement – makes it that *event*, that place of shock, or that place of the invention of ourselves. The event is the place where the rethinking and reformulation of the different elements of architecture (many of which have resulted in, or added to, contemporary social iniquities) may lead to their solution. By definition, it is the place of the combination of the difference.

Of course, it is not by imitating the past and 18th-century ornaments that this will happen. It is also not going to happen by simply commenting through design on the various dislocations and uncertainties of our contemporary condition. I do not believe it is possible, nor that it makes *sense,* to design buildings that *formally* attempt to blur traditional structures, ie which display forms that lie somewhere between abstraction and figuration, or somewhere between structure and ornament, or that are cut-up, dislocated for aesthetic reasons. Architecture is not an illustrative art; it does not illustrate theories (I do not believe you can design deconstruction). You cannot design a new definition of the city and its architecture. But you may be able to design the conditions that will make it possible for this non-hierarchical, non-traditional society to happen. By understanding the nature of our contemporary circumstances and the media processes that go with it, architects are in a position to construct conditions that will create a new city and new relationships between spaces and events.

Architecture is not about the conditions of design, but about the design of conditions. Or, to paraphrase Paul Virilio, our object today is not to fulfil the conditions of construction, but to achieve the construction of conditions that will dislocate the most traditional and regressive aspects of our society and simultaneously reorganise these elements in the most liberating way, where our experience becomes the experience of events organised and *strategised* through architecture. *Strategy* is a key word today in architecture. No more masterplans, no more locating in a fixed place, but a new heterotopia; that is what our cities are striving towards, and here we architects must help them by intensifying the rich collision of events and spaces.

Tokyo and New York only *appear* chaotic; in reality they mark the appearance of a new urban structure, a new urbanity. Their confrontations and combinations of elements may provide us with the event, the *shock*, that I hope will make the architecture of our cities a *turning-point* in culture and society.

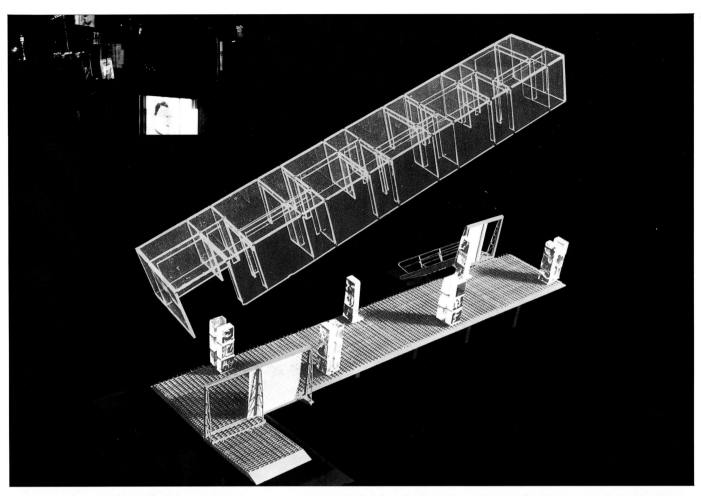

BERNARD TSCHUMI

CHARTRES MASTERPLAN

This international competition by invitation was for a major office development with leisure facilities and housing on the outskirts of the town of Chartres.

The brief was devised in the following four sections: a) a new masterplan for the economic and spatial extension of Chartres to the east (towards Paris), the site being 450 acres; b) an office development for large firms and corporations (300,000 square metres) with 150 housing units; c) leisure facilities, to include indoor sports facilities, meeting halls and restaurants (20,000 square metres) and, finally, d) a 250-acre park with sports grounds and a golf course.

See page 224

GLASS VIDEO GALLERY, GRONINGEN

The invitation extended by the city of Groningen to design a special environment for viewing pop music video clips was an opportunity to challenge preconceived ideas about television viewing and about privacy. We proposed the Glass Video Gallery: a 3.6 x 2.6 metre, tilted, inclining, transparent glass structure, containing a series of inter-locking spaces defined only by a labyrinth of structural glass 'fins' and by the points of metal clip connections. Isolated in this labyrinth are six banks of video monitors for displaying video clips. The gallery and urban space also have the distinct duality of containing both video objects on display and objects for displaying. They encompass monitor walls viewed through TV dealership storefronts on the street, and also exhibit events like those in plastic sex-clip galleries of urban red-light districts. In this new video plaza, one watches and is watched simultaneously.

See opposite

ZKM, KARLSRUHE

Architecture and urbanism are now undergoing profound changes that are closely intertwined with the broader questions of society, its art and technology. Karlsruhe and its new Centre for Art and Media Technology, ZKM, are characteristic of that condition. Our proposal for Centre ZKM reflects this through the project's four components.
1. The urban line of exchange: we suggest a new linear public passage of intense interchange and communication, alternative to the Baroque Karlsruhe. This line will provide a new urban system at the historical edge of the city by turning the old limit into a new line of exchange.
2. The linear core: at the centre of the building, we propose a linear public space of maximum visibility and excitement. This core and its balconies give access to all parts of the ZKM. Its ground floor serves most performances,

exhibitions and seminar spaces. Giant video screens, suspended passerelles and stairs, a tensile glass elevator and two rooms floating in mid-air activate an extensive and colourful foyer for the general public.
3. The two compartments: on each side of the linear core are two simple compartments, each with specialised spaces. The one on the north side contains most of the larger spaces, the media theatre, the Museum of Contemporary Art and the large studio (ellipsoid). The south-side compartment has most of the smaller spaces, laboratories, offices and artists' studios, and the media gallery. On both sides, more public spaces are on the lower floors and more specialised spaces on the upper.
4. The casing: the tight functional structure is enclosed on the south side by an everchanging, photo-electronic, computer-animated, double-glazed skin that can react to external light and sound variations. The skin is seen to emerge from a solid, protective, perforated, stainless steel enclosure (north side), with a copper-clad ellipsoid (containing the multi-purpose studio).

See pages 230-231

KYOTO STATION

The competition for the railway station in Kyoto was characteristic of new hybrid mega-projects in the 1990s: a single complex containing a convention centre, a 600-room hotel, a ten-storey department store, a 2,000-car parking area, a cultural centre and cultural plaza – all on top of a major railway station. Special functions included image theatres, sky restaurants, health clubs, wedding rooms, amusement arcades, a gourmet town and even an Emperor's waiting room. With over 250,000 square metres (1,000 percent larger than the site area) and over a billion dollars estimated construction cost, such a huge facility with complex functions has no precedent.

We began by decomposing the programme into its main constituent elements and aligning them with the Kyoto block grid. These strips intentionally reinforced Kyoto's current building height so that the new building – despite its mass – would not act as a barrier but as a transition between the older and newer parts of the city. At the same time, we extracted from the programme those required functions we felt to be particularly pointed – those utilitarian aspects which, when combined with one another, could aspire to the symbolic. Besides extreme programmatic intensity, the skyframe, with its long cantilevered space and slender glass towers ('seven gates'), was to give Kyoto a new heterogeneous sign, to be superimposed on the temple landscape without obliterating it.

See pages 232-237

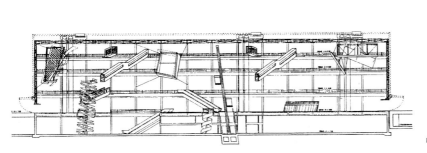

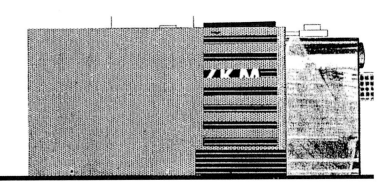

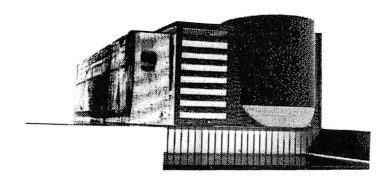

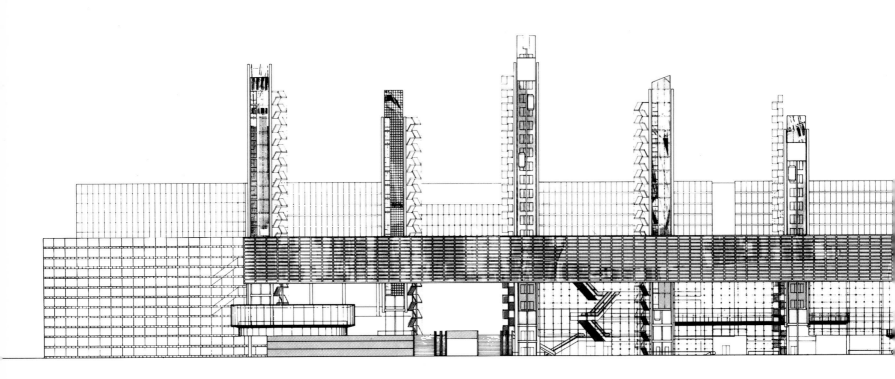

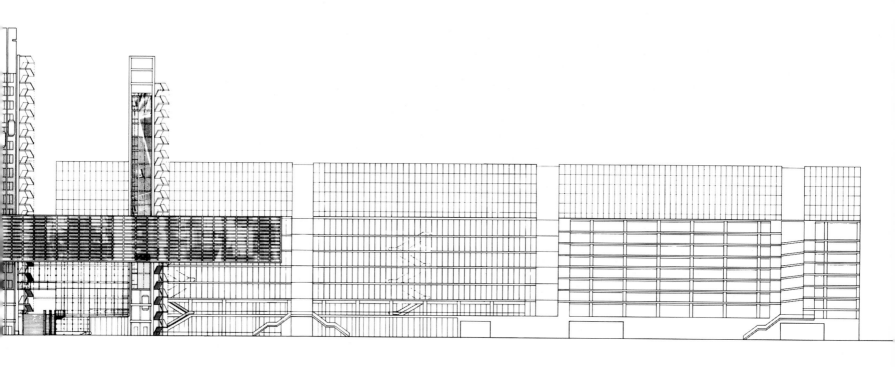

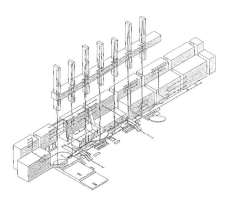

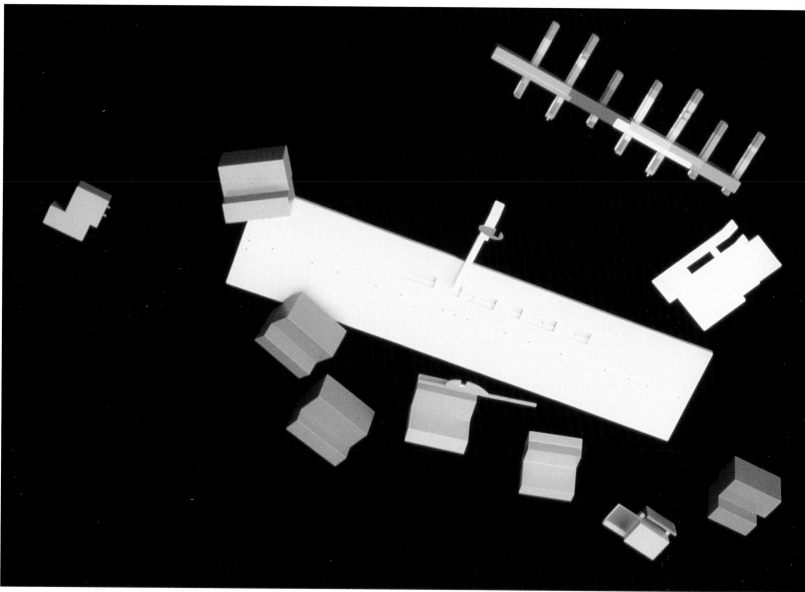

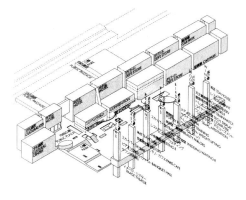

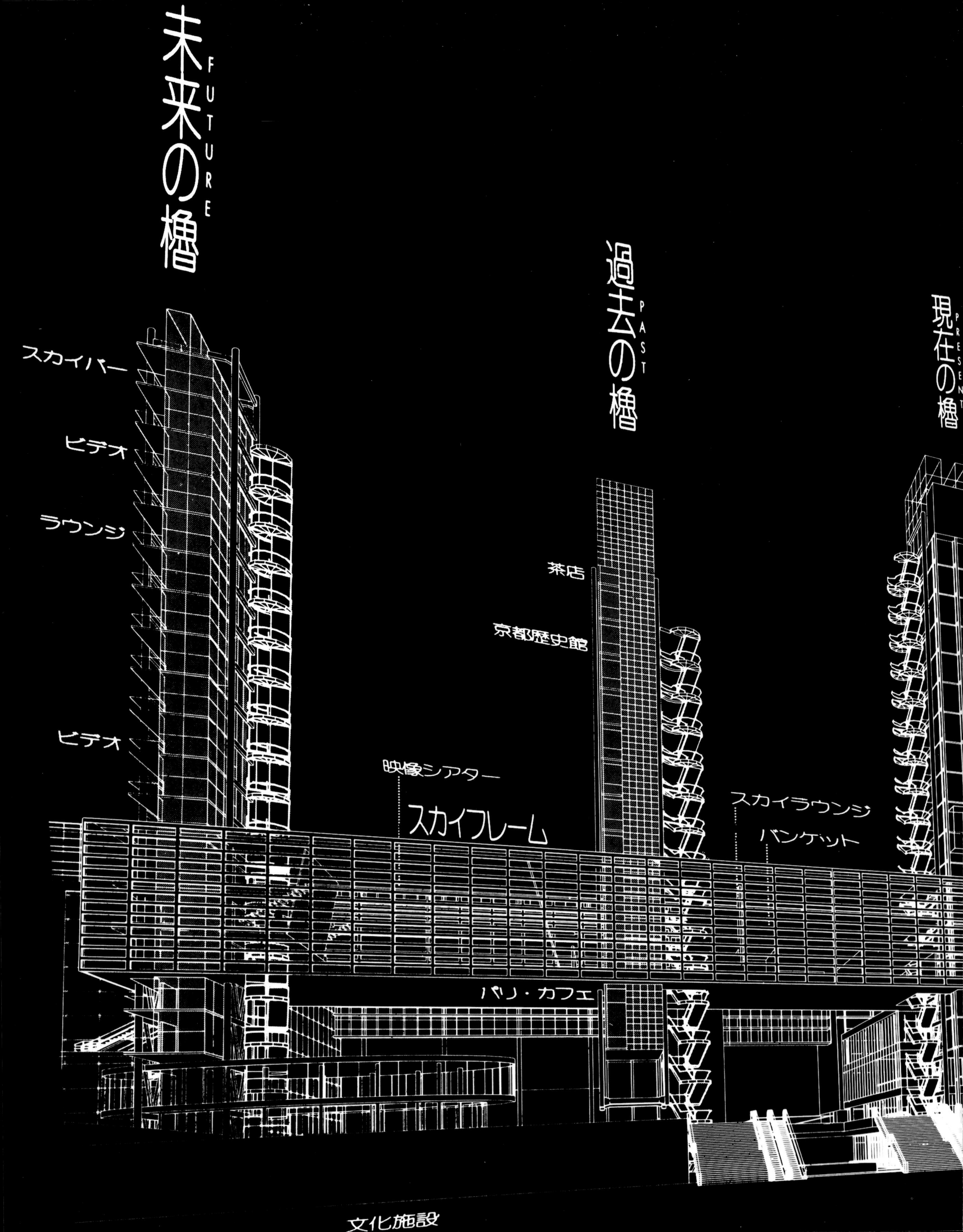

未来の櫓 FUTURE

過去の櫓 PAST

現在の櫓 PRESENT

スカイバー

ビデオ

ラウンジ

ビデオ

茶店

京都歴史館

映像シアター

スカイフレーム

スカイラウンジ

バンケット

パリ・カフェ

文化施設

スカイバー

レストラン

小会議室

スカイレストラン

ブライダル

ホテル

花の櫓 FLOWERS

鳥の櫓 BIRDS

月の櫓 MOON

風の櫓 WIND

読書室

着付室

美容室

ウエディング
控室

メディテーション

サウナ

トレーニング

アスレテック

天文観察室
貴賓待合室

トレイン
ウォッチング

ハイテク
展示室

コンピュータ

書店

レストラン

待避プルメ街

アミューズメント

駅

デパート

PETER WILSON

BLACKBURN HOUSE, LONDON

The brief for this house consisted of transforming a run-down range of prosaic mews buildings into two spaces for housing a substantial collection of contemporary art and furniture – a gallery flat on the first and second floors above the client's office on the ground floor. The clients, David and Janice Blackburn, both have a strong involvement in the contemporary art world – Janice Blackburn at the Saatchi Collection and David Blackburn with the commissioning of art within the Broadgate office complex in the City of London. The architect states:

'To cancel the original inconclusive volume a new white box was created (walls raised and windows closed). Each element added to this white frame tells its own story. The large window breaks out, the view is not good so the glass is opaque, blinded. Only fragmented views are available through small, clear areas of glass. A negative drawing on a window surface. The window shares the facade with the second practical opportunity, the Totem, a stainless steel and welded plastic column that carries clean water into the house and dirty water away. A guardian of entrance.

'Much of the architecture is on the level of interior detail. Door handles, supporting column and cantilevered balcony all in the same structural steel. A vitrine, a handrail in the middle of the upper gallery. Each piece has an autonomous narrative as well as a family resemblance to its neighbours through the use of a limited range of materials: tough steel, refined wood, one colour and the white of the box that contains them.

'The visitor only finally understands the house when he arrives at the top floor. This large, single space with a double-height void inside the big window is the gallery/living room. Light comes from above or near the floor, no views out are available but the space hovers. The back wall is entirely blank – for pictures. In the middle between dining and living space floats the Barge Seat. Sitting here, the visitor finally reaches the centre of the house – hovering like the house hovers, not quite part of London.'

Clients David and Janice Blackburn explain: 'Our primary objective was always to create what we wanted to be an exciting contemporary setting for our contemporary things. So Peter understood the prospective relationship between his architecture and our collection from the outset. As the project developed we came to see the architecture as very much part and parcel of what we were collecting. In designing Peter had the advantage that we weren't planning to live in the gallery flat. We were certainly not building something that could not be lived in but we were able occasionally to go ahead with an idea that seemed to take us right up to the limit of practicability.

'We think Peter liked the challenge. Even though we are both quite strong and have very definite ideas, everything was discussable and the plans for the furniture and art always added an additional dimension to the architectural issues. No idea was ever just rejected either by Peter or us. Eventually we agreed on almost everything. So it was a very good relationship. Most people don't have this kind of relationship with their architects – especially not after the job is finished. If Peter were living in England and we were to do another house we would certainly use him again.

'We decided at a very early stage, after a few discussions with Peter weighing up pros and cons, that we wanted to create a double-height space. The attraction was that we could have the opportunity of a very large feature window and create a dramatic sculptural volume which would impact on all the surrounding spaces. However, there was very little floor space in the whole building and we were taking some of it away. We decided to sacrifice the floor space and get the benefit of the double-height. That was a very early 'joint' decision between ourselves and Peter. The concept of creating the double-height space in the form of a volume skewed out from the basic box of the building was totally Peter's and was the first introduction to the design of the 15-degree angle which seems to be something of a 'signature' for him.

'The study on the first floor was a case of making a virtue out of necessity. The constraints of the site and the basic form of the building envelope left us with what seemed a hopelessly narrow room. Peter's response was to make the room even narrower! He resorted again to the 15-degree angle theme and simply created two wedge-shaped volumes which he removed from the room to form cupboards along approximately half the length of the long sides. The result was a dramatic bottle-shaped space which he further accentuated by placing a floor to ceiling slot window at the narrow end.

'As far as our furniture and art works are concerned, in design or aesthetic terms we certainly don't see everything as frozen. Very few of the pieces that weren't 'built-in' by Peter are totally site specific, but almost every one was commissioned or acquired with a particular location in mind and to interact in terms of form, material and colour with others. We've always seen the grouping and bringing together of the pieces as an added bonus. The prospect of rearrangement and substitution is very exciting. We're sure that as time passes it will open up a whole new range of aspects and implications of the architecture.'

See opposite and pages 240-241

LEBBEUS WOODS

HETERARCHY OF URBAN FORM AND ARCHITECTURE

For the past three years I have studied a new type of urban pattern and form – the heterarchy – and the architectural elements that are its tissue and content. My purpose has been to envision an urban way of living that frees individuals within a community from restricting conventions of thought and action, in order to answer, more fully than is presently possible, the question, 'What is human?' This is an answer individuals must devise for themselves, because individuals, not communities or societies, are the highest and most complete embodiment of the human. So long as the individual is conditioned or controlled by conventions invented as the ethical and physical structure of society, he or she will only be able to give a partial or distorted answer in terms of the social apparatus itself and not from a deeper level of personal experience. As to why this answer is important at all, it can only be said here that based upon it (distorted or not) the entire shape and substance of human communal and private life is, and always has been, determined.

The projects of these past three years are *Underground Berlin* (1988), *Terra Nova* (1988), *Aerial Paris* (1989), *Berlin-Free-Zone* and *Zagreb-Free-Zone* (1991). The ideas and factors influencing the development of these projects can be briefly summarised as follows.

The electronic revolution is breaking down the traditional boundaries between global, national, regional and even local social groups, by the indiscriminate proliferation and dissemination of information. As a result, new social groupings and new types of social groupings are now forming. These tend to be loosely-knit, continually shifting networks (heterarchies), governed by the present and changing needs of their constituents, rather than by rigid attitudes determined by traditions and enforced by fixed structures of authority (hierarchies).

Political liberalisation is growing in advanced technological societies, resulting (in its most advanced stages) in the relative autonomy of individuals within their social groups, requiring of these individuals ethical self-sufficiency and highly developed living and working skills in an ever more competitive and present-oriented economic, political and social milieu.

The revolution in science in this century has not only greatly expanded what is known, but has also fundamentally changed ideas of knowledge itself. The most profound change has been in the introduction of *self-referentiality* into philosophy (epistemology), physics (quantum theory), and related fields such as neurophysiology and cognition studies, as well as into cybernetics, a developing transdisciplinary field considering the relationships between mental processes and machines.

Precedents for heterarchies in architectural history are limited to certain aspects of Medieval town configurations and other vernacular town forms and architecture. However, these examples are products of hierarchical societies that lacked modern technologies. A modern example exists in the ultra-Cartesian concept of 'universal space' (Mies van der Rohe). Any other, less neutralising concept of heterarchy, as applied to the design of architecture and urban form, remains to be invented. Useful in this task will be reference to models of social grouping of autonomous, highly skilled individuals, which are formed, and sustained, by free choice and co-operation, such as utopian communities.

A number of my former projects have contributed conceptually to the present one [*Zagreb-Free-Zone*] with regard to the idea of heterarchy. *Environmental Theater* (1972-74) proposes a cacophonous city of disparate parts, unified (if at all) only by fleeting individual experiences. *The Cybernetic Circus* (1973) similarly deals with circular systems of meaning within apparently disorderly, urban landscapes; the idea of circus referred both to these systems and their genesis, and to a model for autonomous individuals joining together from free choices under conditions of transient equality. *Architecture-Sculpture-Painting* (1978-79) extends the ideas of *Environmental Theater* in terms of a juxtaposition of the three traditional plastic arts. *Four Cities* (1981) derives a diversity of urban form and space from cycles in nature and primordial states of matter and energy. *A City, Sector 1576N* (1985-86) developed complex urban form and architecture from a network of interconnected, yet independent, centres. *Centricity* (1987) is a city (network of cities) of interconnected, autonomous centres, disturbed by non-Euclidian, indeterminate forces, spaces and forms, the composite becoming ambiguous and complex. *Underground Berlin* (1988), proposes a community of free individuals beneath the divided city, creating an urban network based on fleeting personal experience of subtle physical forces active in the earth's planetary mass. *Terra Nova* (1988) develops the idea of a 'new nature – a second nature', in the form of a new layer of earth, reconstituted and re-formed by its inhabitants, in the Korean DMZs. *Aerial Paris* (1989) extends the *Underground Berlin* project and its concepts, by assembling the fragments of its existential culture into kinetic structures in the sky over Paris, becoming a community of aerial performers, an aerial circus, a heterarchy of gypsy experimenters in experience. The *Berlin-* and *Zagreb-Free-Zone* projects take this former project to the surface of two cities, now undergoing profound changes, and represent my first attempt in 18 years to place my ideas and work directly into contemporary urban conditions.

Architectural dynamics, in the context of the preceding ideas and conditions, refers to fluidity and indeterminacy in programmes for architectural design and building, as well as for habitation. Architecture and the urban field are animated in a conceptual or physical sense, achieving dynamic (rather than traditionally static) equilibrium.

Speaking for myself, the answer to 'What is human?' is a quality of becoming that is highly paradoxical, if stated in terms of any existing mode of expression. This is because the human transcends limits, schemes, boundaries of every kind. Even this statement is a kind of boundary that, at the least, must be contradicted: the human can exist only within precise limits formed, and reformed, by the uniquely human critical intelligence. It is, in my opinion, only in the field of sensate, sensual experience – the field embraced by the idea of architecture and city – that these, and other self-contradictory attempts to understand and state the human, can find their common, exalted basis. I have written of a new, still dreamt-of poetic science – a universcience – that will establish in the fleeting moment of the present, the architecture of a landscape suffused with the cool light of self-conscious intelligence and the radiance of transcendent love. It is this ideal alone that lures me on.

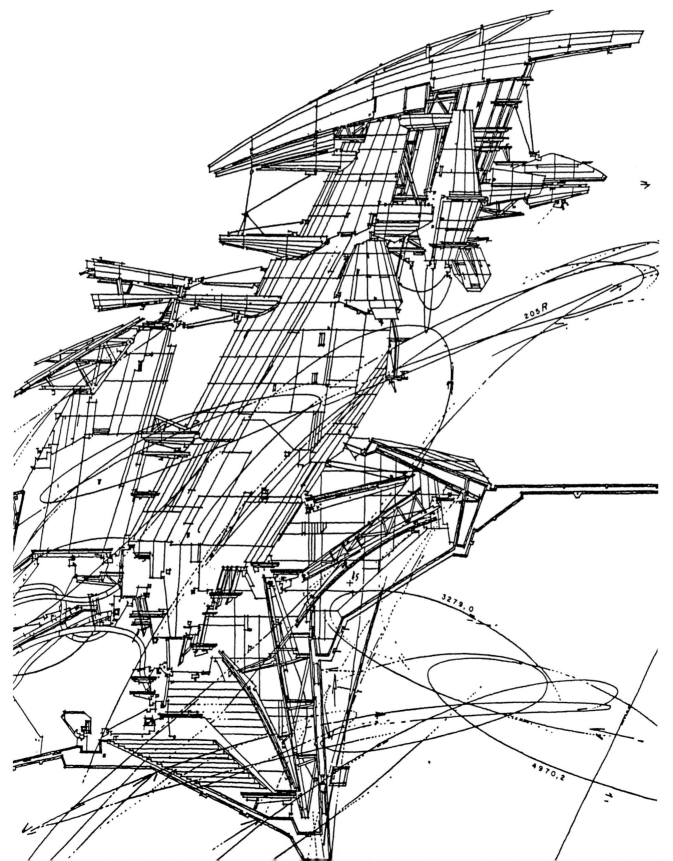

LEBBEUS WOODS

UNDERGROUND BERLIN

Underground Berlin refers to a subterranean community along the lines of the U-Bahn beneath the centre of Berlin. The original impetus for this project was the Wall – physical and ideological – dividing East and West Berlin. Since the project's inception the reunification of Berlin and Germany has been accomplished, by quite different means, but what remains of interest politically in this project is its subversion of an existing authoritarian system of social control by strictly architectural means.

Subversion by constructive means implies an affirmation of the (albeit undefined) order replacing the one subverted. The construction of a new city within and in opposition to an existing one amounts to a profound act of renunciation and even violence, more lasting in its effects than those achieved by the gun. One need only compare the changes made to cities by modern war and by modern architecture to confirm this. The process of changing from one type of order to another is always violent. Over time, architecture can be the most potent weapon of change.

The architectural means of subversion proposed begin with the occupation of territory in the city previously neglected, abandoned or ignored by existing institutions of authority, public and private. In this project, this is the space in the earth beneath Berlin. The construction there of spaces for communal and private life undermines the authoritarian structure above, at the same time affirming an entirely new set of living conditions, resulting from the physical climate of forces – geomechanical and geomagnetic – active within the planetary mass of the earth.

From these new conditions comes this project's non-hierarchical urban form, a linear network of autonomous living and working structures that interact with the earth forces in ways possible only within the mass of the earth: resonantly, harmoniously, comparably with the ways the architecture of the surface city interacts with the forces of the atmosphere into which it projects, the climate formed by the forces of air and wind, of the sun and moon. The architecture of a subterranean world interacts with extremely subtle electrical and seismic fields, the basis of an equally subtle and experimental way of living. The light and loosely-knit metal construction of the network living and working spaces and the living laboratories enables their interaction with the precise, but mathematically indeterminate complexities of the earth's inner climate. The projection towers are architectural weapons *par excellence*. They have every intention of disrupting, of tearing the fabric of the surface city and its way of life.

See opposite and pages 242 and 245

BERLIN-FREE-ZONE

This project proposes the construction of a hidden city within the one now being shaped at the centre of a reunited Berlin. The hidden city is composed of a series of interior landscapes, Freespaces, joined only by the electronic instrumentation of speed-of-light communications, in ever-changing interactions with one another and the community of inhabitants created through the indeterminacies of dialogue. This hidden city is a Free-Zone because it provides unlimited free access to communications and other, more esoteric networks at present reserved for the major institutions of government and business – but also because interaction and dialogue are unrestricted by conventions of use and behaviour enforced by these institutions.

The spatial forms of Freespaces render them unsuitable for conventional types of occupation, and demand instead the invention of new ways of living, even new types of activities: hence they are free in a deeper sense as well: free of pre-determined meaning and purpose. A subtle and dynamic relationship between the material realm of architecture and the dematerialised realm of electronic instrumentation is in this way established. This relationship becomes *cybernetic* through the continuous act of inventing reality.

The definition of purposes for the Freespaces and the Free-Zone itself can only be done at present by negatives, by saying what they are not, in terms of the highly deterministic language now serving the institutions seeking future prediction and the control of human activities within Berlin and the other cities. The Freespaces are *useless* and *meaningless* spaces. The Free-Zone is *dangerous, subversive*, an anarchic event occurring at the very heart of the new Berlin and the new Germany. It undermines all carefully laid plans and carefully preserved values. The Free-Zone is *anti*-control, *anti*-deterministic, *anti*-institutional.

Yet the Free-Zone in Berlin also presents a new matrix of potentialities and possibilities. Built on the free dialogue of self-inventing individuals (not all of whom will be criminals), nurtured by their continual spontaneity and play, the Free-Zone is a parallel culture, by definition challenging one of conformity and predictability. But it will be tolerated only so long as it can remain hidden. It will survive in the new, commercialised centre of Berlin only as long as its inhabitants maintain their wit and quickness, so long as they are free performers in a self-sustaining and secret circus, a cybernetic circus.

See pages 248-251

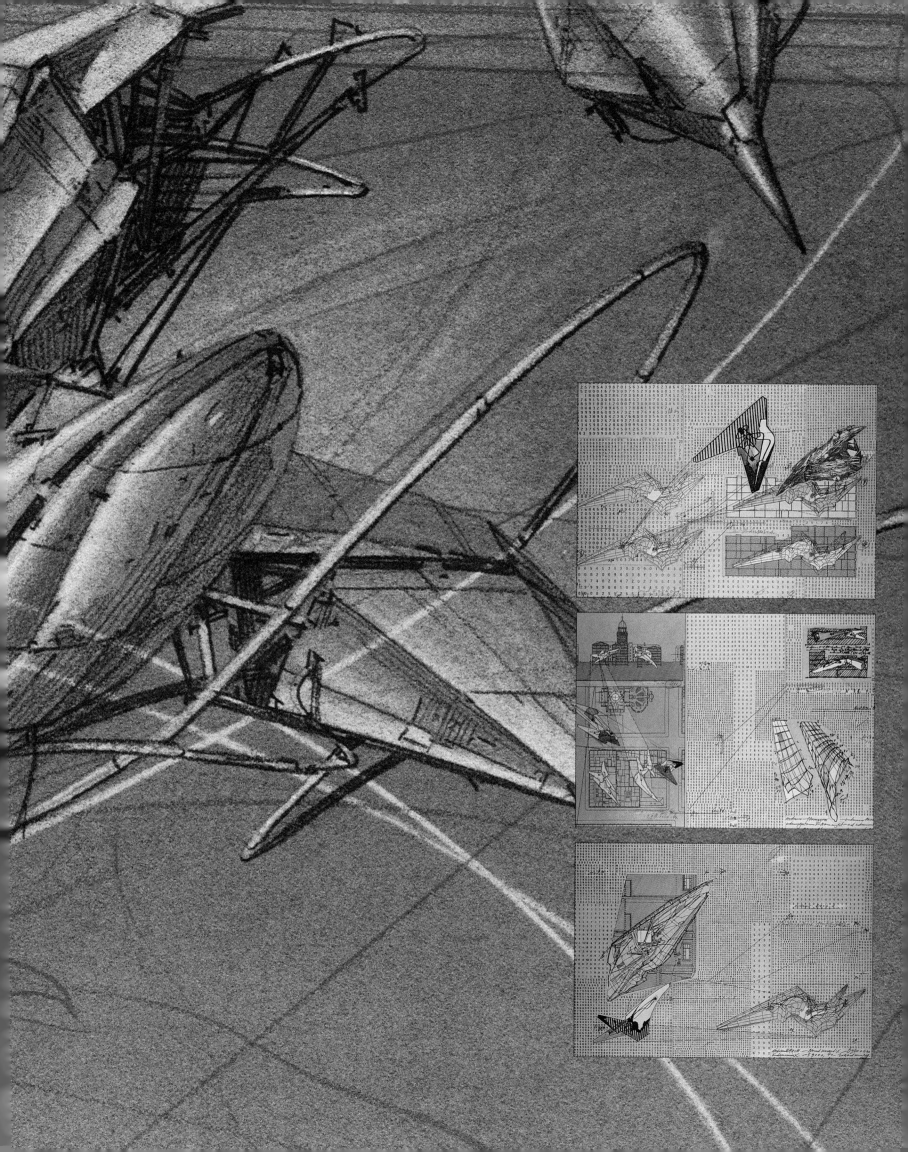

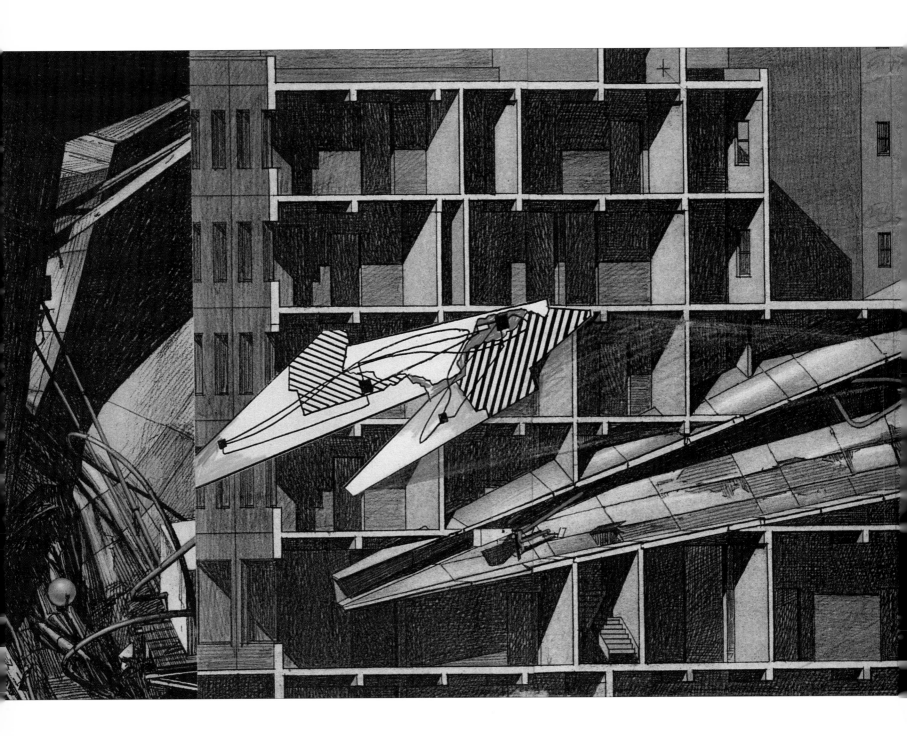

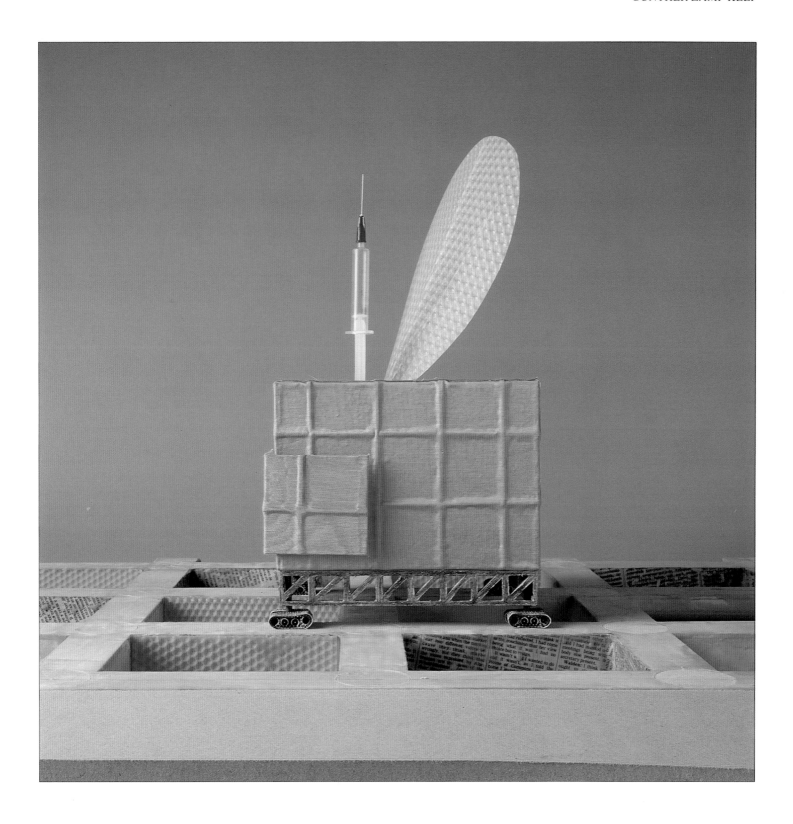

ARCHITECTS' BIOGRAPHIES

WILLIAM ALSOP

William Alsop was born in Northampton in 1947. He graduated from the Architectural Association, London, in 1973, and went to work for Maxwell Fry and Cedric Price. In 1981 he formed a partnership with John Lyall, and subsequently with Jan Stormer. He became a lecturer at St Martin's School of Art in 1974, and has also been a Unit Master at the AA and professor at the College for Art and Music, Bremen, Germany. *Selected buildings and projects:* (1971) Centre Georges Pompidou, competition entry; (1976) Riverside Studios Bookshop, London; (1986) 'Spinal Tap', Melbourne Bay, project; (1988) Sherringham Leisure Pool, Norfolk; (1989) Expo 92 British Pavilion, runner-up, competition entry; Hamburg Ferry Terminal; Hafenstrasse Workshops and Apartments, Hamburg; Cardiff Bay Visitor Centre; (1989) Thamesmead Town, London; (1990) Hôtel du Département des Bouches du Rhône, Marseilles, competition winner; (1991) Museum of Scotland extension; 'Kiss', Nantes urban regeneration programme; Potsdamer-Leipziger Platz, Berlin, urban regeneration proposal, invited competition entry. *Major exhibitions:* (1975) 'A Space: A Thousand Words', Royal College of Art, London; 'Art Net', London; (1990) 'Current Projects', Aedes Galerie and Architekturforum, Berlin.

ARQUITECTONICA

Bernardo Fort-Brescia, co-founder of Arquitectonica, was born in Lima, Peru. He received his BA in Architecture and Urban Planning from Princeton University in 1973 and his master's in Architecture from Harvard University in 1975. Soon afterwards he moved to Florida to teach Architecture at the University of Miami. He practises with his wife and partner at Arquitectonica, where he has been a principal since its founding in 1977. Laurinda Spear grew up in Miami, Florida. She took her BA at Brown University in 1972, and her master's in Architecture at Columbia in 1975. In 1978 she was awarded the Rome Prize for Architecture. She has been a principal at Arquitectonica since its founding. *Selected buildings and projects:* (1976) Spear House, Miami; (1978) Babylon, Miami; (1979) The Palace, Miami; (1980) The Square at Key Biscayne, Florida; The Atlantis, Miami; Overseas Tower, Miami; Decorative Arts Plaza, Miami; (1981) The Imperial, Miami; The Helmsley Center, design proposal; (1982) Maba House, design proposal; Taggart Town Houses, Houston, Texas; Haddon Town Houses, Houston, Texas; Mandell Town Houses, Houston, Texas; Horizon Hill Center,

design proposal; (1983) Banco de Credito del Peru, Lima, Peru; Mulder House, Lima, Peru; (1984) North Dade Justice Center, Miami; South Ferry Plaza Center, competition entry; (1985) Creditbank Tower, Miami; Walner House, Glencoe, Illinois; Rio, Atlanta, Georgia; Miracle Center, Miami; Center for Innovative Technology, Herndon, Virginia; (1986) Kushner House, Northbrook, Illinois; (1987) Sawgrass Mills, Sunrise, Florida; Vintage Park, Foster City, California; Washingtonian Center, Gaithersburg, Maryland; House in Coconut Grove, Coconut Grove, Florida; (1988) International Swimming Hall of Fame, Fort Lauderdale, Florida; Hannah Winery, design proposal; Three Palms, Jupiter, Florida; Yerba Buena Gardens Office Building, competition entry; Bank of America, Beverly Hills, California; Commercial Place, Fort Lauderdale, Florida; (1989) US Pavilion, Seville Expo 92, competition entry; Bibliothèque de France, competition entry; Banque de Luxembourg, Luxembourg; Amir House, Beverly Hills, California; Arbed Headquarters, competition entry; Private Residence, Hillsborough Beach, Florida.

GÜNTER BEHNISCH

Günter Behnisch was born in 1922 in Lockwitz, near Dresden, and educated at the Technische Hochschule in Stuttgart. From 1952 to 1956 he was in partnership with Bruno Lambart, and since that time has had his own practice. In 1966 he formed Behnisch and Partners. He became a professor at the Technische Hochschule in Darmstadt in 1967. *Selected buildings and projects:* (1986) Sporthalle, Bruchsal; Aufstockung Analysegebäude, Firma Leybold-Heraeus, Hanau; Erweiterung Fachhochschule, Ulm; (1987) Zentralbibliothek, Katholische Universität, Eichstätt; Hysolar Forschungs- und Institutsgebäude der Universität, Stuttgart-Vaihingen; Büro- und Produktionsgebäude, Leybold AG, Alzenau; (1990) Deutsches Postmuseum, Frankfurt/Main; Kindergarten, Stuttgart-Luginsland; (1991) Bahnhofsvorplatz, Stuttgart-Feuerbach; Albert-Schweitzer-Schule, Bad Rappenau; (1992) Erweiterung Gießerei, Roboter- und Sensortechnik, Fachhochschule Aalen; Wohnhaus Behnisch, Stuttgart-Sillenbuch, im Bau; Umbau und Sanierung, Gemeindehaus, Gorch-Fock-Str 30, Stuttgart-Sillenbuch, im Bau; Bundesbauten, Bonn, im Bau; Kaufmännische Berufsschule mit Wirtschaftsgymnasium und Sporthalle, Öhringen, im Bau; Erweiterung Volksschule, Lorch, im Bau; Geschwister-Scholl-Schule, Frankfurt/Main, im Bau; Erweiterung, Deutsche Bundesbank, Frankfurt/Main; Wiederaufbau Frauenkirche, Dresden.

NIGEL COATES

Nigel Coates was born in Malvern, Worcestershire in 1949. He went to Nottingham University, then studied for a diploma at the Architectural Association, London, from 1972 to 1974. He taught at the AA from 1974, becoming Unit Master of Unit 10 in 1979. He formed NATO (Narrative Architecture Today) in 1983, with Catrina Beevor, Martin Benson, Peter Fleissig, Robert Mull and Carlos Villanueva, editing the first *NATO* magazine. In 1983 he formed Nigel Coates Architecture, and in 1985 Branson Coates Architecture with Doug Branson. *Selected buildings and projects:* (1985) House for Jasper Conran, London; Metropole Restaurant, Tokyo; (1986) Jasper Conran shop, London; Takeo Kikuchi shop, barbershop and Bohemia Jazz Club, Tokyo; Caffé Bongo for Parco, Tokyo; Furniture Rockstone, Tokyo; (1987) Ashiya Pavilion Commercial Building, Ashiya (unbuilt); Silver jewellery shop, London; Jasper Conran shop, Dublin; (1988) Dunhill International Exhibition, London and Toronto; Jigsaw shops in London and Bristol; Katharine Hamnett shops, Glasgow and Sloane Street, London; Nigel Coates Furniture SCP, London; SCP furniture launch at Salone del Mobile, Milan; Arca di Noè restaurant building, Sapporo; (1989) Jasper Conran shop, Tokyo; Stonehenge shop, Stonehenge, Salisbury; Situationist International Exhibition for the Centre Georges Pompidou, Paris, the ICA in London and the ICA in Boston; Hotel Otaru Marittimo, Otaru, Japan; Poltronova furniture launch at Salone del Mobile; (1990) Hamnett Active, Tokyo; Nishi Azabu Wall, Commercial Building, Tokyo; No Furs Shop, Habitat and Identita Exhibition, Arezzo, Italy; (1991) Taxim, restaurant, bar and night club, Istanbul; Mayflower Golf Club, Japan; Debating Chamber for weekly current affairs programme *La Cinq TV*, Paris. Current projects: Art Gallery Tower Nishi Azabu, Tokyo; Strategic study, Liberty, Regent Street, London and other branches; Airside Passenger Restaurant and Bars, Schiphol International Airport, Amsterdam; Restaurant, Holland Park, London. *Selected writings:* (1976) 'L'Art, Le Sphinx', *Artscribe* 3; (1981) 'Modern Life and the Impact of Architecture', Architectural Association, London; (1982) 'Giant Sized Baby Town', Architectural Association, London; (1983) *Albion*, Architectural Association, London; (1984) 'Cook's Chefs-d'oeuvre', *The Architectural Review*, CLXXV, 1045; (1984) 'Voxhall', Architectural Association, London' (1985) 'Trading Spaces', Architectural Association, London; (1988) 'Iron Curtain Goes Up', *Blueprint* 46.

COOP HIMMELBLAU

Coop Himmelblau, the 'Blue-Sky Co-operative', was formed by Wolf Prix and Helmut Swiezinsky in 1968. Prix was born in Vienna in 1942, Swiezinsky in Poznan, Poland, in 1944. *Selected buildings and projects:* (1980) 'The Blazing Wing', an architectural happening (Günther Domenig invited Coop Himmelblau to the University at Graz, where they ignited a one-and-a-half ton, 50-foot-high steel structure); (1984-88) Baumann Studio, Vienna; (1985) Skyline, Hamburg, Germany; (1986) Apartment Building, Vienna; (1988-89) Funderwerk 3, factory; (1989) Ronacher Theatre, Vienna; (1989) Rooftop Remodelling, Vienna; (1991-) Anselm Kiefer's Studio. *Selected writings:* (1978) *The Poetry of Desolation*; (1980) *Architecture Must Blaze*; (1990) 'On the Edge' (edited version of a lecture given at the Royal Institute of British Architects), 'Deconstruction III', *Architectural Design* 60, 9/10; (1991) Prix, Wolf, 'An Architectural Design Interview', 'New Museums', *Architectural Design* 61, 11/12.

DILLER + SCOFIDIO

Diller + Scofidio, a collaborative cross-disciplinary team working with architecture, performance and the visual arts, was formed in 1979 by Elizabeth Diller and Ricardo Scofidio. Diller was born in Lodz, Poland, in 1954. She attended the Cooper Union school of Art and Cooper Union School of Architecture, and was awarded a B Arch in 1979. She has been Assistant Professor at Princeton University since 1990, and has taught at Cooper Union, Harvard, Columbia Graduate School of Design and the Institute for Architecture and Urban Studies. Scofidio was born in New York in 1935. He attended Cooper Union School of Architecture and Columbia University, taking his B Arch in 1960. He has been professor at Cooper Union since 1967, and has taught at the universities of Harvard and Illinois. Diller + Scofidio won First Prize in the Nature Morte Competition, 1988, a Tiffany Foundation Award for Emerging Artists in 1990, and the Progressive Architecture Award in 1991. *Selected projects and exhibitions:* (1986) *Urban, Suburban, Rural Windows*, installation for the Domestic project, 17th Milan Triennale; (1987) *The withDrawing Room*, installation at Capp Street project, San Francisco; The Rotary Notary and his Hot Plate, stage set and costumes, Painted Bride Art Center, Philadelphia, La Mama Etc, New York, and the Southern Theater, Minneapolis; (1988) *Investigations*, installation at the Institute for Contemporary Art, Philadelphia; (1989) *Para-Site*, installation at the Museum of Modern Art, New York; (1991) *Tourisms; suitCase Studies*, installation at the Walker Arts Center, Minneapolis, List Center for the Visual Arts, Cambridge, Massachusetts, and Wexner Art Center, Columbus, Ohio; (1992) 'Non-Sequiturs', Sadock & Uzzan Galerie, Paris; *The Desiring Eye: ReViewing the Slow House*, installation, Gallery MA, Tokyo; Headquarters for creative Time and Dance Theater Workshop, Battery Maritime Building, New York (in progress); The Slow House, family residence, Long Island, New York (in progress).

GÜNTHER DOMENIG

Günther Domenig was born in Klagenfurt, Germany, in 1934, and studied Architecture at the Technical University, Graz. In 1963 he went into partnership with Eilfried Huth, and in 1973 started his own office. Since then he has established architectural bureaux in Klagenfurt, Graz and Vienna. In 1980 he became a professor at the University in Graz, and he has held guest professorships, attended seminars and lectured in Germany, Italy, France, Belgium, UK, Turkey and the USA. *Selected buildings and projects:* (1963-68) Teachers' College, Graz-Eggenberg; (1964-69) Zellflex Zeltweg, project; (1965-69) Roman Catholic Church, Oberwart; (1965-69) Stadt Ragnitz, project; (1967) Entrance area for the Trigon Exposition; (1967-68) Artiflex I, project; (1969-73) Research and Calculation Centre, Leoben; Simulator models, project; (1970-72) Pavilion Indoor Pool, Munich; Restaurant Nord, Munich; (1970-73) Centre for Apprentices, Graz; (1970-73) Medium Total, project; (1971-72) Floraskin, project; (1973) University of Vienna addition, project; (1974-77) Multi-purpose Hall, Graz-Eggenberg; (1974-79) Central Savings Bank Favoriten, Vienna; (1975) Ballhausplatzverbauung, Vienna, project; (1977) Elephant Bar, project; (1979) Laying-out Hall Velden, project; Capitalo shops, offices and hotel centre, project, Caracas, Venezuela; (1979-78) Humanic shoeshops; (1979-82) Shipyard Klagenfurt; (1983) Rikki Reiner fashion shop, Klagenfurt, structural conversion; (1983-) Addition to the Technical University of Grax, Technikerstr, project; (1984-89) Addition to the Technical University Graz, Steyrergasse; (1985-) 'Resowi' addition to the University of Graz, project; (1986-88) Housing Neufeldweg, Graz; (1986) Court in front of the railway station, Salzburg, project; (1986-) Steinhaus (Stonehouse) in Steindorf, Carinthia; Central Savings Bank of Vienna, 'ZVZ' structural conversion, project; 'Meini Plaza', hotel and congress centre conversion, project; (1987) Founder Exposition Hall, structural conversion, St Veit, Carinthia; (1987-) Hospital Bruck an der Mur, project; (1988-89) Power Station Unzmarkt, Styria; (1989) Bibliothèque de France, Paris, project; (1990) Hotel, sports and congress centre, project, Sotschi, Russia. *Major exhibitions:* (1968) 'Urban Fiction', Vienna; (1969) 'Urban Fiction', La Chaux de Fonds, Grenoble and Rome; (1970) 'Medium Total', Gallery nächst St Stephan, Vienna; (1974) 'Architektur zum Jahr 2000', Akademie der Schöen Künste; (1979) 'Transformations in Modern Architecture', Museum of Modern Art, New York; (1984) 'Architeckturvisionen', Styrian Autumn; (1985) Venice Biennale; (1986) 'Günther Domenig', Architectural Association, London; (1989) 'Günther Domenig: Das Steinhaus', Museum für Angewandte Kunst, Vienna. *Awards:* (1969) The Grand Prix International d'Urbanisme et d'Architecture, Cannes, project Ragnitz; (1975) Prix European de la construction Metallique. *Selected writings:* (1988) *Das Steinhaus* (The Stonehouse), Österreichisches Museum für angewandte Kunst, Wien. *Steinhaus: Zeichnungen und Modellen*, Ritter Verlag, Graz.

PETER EISENMAN

Peter Eisenman was born in Newark, New Jersey in 1932. He proceeded Bachelor of Architecture, Master of Architecture, and PhD, from the universities of Cornell (1955), Columbia (1960) and Cambridge (1963) respectively. He was Architectural Designer first at Percival Goodman, FAIA, New York, 1958-59, and then at The Architects' Collaborative, Cambridge, Massachusetts, 1959. He founded his own firm in New York in 1963, and became a partner of Eisenman/Robertson Architects, Design Development Resources in 1980; in 1987 he formed his current firm, Eisenman Architects, New York. From 1967 to 1982 he was an editor of Oppositions Books, and from 1975 to 1982 Editor of *Oppositions* magazine, for The Institute for Architecture and Urban Studies, New York. He has held professorships at the University of Maryland, Yale University School of Architecture, Harvard University Graduate School of Design, Ohio State University and the University of Illinois. He was awarded the Stone Lion (first prize) at the Venice Biennale in 1985, the American Institute of Architects Honor Award in 1988 and the Fifth World Biennial of Architecture Interarch Gold Medal in 1989. *Selected buildings and projects:* (1960) Liverpool Cathedral, commended competition entry; (1963) Boston Architectural Center, competition entry with Michael Graves; (1965) University of California Arts Center, competition entry with Michael Graves; (1966) Manhattan Waterfront, project with Michael Graves; (1967-78) Houses 1-11a; (1980) House El Even Odd; (1981) International Bauausstellung, Berlin 1984, South Friedrichstradt, West Berlin; (1981-82) New Brunswick Theological Seminary, New Jersey; (1981) Cummins Engine Company, Madison Components Plant, Indiana; (1982-86) Berlin Housing, South Friedrichstradt, West Berlin; (1982) Beverly Hills Civic Center, California; (1983-85) Engine Co 233/Ladder Co 176, Fire Station in Brooklyn, New York; (1983) Fin d'Ou T Hou S; (1985) 'Moving Arrows, Eros, and Other Errors: An Architecture of Absence', project; (1986) 'Casa Che Cresca', project; (1986) University of Cincinnati College of Design, Art, Architecture, and Planning; (1986) California State University at Long Beach Art Museum, Programming and Design; Progressive Corporation, Cleveland, Ohio; Tokyo Opera House, competition entry; Rovereto Museum of Futurism, Italy; Parc de la Villette, Paris, garden design; (1988) Guardiola House, Cadiz; (1988-90) Koizumi Sangyo Office Building; (1989) Banyoles Olympic Hotel, Spain; (1989) Housing at the Hague, for the 200,000th Home Festival; (1989) Cooper Union Student Housing competition entry; (1990) Groningen Video-Music Pavilion, Netherlands; (1990) Atocha 123, Apartments, Madrid; (1990) Nunotani Office Building, Tokyo; (1990) Alteka Office Building, Tokyo; (1990) Rebstock Park Master Plan, Frankfurt; (1991) Emory University Arts Center, Atlanta. *Major exhibitions:* (1966) 'Forty Under Forty', Architectural League, New York; (1973) 'Another Chance for Housing: Low-Rise Alternatives', Museum of Modern Art, New York; Milan Triennale;

(1975) 'The New York Five', Art Net, London; (1976) Venice Biennale; (1980) 'Autonomous Architecture', Harvard University, Fogg Museum; (1983) *Beyond Utopia, Changing Attitudes in American Architecture*, a film by Michael Blackwood Productions, screened at the Museum of Modern Art; (1984) 'Cite Un Seen I', Architeckturmuseum, Frankfurt; (1985) Venice Biennale; (1986) Milan Triennale; (1991) Venice Biennale. *Selected writings:* (1982) *House X*, Rizzoli, New York; (1985) *Fin D'Ou T Hou S*, Architectural Association, London (with Jeff Kipnis and Nina Hofer); (1986) *Moving Arrows, Eros, and Other Errors: An Architecture of Absence*, Architectural Association, London; (1988) *Houses of Cards*, Oxford University Press, New York. Forthcoming: *CHORA L WORKS*, Architectural Association, London (with Jacques Derrida and Jeff Kipnis); *Giuseppe Terragni: Transformations, Decompositions, Critiques*, Rizzoli, New York.

MARK FISHER

Mark Fisher was born in 1947, and studied at the Architectural Association, London, from 1965 to 1971. He entered private practice in 1971, designing and building inflatable, tension and other lightweight portable structures for the entertainment industry, then taking the resulting artefacts out on tour with the client, for example the Rolling Stones. He was Unit Master at the AA from 1973 to 1977, taught at various universities in the USA and Canada from 1977 to 1979, and has been a part-time tutor at the AA since 1986. In 1984 he founded Fisher Park with Jonathan Park. *Selected writings:* (1990) 'It's Only Rock 'n' Roll: The Steel Wheels North American Tour', 'New Architecture: The New Moderns and The Super Moderns', *Architectural Design* 60, 3/4; (1992) 'Pop Architecture: A Sophisticated Interpretation of Popular Culture', *Architectural Design* 62, No 7/8.

HIROMI FUJI

Hiromi Fuji was born in Tokyo in August 1935. He graduated from Waseda University in 1958, and studied in Milan and London from 1964 to 1967. In 1968 he established Hiromi Fuji, Architect and Associates. He has lectured at Harvard, Columbia, Kentucky, Illinois, Rice, and other American universities, and is currently professor at the Shibaura Institute of Technology. *Selected buildings and projects:* (1980) Miyata House; (1985) The Ushimado International Arts Festival Center; (1986) Second Gymnasium at the Shibaura Institute of Technology; (1988) House Mizoe-1; (1989) *The Nave of Signs*, installation. *Major exhibitions:* (1987) exhibit at Harvard and Columbia universities; (1988) GA Japan 88, Tokyo, and Europalia Exhibition, Belgium; (1990) GA Japan 90, Tokyo; (1991) Fifth Venice Biennale, special workshop award; London Japan Festival, Architectural Association, London; (1992) GA Japan 92, Tokyo.

FRANK GEHRY

Frank Gehry was born in Toronto in 1929. He studied at the University of Southern California, 1949-51, and Harvard, 1956-57. In the 1950s he

worked for Victor Gruen, Hideo Sasaki, Pereira and Luckman, and André Remondet in Paris. He has taught at the University of Southern California (1972-73), Rice University (1976), California University (1977-79), Yale (1982-88), Harvard (1983), and UCLA (1988-89). *Selected buildings and projects:* (1964) Danziger Studio-Residence, Hollywood; (1968) O'Neill Hay Barn, San Juan Capistrano, California; Bill Al Bengston; Los Angeles County Museum of Art; Joseph Magnin Stores, Costa Mesa and San José, California; (1972) Ron Davis Studio, Malibu, California; (1973) Santa Monica Place, Santa Monica, California; (1974) Rouse Company Headquarters, Columbia, Maryland; (1975) Concord Pavilion, Concord, California; Main Street, Venice, California; (1976) Jung Institute, Los Angeles; (1977) Law offices, Los Angeles; Ron Davis Studio addition, Malibu, California; Gehry House additions, Santa Monica, California; (1978) Gunther House, Encinal Bluffs; Wagner House, Malibu, California; Familian House, Santa Monica, California; De Menil House, New York; Mid-Atlantic Toyota, Glen Burnie, Maryland; (1979) Cabrillo Marine Museum, San Pedro, California; (1980) Spiller House, Venice, California; Chicago Tribune Tower; (1981) Benson House, Calabasas, California; Indiana Avenue Houses, Venice, California; House for a Filmmaker, Los Angeles Smith House, Brentwood, California; (1981) Loyola Law School, Los Angeles; (1982) California Aerospace Museum, Los Angeles; Wosk Residence, Beverly Hills; (1983) Norton House, Venice, California; Frances Howard Goldwyn, Regional Branch Library, California; Fish and Snake Lamps; (1984) Il Corso del Coltello, Venice; Médiathèque, Nîmes, France; Borman House, Malibu, California; Sirmai-Peterson House, Thousand Oaks, California; Rebecca's, Venice, California; Camp Good Times, Santa Monica Mountains, California; (1985) Yale Psychiatric Institute, New Haven, Connecticut; (1986) Fishdance Restaurant, Kobe, Japan; Winton Guest House, Wayzata, Minnesota; Santa Monica Airport Park, California; (1988) Walt Disney Concert Hall, Los Angeles; Edgemar Development, Santa Monica, California; 360 Newbury Street, Boston; King's Cross Development, London; Canary Wharf, London; Madison Square Garden, New York; (1989) Vitra Museum, Weil am Rhein, Germany; Herman Miller Industrial Complex, Rocklin, California; Schnabel Residence, Brentwood, California; Main Street Building, Venice, California; Turtle Creek Development, Dallas, Texas; Iowa Laser Laboratories, Iowa City; Toledo Art Museum School, Ohio; (1989) American Center, Paris; Concert Hall Hotel, Los Angeles; (1990) EuroDisney Leisure Center, Paris; New Headquarters for Vitra, Basle, Switzerland; University of Minnesota Art Museum, Minneapolis.

ZAHA HADID

Zaha Hadid was born in Baghdad in 1950. She took a Maths degree at the American University of Beirut in 1971, and studied at the Architectural Association, London, from 1972 to 1977, obtaining a Diploma Prize. In 1977 she joined OMA

(Office of Metropolitan Architecture) and in 1980 she began her own practice. From 1977 to 1987 she was Unit Master at the AA, in 1987 she was Visiting Professor at Columbia University, New York, and in 1988 she was Visiting Design Critic at Harvard. *Selected buildings and projects:* (1978) Dutch Houses of Parliament Extension in the Hague, project; (1981) Irish Prime Minister's House and State Guest House, project; (1982) Apartment Conversion, 59 Eaton Place, London, project; Parc de la Villette, project; (1983) The Peak, Hong Kong, prizewinning competition entry; (1985) Grand Buildings, Trafalgar Square, London, competition entry; (1986) Kurfürstendamm Office Building, Berlin, first-prizewinning competition entry; (1986) IBA Housing project, Berlin; (1987) West Hollywood Civic Center, California, project; (1988) Al Wadha Sports Stadium, Abu Dhabi, project; Victoria City Area, Berlin, project; (1989) Office/Housing project, Hamburg Hafenstrasse; Hamburg Docklands, Bauforum 2, project; Bordeaux Docklands, project; Tokyo Forum, project; (1990) Music-Video Pavilion, Groningen, Netherlands; Moonsoon Restaurant, Sapporo, Japan; Folly Three, Expo 90, Osaka; Vitra Fire Station, Weil am Rhein, project; Azabu-Jyuban Building, Tokyo, project; Glunz Wood Exhibition Pavilion, Cologne, project; 'London 2066' for *Vogue*'s 75th Anniversary, project; Cwmdu Site Masterplan, Swansea, mixed use development project; Villa, The Hague, project; (1992) Zollhof 3 Media Centre, Dusseldorf; Hotel Billie Strauss, Stuttgart, project. *Major exhibitions:* (1978) OMA Exhibition, Frankfurt, Guggenheim Museum, New York; (1980-81) 'Planetary Architecture', Van Rooy Gallery, Amsterdam; (1982) '59 Eaton Place', AA and RIBA, London; (1983) 'Planetary Architecture Two' (retrospective), AA, London; (1984) Aedes Gallery and IBA, Hamburg, Munich, Berlin; (1985) Milan Triennale; Paris Biennale; Phillippe Bonnafont Gallery, San Francisco; (1986) National Museum of Art, Kyoto; Grey Art Gallery, New York; (1987) 'Corbu Vu Par', Institut Français d'Architecture, Paris; Max Protetch Gallery, New York; (1988) 'Deconstructivist Architecture', Museum of Modern Art, New York; Arts Council, Rotterdam; (1989) 'Wild and Uncertain Times', IFA, Paris; 'Private Lives', Museum of Architecture, Frankfurt; (1990) 'Leicester Square; Rediscovering the public realm', Heinz Gallery, London; (1991) 'New Berlin', Deutsches Architektur Museum, Frankfurt; 'Osaka folly', AA.

ITSUKO HASEGAWA

Itsuko Hasegawa graduated from the Department of Architecture, Kanto Gakuin University, in 1964. From 1964 to 1969 she worked in the office of Kiyonori Kikutake, and from 1969 to 1971 was a research student in the Department of Architecture, Tokyo Institute of Technology. She worked as an assistant at the Kazuo Shinohara Atelier, Tokyo Institute of Technology, 1971-78, and established Itsuko Hasegawa Atelier in 1979. In 1988 she was a lecturer at Waseda University, and in 1989 at the Tokyo Institute of Technology. She received the Japan Cultural Design Award in

1986 and the Avon Arts Award in 1990. *Selected buildings and projects:* (1972) House One at Yaizu; (1975) House at Kamoi; House at Midorigaoka; (1978) Stationer's shop at Yaizu; (1979) Tokumaru Children's Clinic; (1980) House at Duwahara, Matsuyama; (1982) Aono Building; (1983) NC House; (1984) Bizan Hall; (1985) By House; House at Oyama; (1986) Tomigaya Atelier; Sugai Internal Clinic; House at Nerima; House at Kumamoto; (1987) House at Higashitamagawa; (1988) Uraoka clinic; (1989) Nagoya Design Expo, interior pavilion; (1990) Cona Village; Shonandai Cultural Centre, Fujisawa, first-prizewinning competition entry; STM House. *Major exhibitions:* (1978) 'Post-Modernism', London; (1982) Paris Biennale; (1983) 'Japan Design', Moscow; (1984) Japan Festival, Rotterdam; (1987) exhibition at Gallery Rom, Oslo; (1988) exhibition at Mosegards Gallery in Århus, Denmark; 'Autobiographical Architecture', Heerlen, Netherlands; (1989) 'Architecture as a Second Nature "Hanging Garden"', Gallery MA, Tokyo; (1989) exhibition in MIT Gallery, Boston; Urban Scape, Shigama, first-prizewinning competition entry; (1990) Sumida Cultural Centre, Tokyo, first-prizewinning competition entry; (1991) exhibition in Avery Hall, Columbia University, New York

JOHN HEJDUK

John Hejduk was born in New York in 1929. He attended the Cooper Union School of Art and Architecture from 1947 to 1950 and then worked in various architectural offices in the city. He took his B Arch from the University of Cincinnati in 1952, and his M Arch from the Harvard Graduate School of Design in 1953. In 1954 he went to the University of Rome on a Fulbright Scholarship, and from 1954 to 1956 he was Instructor in Architectural Design at the School of Architecture, University of Texas. He worked for IM Pei in New York, 1956-58, and was Assistant Professor of Architecture at the Cornell University School of Architecture, 1958-60. From 1961 to 1964 he was Critic in Architectural Design at the Yale Graduate School of Design, and since 1964 he has been Professor of Architecture at the Cooper Union School of Architecture. He has had a private practice since 1965, and has been Dean of the Cooper Union School of Architecture since 1975. *Selected buildings and projects:* (1954) Skinner Duplex Apartments, Austin, Texas, project, with Bernard Hoesli; (1959) Friedlander House, Waverly, New York, project; (1960) Demlin House, Locust Valley, Long Island; (1967) installation design for 'The Diamond in Painting and Architecture', Architectural League of New York, project, with Robert Slutzky; (1968) Bernstein House, Mamaroneck, New York, project; (1971) installation design for 'Education of an Architect', Museum of Modern Art, New York; (1972) installation design for 'Projects, John Hejduk, Architect', Le Corbusier Foundation, Paris; (1973) Bye House, Ridgefield, Connecticut, project; (1975) Foundation Building, Cooper Union, New York, renovation and restoration, with Peter Bruder and Edwin Aviles; (1984) Studio for a Painter, Handcart and

Studio for a Musician, design and construction of elements from Victims project, Internationale Bauausstellung Berlin, Martin Gropius Bau, Berlin, West Germany; (1986) The Collapse of Time, clock element from Victims project, Architectural Association, London; (1987) Subject/Object, two elements from Riga project, The University of the arts, Philadelphia, Pennsylvania; (1988) Tegel Housing, IBA Social Housing, Berlin; Kreuzberg Tower and Wings, IBA Social Housing, Berlin; (1989) Security, element from Victims project, Oslo School of Architecture, Norway; (1990) The House of the Suicide/The House of the Mother of the Suicide, elements from Lancaster/Hanover Masque, Georgia Institute of Technology, Atlanta, Georgia, and (1991) Prague Castle, Prague, Czechoslovakia; Tower of Cards, Groningen City Marker, Groningen, Netherlands.

PHILIP JOHNSON

Philip Johnson was born in Cleveland Ohio in 1906. He was educated at Harvard, where he took his BA in 1930 and his master's in Architecture in 1943. He was instrumental, in his capacity as the founder and director of the Department of Architecture at New York's Museum of Modern Art, in first introducing to a generation of American architects the radical approaches to design of such modern masters as Mies van der Rohe and Le Corbusier, in particular through his landmark exhibition of 1932, 'The International Style'. Johnson was also closely associated with the reintroduction of a range of historical styles into modern architecture, as marked by the AT&T Corporate Headquarters building, New York, 1984, designed with John Burgee, with whom Johnson went into partnership in 1967. Since 1991 he has been working as Philip Johnson Architects, with clients including the Sony Corporation and the University of Houston. He has recently been commissioned to design a mixed-use office building in Berlin. *Selected buildings and projects:* (1949) Glass House; (1950) The Rockefeller Guest House, New York; Annex to the New York Museum of Modern Art; (1953) New York Museum of Modern Art, Abby Aldrich Rockefeller Sculpture Garden; (1956) Kneses Tifereth Israel Synagogue, Port Chester, New York; (1958) Seagram's Building (with Mies van der Rohe); (1959) The Four Seasons Restaurant in the Seagram's Building (1960) The Roofless Church in New Harmony, Indiana; (1963) The Museum for Pre-Columbian Art, Washington DC; (1964) The New York State Theater (with Richard Foster); New York Museum of Modern Art, East Wing and Garden Wing (1973) The Elmer Holmes Bobst Library for the New York University Campus, with Richard Foster; Minneapolis IDS Center; (1975) Avery Fisher Hall, New York; (1976) Pennzoil Place, Houston; (1980) Garden Grove Community Church, California; (1982) Dade County Cultural Center (1984) corporate headquarters for Pittsburgh Plate Glass; NCNB Center, Houston; (1983) The New Cleveland Play House, Cleveland (1984) AT&T Corporte Headquarters Building; (1985) Transco Tower, Houston; University of Houston, College of Archi-

tecture (1987) Atlantic Center, Atlanta; Momentum Place, Dallas (1988) 500 Boylston Street, Dallas; (1992) CBC Building in Toronto, Singapore Retail Mall, Singapore. *Awards:* (1978) AIA Gold Medal; Bronze Medallion of the City of New York; (1979) Pritzker Architecture Prize for a Distinguished Career in Architecture. *Publications:* (1932) *The International Style: Architecture Since 1922*; (1947) *Mies van der Rohe*; (1931-1975) *Philip Johnson Writings*.

KRUEGER AND KAPLAN

In 1984 Ted Krueger and Ken Kaplan graduated from the Columbia University Graduate School of Architectural Planning and Preservation. Both trained originally as social scientists, gaining 15 years of clinical and research experience, Kaplan as a psychiatric social worker at New York University, Krueger receiving his BA from the University at Wisconsin. In 1985 the Krueger and Kaplan Research Development was founded, which has since received awards and grants from the New York State Council of the Arts, the New York Foundation for the Arts, the Research Institute for Experimental Architecture and Art Matters Inc. Present projects include the preparation of a text, *The Renegade Cities. Major exhibitions:* (1986) 'Building: Machines', PS 1, Long Island City, New York; 'Retrospective of Storefront', Storefront for Art and Architecture, New York; 'From Here to Eternity', Artists' Space Gallery, New York; ASR Benefit Auction, Max Protetch Gallery, New York; 'Behind Closed Doors', the Urban Center, New York; (1987) 'Mechanisms', an installation at Columbia University, New York; 'Art on the Beach', in collaboration with J Croak, Long Island City, New York; 'Future of Storefront', Storefront for Art and Architecture, New York; (1988) 'Project DMZ', Storefront for Art and Architecture, New York; 'Spirit of Design', Interior Center, Tokyo and the University of Ashikaea, Hokkaido, Japan; 'New York Newsstands', in collaboration with A Blum; ASR Benefit Auction, Max Protetch Gallery, New York; (1989) 'Exhibition Diomede', the Clocktower, New York; 'Renegade Cities', Fenster Gallery, Frankfurt am Main, Germany; Grant, Research Institute for Experimental Architecture and Grant, Art Matters, Inc; 'Renegade Cities', installation at the Storefront for Art & Architecture, New York; (1990) 'Post-Consumerism', Storefront for Art & Architecture, New York; 'Interventions', exhibition at 2 AES, San Francisco; 'RIEA: Experimental Architecture', Aedes Gallery, Berlin; Installation at Artpark, Lewiston, New York; 'Renegade Cities', Galerie Ulla Klodt, Hamburg, Germany; (1991) 'Free-Zone, Zagreb', Arts and Crafts Museum and the Zagreb Society of Architects, Zagreb, Yugoslavia; 'Architects & Artifacts', Society for Art in Crafts, Pittsburgh, Pennysylvania; 'Critical Mass', Maryland Institute College of Art, Baltimore, Maryland.

DANIEL LIBESKIND

Daniel Libeskind was born in Poland in 1946. He first studied music in Israel, and later gained his degree in Architecture from Cooper Union, New

York, where he studied under John Hejduk. He subsequently took a postgraduate course in the History and Theory of Architecture at Essex University. Between 1978 and 1985 he was Head of the Department of Architecture at Cranbrook Academy of Art, and visiting professor at the universities of Harvard, Ohio State, the Danish Academy of Art, Copenhagen, and the University of Naples. He was also Louis Sullivan Professor at the University of Illinois, Chicago. Invited by the John Paul Getty Foundation to become a Senior Scholar, he pursued his work at the Center for Arts and Humanities, 1986-89. In 1991 he was appointed Banister Fletcher Professor at London University. Selected buildings and projects: (1985) 'Three Machines for Palmanova', Venice Biennale; (1986) 'House Without Walls', Milan Triennale; (1987) 'The City Edge', housing and commercial project, IBA Flottwellstrasse, Berlin; (1988) Housing Villa, Luxowplatz; New City Plan, Berlin; Yatai Architecture Nagoya, Japan; (1989) Extension to Berlin Museum, including the Jewish Museum; Folly, Expo 90, Osaka, Japan; urban design for Potsdammerplatz, Berlin; (1990) planning proposals for Berlin. Selected writings: (1981) Between Zero and Infinity, Rizzoli, New York; (1983) Chamber Works, Architectural Association, London; (1985) Theatrum Mundi, Architectural Association, London; (1988) Line of Fire, Electa, Milan; Threshold, Rizzoli, New York; Arquitecture, Madrid; (1990) Marking the City Boundaries: Groningen, The Netherlands, MIT Press, Boston; (1991) Berlin Morgen-Ideen Fur das Herz Einer Groszstadt, DAM.

MORPHOSIS

Morphosis was formed by Thom Mayne and Michael Rotondi in Santa Monica, California, in 1975. The partnership lasted until November 1991, when Rotondi left to establish a different group, ROTOndi. Thom Mayne was born in 1944 in Connecticut; he received his BA from the University of Southern California School of Architecture in 1968, and became Master of Architecture, Harvard University, Graduate School of Design, in 1978. He was a Founding Board Member of the Southern California Institute of Architecture in 1972. He has taught at the California State College at Pomona, Miami University, Ohio, the University of Texas at Austin, UCLA, Columbia University, the University of Cincinatti and the Academy of Applied Arts, Vienna. He received the Rome Prize Fellowship, American Academy in Rome, in 1987, and was appointed to the Elliot Noyes Chair, Harvard University, in 1988, and the Eliel Saarinen Chair, Yale University, in 1991. Since Rotondi's departure Morphosis Architects have built the Salick Health Care Corporate Headquarters, 1992. Michael Rotondi was born in 1949 in Los Angeles, and received his B Arch from SCI-ARC in 1973. He worked as a designer with Daniel, Mann, Johnson and Mendenhall (DMJM) in Los Angeles from 1973 to 1976, and from 1974 to 1976 established an independent practice and freelance collaboration with Peter de Bretteville and Craig Hodgetts.

From 1976 to 1987 he was Director of the Graduate Programme/Graduate Design Faculty at SCI-ARC, and in 1987 was appointed Director, Board Member, Faculty (SCI-ARC). He has taught architecture at the University of Texas at Austin, the University of Pennsylvania, UCLA, Columbia University, the University of Minnesota and the University of Moscow. He became Principal of ROTOndi in 1991, since when he has built the CDLT building, Los Angeles (1992). Rotondi received the Progressive Architecture Award, CDLT, in 1992, and the American Academy of Arts & Letters Award in Architecture the same year. Selected works and buildings: (1978) 2-4-6-8 House, Los Angeles; (1980) Sedlak Residence, Venice, California; (1981) Competition entry for Vietnam Veterans Memorial, Washington; (1983) 72 Market Street, Venice, California; (1984) Hennessey and Ingalls Bookstore Façade, Santa Monica, California; (1986) Kate Mantilini Restaurant, Los Angeles; (1987) Gonfiantini Residence (Reno House), Reno, Nevada (project); (1988) Sixth Street House, Santa Monica, California; (1989) Cedars-Sinai Comprehensive Cancer Center, Los Angeles; (1990) San Fernando Valley Arts Park, Performing Arts Center, Los Angeles, under construction. Major exhibitions: (1988) 'Morphosis', 2 AES Gallery, Art and Architecture Exhibition Space, San Francisco; (1989) 'Three Houses', Walker Arts Center, Minneapolis, Minnesota; (1990) 'Parallel Activities', Gallery MA, Tokyo; (1991) 'Morphosis: Making Architecture', Laguna Art Museum, Laguna, California; (1992) 'Current Research 1', Yokohama Pacifico Hall Center, Yokohama, Japan. Awards: (1974) Progressive Architecture Award, Sequoyah Educational Research Center; (1977) Progressive Architecture Award, Riedel Medical Building; (1980) Progressive Architecture Award, Flores Residence; (1981) AIA Award, Sedlak House; (1982) Progressive Architecture Award, Western-Melrose Office Building; (1984) Progressive Architecture Award, Hermosa Beach Commercial Center; (1985) AIA Award, Bergren Residence, Lawrence Residence and 72 Market Street; (1986) AIA Award, Angeli Restaurant; (1987) AIA Award, CCAIA Award, P/A Award, Kate Mantilini Restaurant; (1988) AIA Award, Cedars-Sinai Comprehensive Cancer Center; (1989) Progressive Architecture Award, Higashi Azabu Tower; (1990) CCAIA Award, Interior Award, Leon Max Showroom.

ERIC OWEN MOSS

Eric Owen Moss was born in 1943. He took a BA from UCLA in 1965, an MA from Berkeley in 1968, and an M Arch from Harvard in 1974. Since then he has lectured at SCI-ARCH and at a number of other universities, including Yale. Selected buildings and projects: (1977) Playa del Rey Duplex, Los Angeles; (1978) Morgenstern Warehouse, Los Angeles; (1982) Petal House, Los Angeles; Pin Ball House, Los Angeles; (1983) Fun House, Los Angeles; (1984) World Savings and Loan Interiors, Los Angeles; (1987) Uehara House, Los Angeles; (1988) 8522 National Office Complex, Los Angeles; (1989) Central Housing Office

Building, 3964 Ince Boulevard, Los Angeles; (1990) Paramount Laundry Building, Los Angeles; (1991) QRC Interiors, Los Angeles; Gary Group, Los Angeles; Golen Group, Los Angeles; SMA, Los Angeles; Lindblade Tower, Los Angeles; (1992) P&D Guest House, Los Angeles; Samitaur Office Building.

JEAN NOUVEL

Jean Nouvel was born in France in 1945. He was awarded First Class admission to the ENSBA, and in 1971 received his DPLG Diploma and Chevalier de l'Ordre du Mérite. In 1976 he co-founded the French architectural movement 'Mars 1976', and in 1979 co-founded the Syndicat de l'Architecture, also working as the main organiser of the international committee for the redevelopment of the Les Halles area of Paris. In 1980 Nouvel founded the Architectural Biennale within the Paris Biennale, and in 1991 he became Vice President of the Institut Français d'Architecture. Selected buildings and projects: (1974) Ecole Maternelle, Trélissac, Dordogne; (1982) Renovation of Parc de la Villette, Paris, prizewinning project; (1983) 'Tête Défense', Paris, project; (1984) Les Godets, Antony, leisure centre, Hauts de Seine; Médiathèque, contemporary arts centre, Nîmes, prizewinning project; (1987) Arab Institute, Paris; Opéra de Tokyo, prizewinning project (with Philippe Starck); (1989) ONYX, St Herbiain, cultural centre, Nantes/Loire Atlantique (with Myrto Vitard); Cartier ADP, Paris; Hôtel Amat, Bordeaux; INIST, Nancy, CNRS Documentation Centre; World Harbour Centre, Rotterdam; (1990) Aix Sextius-Mirabeau, project; French Pavilion, Venice Biennale, first-prizewinning competition entry; Expo 95, Vienna, competition entry; (1991) La Grande Arche, La Défense, Paris, EPAD, project; Médiapark Bloc 1, Cologne, hotel, commercial premises, residential quarters and offices, project; Galeries Lafayette, Berlin, prizewinning competition entry. Awards: (1983) Chevalier des Arts et Lettres; Académie d'Architecture silver medal; 'Honoris Causa' doctorate at the University of Buenos Aires; (1987) Awarded the Grand Prix d'Architecture; Prix Aga Khan special mention; L'Equerre d'Argent for the Arab Institute as the best French building; Designer of the Year, Salon du Meuble, Paris; (1990) Architectural Record prize for the St James Hotel. Selected writings: 'L'Avenir de l'Architecture n'est plus architectural', Le Cahiers de la Recherche Architectural 6-7; (1987) 'Les Cinéastes? Sur des choses certaines ils m'entrouvent les yeux', Cités-Cinés, Ramsay; (1987) Jean Nouvel and Associates, Philippe Starck, Nouveau théâtre national de Tokyo, Champ Vallon.

OMA

OMA was co-founded by Rem Koolhaas with Madelon Vriesendorp and Elia and Zoe Zenghelis. For the first five years OMA was occupied with competitions, theoretical work and research. During this time Koolhaas taught in the US at UCLA, Columbia University and the Institute for Architecture and Urban Studies, and in Europe at the

AA School and Delft University. In 1978 *Delirious New York: A Retroactive Manifesto for Manhattan* was published in New York, London and Paris, coinciding with the exhibition 'The Sparkling Metropolis' at the Guggenheim Museum. The book combined Koolhaas's research on Manhattan's 'culture of congestion' with a series of theoretical projects researched with Vriesendorp and the Zenghelises. OMA's attention then shifted back to Europe. A prize *ex-aequo* in the competition for the extension to the Dutch Parliament (1978) led to several significant commissions in the Netherlands, and the opening of the Rotterdam office. In 1987 OMA completed their first major building, the Netherlands Dance Theatre in the Hague. Throughout the 80s, the office continued to participate in competitions. Their 1982 prize-winning entry for a park for the 21st century at La Villette in France – OMA's first important urbanistic project – studied 'invisible congestion', or 'density without architecture'. The firm's studies in urbanism developed further with a project for Melun Senart, 'To Imagine Nothingness', in 1987. Shortly after, OMA were commissioned as the urban planners for the new city centre of Lille in France, where the revolutionary structure of the TGV station and the Channel Tunnel will create a new centre of the Paris-London-Brussels triangle. As urban planners for Lille, OMA are supervising projects by Nouvel, Portzamparc, Shinohara and Vasconi, and have been commissioned as architects of the Congrexpo Building, a 34,000-square-metre congress/exposition hall. In the summer of 1988, OMA undertook three important competitions for big buildings, the Bibliothèque de France, the Centre for Art and Media in Karlsruhe, and a sea terminal in Zeebrugge, Belgium. With these three projects OMA rediscovered the ideas explored in *Delirious New York*, and investigated the potential of verticality and 'bigness' in a European context. In the past two years, OMA have completed several other projects, including the Nexus Housing, in Fukuoka, Japan (winner of the Best Building in Japan Award, 1991), the Villa dall'Ava in Paris (winner of the Prix d'architecture du Moniteur, 1991), and Byzantium, an office/apartment building in Amsterdam. The Kunsthal, an art centre, is currently under construction in Rotterdam, to be completed by autumn 1992. Current projects in the design phase include the Educatorium at the University of Utrecht, an urban planning project for the Amsterdam Waterfront, a villa in Holten, Holland, and an office building in La Défense, Paris. Rem Koolhaas is currently working on two books, *OMA by OMA*, and *The Contemporary City*, a study of the emerging landscapes of Atlanta, Tokyo, and *villes nouvelles* surrounding Paris. *Selected Buildings and Projects:* (1972) Exodus, or the Voluntary Prisoners of Architecture (project); The City of the Captive Globe (project); (1973) The Egg of the Columbus Circle, New York (project); (1974) House, Miami, Florida, USA; (1975) Hotel Sphinx, New York (project); Development of Roosevelt Island, New York (competition); New Welfare Island, New York (competition); (1976) The Story of the Pool (project); Welfare Palace Hotel, New York (project); (1978) Extension of the Dutch Parliament, the Hague; Renovation of a Panopticon Prison, Arnhem (project); (1979) Residence for the Prime Minister and Guest House, Dublin, Ireland (competition); (1980) Social Housing, Kochstrasse/Friedrichstrasse, Berlin, competition; Checkpoint Charlie Housing, Berlin; Social Housing Lutzowstrasse, Berlin; Urban Planning, IJ-Plein, Amsterdam; Two Apartment Slabs, IJ-Plein, Amsterdam; School and Gymnasium, IJ-Plein, Amsterdam; Boompjes Tower and Slab, Rotterdam (study); (1981) Netherlands Dance Theatre, Scheveningen, The Hague; Netherlands Dance Theatre, Spui, The Hague; Villas, Antiparos, Greece; (1982) Parc de la Villette, Paris (competition); (1983) Exposition Universelle 1989, Paris (study); (1984) Office Building Churchillplein, Rotterdam (competition); Villa Chalkiades, Mytilene, Greece; De Brink apartment blocks, Groningen; Lintas Dutch Headquarters, Amsterdam; Villa dall'Ava, St Cloud, Paris; Two Patio Villas, Rotterdam; Police Station, Almere, Holland; Planning for Municipal and Public Beaches, Argostoli and Skala, Greece; (1985) Morgan Bank, Amsterdam (competition); Bus Station, Rotterdam; Byzantium Office/Housing/Shops, Amsterdam; Reconstruction, Bay of Koutavous, Argostoli, Greece; Parc Citröen Cevennes, Paris; (1986) Milan Triennale, casa Palestra, Milan; 200,000 Dwelling, Housing Exhibition, the Hague; Kavel 25 housing block; Waterstad (planning study), Rotterdam; Uithof 2,000, extension of university campus, Utrecht (study); City Hall, the Hague (competition); (1987) Scientopia, Science Park, Rotterdam (study); Urban redevelopment, Bijlmermeer district, Amsterdam (study); Kunsthal, Rotterdam; Urban Planning, Ville Nouvelle Melun-Sénart, France; (1988) Oosterflank offices, Rotterdam (study); Parking Garage and Riverside Development, Rotterdam (study); Verbindingskanaal Zone, urban design, Groningen; Offices and Housing, Groningen; Archiparc office, Utrecht, Rijnsweert; Biocenter, laboratories of the University of Frankfurt, competition; Apartment Block, Rotterdam; Apartment Tower, The Hague; Netherlands Architectural Institute, Rotterdam; Renovation Hotel Furka Biick, Furka Pass, Switzerland; Euro-Disney, Marne la Vallée, France (competition); Sports Museum, Flevohof, The Netherlands (study); NS -150, Site Planning and pavilion design for Railroad expo, Utrecht; Urban Planning, International Business Centre, Lille, France; RWA Ateliers for the handicapped, Amersfort, the Netherlands; Museum Park, Rotterdam, the Netherlands; (1989) Sea Trade Centre, Zeebrugge, Belgium (competition); Nexus Housing, Fukuoka, Japan; Office Complex, Frankfurt (competition); National Library of France, Paris; National Bridges and Roads School, Marne la Vallée, France (competition); Centre for Art and Media Technology, Karlsruhe, Germany; (1990) 'Stad aan de Stroom', urban planning, Antwerp, Belgium (competition); Urban Planning, Kortrijk (competition); Hotel and Conference Centre, Agadir, Morocco (competition); Sports Complex, Groningen (study); Hilton Hotel, The Hague (study); Parking Garage, The Hague (study); (1991) Congrexpo Building, Lille, France; Urban Planning, Duisburg, Germany (competition); Transferium, transportation exchange centres (competition); Frankfurt Airport Offices; Office Building Zac Danton, Paris; Leipziger Messe, Expo Halls and grounds, Leipzig (competition); Urban Design Forum, Yokohama, Japan (study); (1992) IJ-Oevers, Urban Planning, Amsterdam.

PHILIPPE STARCK

Philippe Starck was born in France; in addition to his highly accomplished work as an architect he has achieved an international reputation as a versatilen specialist in interior and industrial design. *Selected buildings and projects:* (1987) Lemoult, Construction of a Private House, Paris; (1988) Laguiole, Construction of a Knife Factory, France; (1989) Naninani, Office Building, Show Room, Restaurant, Tokyo; Starck Street, Residential and Office Buildings and Artists' Workshops, Paris; Kotaro Shimogori, ten Residential Units, Los Angeles, USA; (1991) Moondog, Block of Flats, Tokyo; (1992) Le Baron Vert, Office Building, Osaka, Japan. *Interior Design:* (1982) Starck Club, Night Club, Dallas, USA; (1984) La Villette, Interior Design of seven Lecture Rooms in the Science Museum, La Villette, Paris; (1985) Multi-Functional Room, Museum of Decorative Arts, Paris; (1988) Royalton Hotel, New York; (1990-91) Groningen Museum of Modern Art with Mendini and Frank Stella; (1991) Coppola Hairdressing Salon, Milan. *Furniture:* (1983) President of France, Complete Collection for the President; (1985) Elisee Editions, Design of a Carpet; (1986) Vittel, Design of a Bottle of Mineral Water, France; Panzani, Pasta Design, France; (1986-87) Casatec, Furniture Collection, Japan; Vuitton, Design of a Complete Line of Luggage, France; (1988-91) Kartell, Collection, Italy; (1990-91) Vitra, Furniture Collection, Switzerland; Glacier, Design of Mineral Water Bottles, USA; (1991) Design of Two-Wheeled Vehicles; Watch Design; Glasses Design; (1992) Cojo, Design of the Ceremonial Torch for the Jeux Olympiques '92. *Major Exhibitions:* (1985) Museum of Modern Art, Kyoto, Japan; (1986) Neocone 18 Chicago, USA; (1988) Scenery of the Exhibition, '30 Ans de Design Français'; (1990) Venice Biennale.

BERNARD TSCHUMI

Bernard Tschumi was born in Lausanne, Switzerland, in 1944. He was educated in Paris and Zurich (ETH) from 1963 to 1969. He has taught at Portsmouth, the AA, the Institute for Architecture and Urban Studies, NY and Cooper Union. In 1988 he became Dean of Architecture at Columbia Graduate School of Planning and Preservation. He formed Bernard Tschumi Associates, with offices in New York and Paris, in 1983. He has been awarded the Chevalier des Arts et des Lettres and the Chevalier of the Legion of Honour. *Selected buildings and projects:* (1983) Parc de la Villette, Paris, first prize, international competition; (1986) New Theatre and Opera House,

Tokyo, Japan, second prize; Strasbourg County Hall, France; (1987) Conceptual Plan for Flushing Meadows/Corona Park, New York; (1988) Hotel EuroDisney, Marne-la-Valleé, France; Moabiter Werder, Werder, urban and landscape proposal, Berlin; Berlin Library, Ponts-Villes, Lausanne, Switzerland; Kansai International Airport, Osaka, Japan, second prize; (1989) Vieux-Port, Montreal, planning study; National Library of France, Paris; ZKM Centre for Art and Media Technology, Karlsruhe, Germany, third prize; Steelworks, Völklingen, Germany, planning study; (1990) ARBED Headquarters, Esch, Luxembourg; Kyoto Station, Japan; The Glass Video Gallery, Groningen, Netherlands; 'Art et Publicité' installation, Centre Pompidou, Paris, France; (1991) Masterplan, Chartres, France.

PETER WILSON

Peter Wilson was born in Melbourne, Australia in 1950. He studied at the local university, and then from 1972 at the Architectural Association, London, where he then worked as an assistant from 1974 to 1978. From 1978 he ran his own unit at the Diploma School. In 1980 he and his wife, Julia Bolles, set up the Wilson Partnership in Münster, Germany. *Selected buildings and projects:* (1982) Pont des Arts, Paris; (1985) Accademia Bridge, Venice Biennale, competition entry; (1986) Paradiso Bridge, Amsterdam, project; New National Theatre and Opera House, Tokyo, competition entry; Blackburn House, London; (1988) Rotterdam Railway Tunnel Site, urban design proposal; Rosslyn Mews, London (with Chassay Wright); Forum of Sand, Berlin, project; Kindergarten, Frankfurt, Germany; 'Comfort in the Metropolis', competition entry; (1989) Folly, Expo 90, Osaka, Japan; ZKM Center for Art and Media Technology, Karlsruhe, Germany, competition entry, second prize; Bridge Fort, Asperen, Netherlands; Green Homes Offices, Cosmos Street, Tokyo; Kassel Sculpture Hall, Germany, competition entry; (1990) City Library, Münster, Germany.

LEBBEUS WOODS

Lebbeus Woods was born in 1940 in Lansing, Michigan. He was educated at the Purdue University School of Engineering and the University of Illinois School of Architecture. He has been visiting professor of Architecture at Cooper Union, the University of North Carolina, the University of Houston, SCI-ARC and Columbia University. He is Director at the Research Institute for Experimental Architecture (RIEA), a not-for-profit organisation. *Major solo exhibitions:* (1985) 'Origins', the Architectural Association, London; (1986) 'Vision der Moderne', Deutsches Architekturmuseum, Frankfurt; (1987) 'Centricity', AEDES Gallerie, Berlin; 'Zauber der Medusa', Kunstlerhaus, Vienna; (1988) 'Berlin: Denkmal oder Denkmodell', Paris 1989, Berlin 1989, Krakow 1990 and Moscow 1991; (1989) 'Terra Nova', Fenster Galerie, Frankfurt am Main; (1991) 'Berlin-Free-Zone', AEDES Galerie, Berlin; 'Paris: Architecture et Utopie', Paris and Berlin; 'Kunstlerhauser', Deutsches Architekturmuseum, Frankfurt am Main. *Selected writings:* (1985) *Origins*, Architectural Association, London, September; (1987) *Centricity: The Unified Urban Field*, AEDES, Berlin; (1989) *OneFiveFour, 3*, Princeton Architectural Press.

GÜNTER ZAMP KELP

Günter Zamp Kelp was born in Bistritz, Transylvania in 1941. From 1959 to 1967 he studied Architecture at the Technical University of Vienna, and from 1967 to 1969 he was assistant to Professor Karl Schwanzer at the Institute for Building and Design at the university. In 1967 he established Haus Rucker Co with Laurids Ortner and Klaus Pinter in Vienna. In 1969 he moved to Düsseldorf, establishing a Haus Rucker Co studio there, and became a member of the Architectural League and the Society of German Architects (BDA). In 1971 Zamp Kelp went to New York to co-found a studio there, returning to Düsseldorf the next year. In 1981-82 he was a visiting professor at Cornell University and the Hochschule der Künste in Berlin. In 1987 Zamp Kelp became a member of the Architectural League of Berlin, and set up a personal office in Düsseldorf. In 1988 he was visiting professor at Städelsche Kunstschule Frankfurt Am Main, and appointed professor at the Hochschule der Künste in Berlin. He also established a personal studio in Berlin. At present he lives and works in Düsseldorf and Berlin.

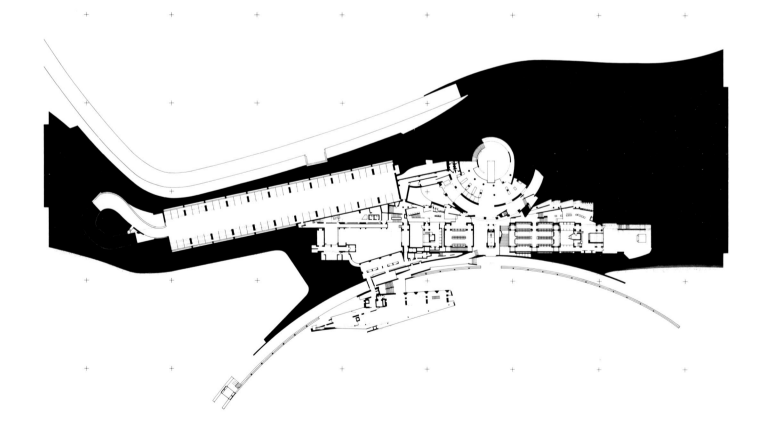

Above: Morphosis, 'Chiba' Project, Tokyo

ACKNOWLEDGEMENTS

Many of the projects presented in this Omnibus volume have previously appeared in *Architectural Design* magazine. References to particular issues are given below. All photographs in the book are courtesy of the architect unless otherwise stated.

Cover: photograph by Hélène Binet; *p5:* photograph by Christian Kandzia of Behnisch and Partners.

Who Are These Spirits Wild and Free? by Geoffrey Broadbent, pp12-37: this essay was specially commissioned for the volume. Photography: *p12:* Tom Bonner, from *AD Modern Pluralism*, Profile No 95; *p14 above:* Michel Clais and E J Ouwerkerk from *AD A New Spirit in Architecture*, Profile No 89; *p15 below:* Gerald Zugmann; *pp16 and 17:* Charles Jencks; *p26:* Andreas Papadakis; *p30:* Gerald Zugmann; *p33:* Dick Frank; *p35:* courtesy of the German Architecture Museum, Frankfurt; *p36:* Udo Hesse.

ARCHITECTS' ESSAYS

WOLF PRIX *On the Edge, pp56-63:* previously appeared in *AD Deconstruction III*, Profile no 87, as an edited version of a lecture given at the Royal Institute of British Architects.

PETER EISENMAN *Visions Unfolding – Architecture in the Age of Electronic Media, pp88-91:* included in *Eisenmanual*, Academy Editions, London, forthcoming.

MARK FISHER *Steel Wheels, p105:* previously appeared in *AD Pop Architecture*, Profile No 98.

CHARLES JENCKS *Frank Gehry: The First Deconstructionist, pp110-115:* previously appeared in *The New Moderns* by Charles Jencks, Academy Editions, London, 1990.

ITSUKO HASEGAWA *Architecture as Another Nature, pp134-137:* previously appeared in *AD Aspects of Modern Architecture*, Profile No 90.

DANIEL LIBESKIND *Fishing From the Pavement, pp164-174:* previously appeared in *Journal of Philosophy and the Visual Arts: Philosophy and Architecture*, London, 1991; *End Space, pp175-177:* previously appeared in *Daniel Libeskind: Countersign*, Architectural Monograph No 16, Academy Editions, London 1991; *Between the Lines pp178-181:* previously appeared in *AD The New*

Modern Aesthetic, Profile No 86, as an edited version of a lecture given at the 'New Moderns' Symposium at the Tate Gallery, London.

BERNARD TSCHUMI *The Architecture of the Event, pp224-227:* previously appeared in *AD Modern Pluralism*, Profile No 95.

LEBBEUS WOODS *Heterarchy of Urban Forms and Architecture, pp242-245:* previously appeared in *AD Free Space Architecture*, Profile No 96.

ARCHITECTS' PROJECTS

ARQUITECTONICA pp40-43: featured in *AD The New Modern Aesthetic*, Profile No 86.

GÜNTER BEHNISCH pp44-49: featured in *AD A New Spirit in Architecture*, Profile No 89. Photographs by Christian Kandzia of Behnisch and Partners.

NIGEL COATES pp50-55: featured in *AD The New Modern Aesthetic*, Profile No 86. Photographs by Paul Warchol and Edward Valentine Hames.

COOP HIMMELBLAU pp64-75: featured in *AD Deconstruction III*, Profile No 87. Photographs by Gerald Zugmann.

DILLER + SCOFIDIO pp76-81: featured in *AD Modern Pluralism,* Profile No 95, and more extensively in *The Journal of Philosophy and the Visual Arts: Architecture • Space • Painting*, London, 1992. 'Para-Site' photographs by Paul Warchol; 'Tourisms' photographs by Glenn Halvorson.

PETER EISENMAN pp92-103: featured in the *AD Wexner Centre for the Visual Arts*, Profile No 82. Photographs by Peter Aaron of Esto, James Freedman and Wolfgang Hoyt, and Dick Frank.

MARK FISHER pp104-107: featured in *AD Pop Architecture*, Profile No 98. 'The Wall' photographs by Paul Slattery; 'Steel Wheels' photographs by Mark Fisher.

FRANK GEHRY pp110-121: featured in *AD Pop Architecture*, Profile No 98. Photographs by Charles Jencks.

ZAHA HADID pp122-133: 'Moonsoon Restaurant' featured in *AD Deconstruction III*, Profile No 87. Photographs by Paul Warchol. 'Vitra Fire Station' and 'Media Park' featured in *AD Free Space Architecture*, Profile No 96. Photographs by Edward Woodman. 'Folly 3' photographs by Hélène Binet.

ITSUKO HASEGAWA pp134-145: featured in *AD Aspects of Modern Architecture*, Profile No 90.

JOHN HEJDUK pp146-153: 'The Potsdam Printer's House/Studio' featured in *AD Berlin Tomorrow*, Profile No 92. 'Groningen City Marker' featured in *AD Free Space Architecture*, Profile No 96, and more extensively in *Art & Design: Marking the City Boundaries*, Profile No 25. Photographs by John Stoel.

PHILIP JOHNSON pp154-159: featured in *The New Moderns* by Charles Jencks, Academy Editions, 1990. Photograph on p155 by Kevin Simpson of John Burgee Architects.

KRUEGER & KAPLAN pp160-163: 'Art Park' featured in *AD Modern Pluralism*, Profile No 95.

DANIEL LIBESKIND pp164-187: featured in the *Daniel Libeskind: Countersign* Monograph No 16, Academy Editions, London, 1991; *AD New Architecture*, Profile No 84; *AD The New Modern Aesthetic*, Profile No 86; and *AD Berlin Tomorrow*, Profile No 92. Photographs on pp175-187 by Udo Hesse.

MORPHOSIS pp188-197: featured in *AD Modern Pluralism*, Profile No 95. Photographs by Tom Bonner.

JEAN NOUVEL pp204-209: featured in *AD Berlin Tomorrow*, Profile No 92. Material courtesy of the German Architecture Museum.

OMA pp210-215: 'Checkpoint Charlie' featured in *AD Deconstruction III*, Profile No 87. Photographs by Michel Claus and E J Ouwerkerk. 'The Byzantium' featured in *AD Modern Pluralism*, Profile No 95. Photographs by Van Vlugt and Claus.

PHILIPPE STARCK pp216-223: featured in *AD A New Spirit in Architecture*, Profile No 89.

BERNARD TSCHUMI pp224-237: 'Chartres Masterplan' and 'Kyoto Station' featured in *AD Modern Pluralism*, Profile No 95; 'ZKM' and 'Glass Video Gallery' featured in *AD Deconstruction III*, Profile No 87.

PETER WILSON pp238-241: featured in *AD A New Spirit in Architecture*, Profile No 89. Photographs by Hélène Binet, Richard Bryant and John Freeman.

LEBBEUS WOODS pp242-251: featured in *AD Free Space Architecture*, Profile No 96.

GÜNTHER ZAMP KELP pp252-255: 'Ornamenta 1' and 'Mekka Medial' featured in *AD A New Spirit in Architecture*, Profile No 89.